THE
DEVIL
DISGUISED AS
ST. ELMO

The Saga of
Pierre Taillandier, SJ

ANTONIO R. SIEVERT with
ELIZABETH POTTER SIEVERT

Other books by the Authors:

ACROSS THE SEAS — Three Brothers Find New Lives in Colonial Philippines
by Antonio R. Sievert
*THE STORY OF ABACA — Manila Hemp's Transformation from Textile to Marine Cordage
and Specialty Paper*
by Elizabeth Potter Sievert

Library of Congress Cataloguing-in-Publication data, Case # 1-11217782651
Sievert, Antonio R. 1942.

COPYRIGHT INFO:
The Devil Disguised as St. Elmo / Antonio R. Sievert, Elizabeth Potter Sievert
Includes bibliographical references and index.

Book Cover Credits:
Galleon in Full Sail by Anton Otto Fischer
Jesuits in Akbar's Court by Nar Singh
The Author in Pondicherry

Title Page Credit:
Theses Opticae et Astronomicae
By Petrus Taillandier and Johannes Baptista Thioly, 1693

Print ISBN: 978-1-66783-374-3

eBook ISBN: 978-1-66783-375-0

CONTENTS

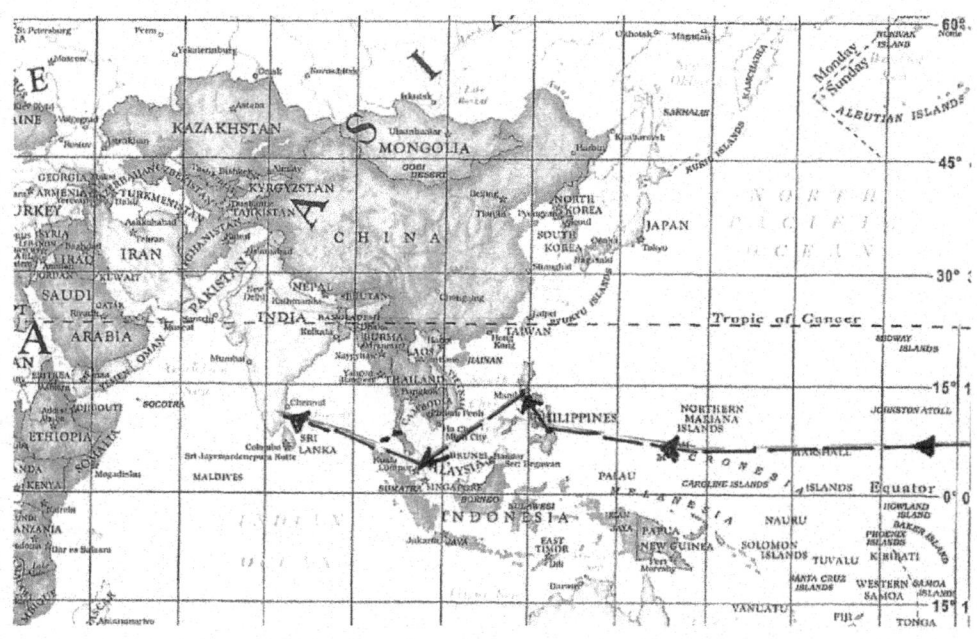

Pierre Taillandier's Route from

~ 1707 to

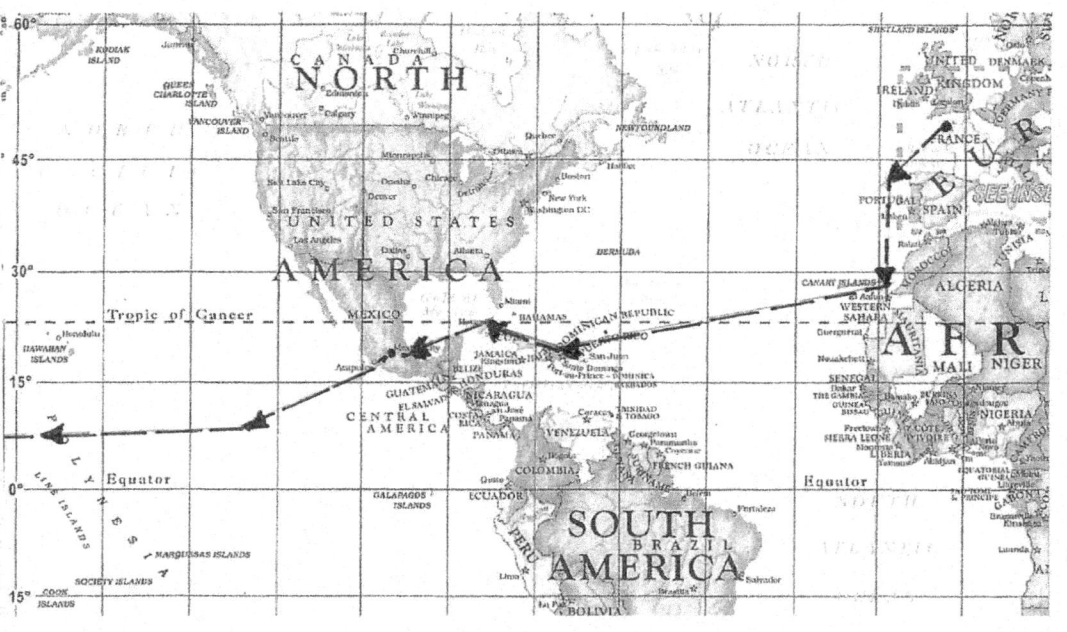

Saint-Malo to Pondicherry

1710 ~

ACKNOWLEDGEMENTS

Writing this book was more difficult than I thought it would be, but it became more rewarding as the years passed. *The Devil Disguised as St. Elmo* would not have been possible had I not received an old parchment-bound book from my son, Kevin Sievert, in 2002. It was an original copy of Volume 7 of Diego Davin's Spanish translation of selected letters from the *Lettres Édifiantes et Curieuses* that was published in 1755 in Madrid. Among the letters was one written from Pondicherry (now Puducherry), India, by Pierre Taillandier. That letter fascinated me and drew me to learn more about the author and his journey to India.

My wife, Betsy, and I decided to follow in Taillandier's footsteps, as best we could, to witness what he described more than 300 years ago and then to place his observations in historical context. In essence our goal was to present a "slice" of history seen through this man's eyes as he pursued his destiny.

One early stop on our journey to uncover Pierre Taillandier's background was his birthplace: Lyon, France. There we were helped immeasurably by Gilles Adam, an astrophysicist with a keen interest in the history of astronomy, especially that of the Lyon Observatory. It was Gilles who arranged for us to visit the Lycée Ampere, formerly the Collège de la Trinité, where Taillandier was educated, entered the Jesuit priesthood, taught, and later became director of its Observatory. Further, Gilles guided us to the Municipal Archives of Lyon and the Archives of the Rhône Department where we found records relating to Taillandier's father and grandfather.

I am grateful to Edward Jeganatham, SJ, who gave us access to the Jesuit Archives of Madurai in Shembaganur (Kodaikanal), India, an impressive depository of documents, some of which date to the 16th century and the time of Francis Xavier.

To Betsy (Elizabeth Potter Sievert), I offer my heartfelt thanks for her dedication during the most trying years of this book's creation. She spent countless hours translating letters and other documents from French, formatting the manuscript, and scouring the internet for historical records and images that would give this narrative added interest and perspective.

PROLOGUE

Since the founding of the Society of Jesus by Ignatius of Loyola, Jesuits have regularly reported on their missionary work, their problems, and their observations of the language, natural history, customs, and mores of the far-flung places where they served by sending letters and accounts back to the Society's central government and to their benefactors. Selected letters written mostly by French Jesuits, were published beginning in 1703 as the *Lettres Édifiantes et Curieuses, Écrites des Missions Étrangères*[1] (*LEC*). The first volume, which contained letters from China, was so well received that it was followed by thirty-three more up until 1776, each with contemporaneous correspondence from missions in Asia, the Levant, and the Americas. It has been said that these reports and the insights conveyed by their Jesuit authors contributed significantly to the Age of Enlightenment in Europe.

From his mission in a foreign land, a Jesuit's primary means of communication with his Order was through letters. From India, for example, he would dispatch accounts of his toils and achievements aboard the next vessel bound for Europe—a sailing ship that, if fortunate, arrived safely and returned once a year with mail from home and supplies required to maintain the missions. But just as importantly, a returning ship would also have brought replacements—men molded in the Ignatian spirit who would assume responsibilities in lands that lacked missionaries or had lost them due to sickness, adversity, or martyrdom.

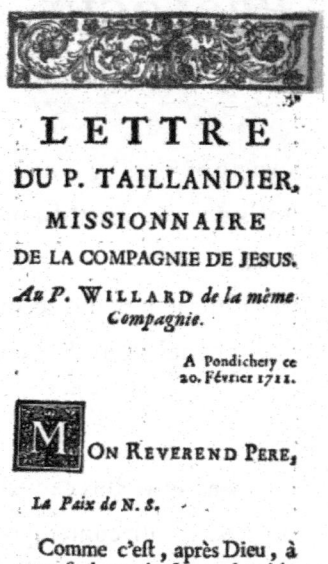

Father Taillandier's letter, 20 February 1711.

One of the letters published in the 11th volume of the *LEC* was written by Father Pierre Taillandier,[2] a thirty-four-year-old Jesuit and astronomer from Lyon, France. In it, he described his epic two-and-a-half-year journey to Pondicherry, India. Unlike those of many of his colleagues, Taillandier's letter was long, technical, and sprinkled with the excitement of adventure and peril. However, it was maddeningly silent about his life in India. Sometime between 1711 and 1713, he departed Pondicherry with two catechists for Golconda, a fortified city founded by Persian Shia Muslims in the 14th century. While en route, Taillandier died mysteriously. The precise circumstances of his death are unclear, but we will relate the facts and the hypotheses surrounding his disappearance in the region called South India.

Taillandier's journey began in 1707 when he boarded a French corsair in Saint-Malo, a wind-swept and rock-strewn fortified city on Brittany's north coast. At that time a war[3] involving Europe's premier sea-faring nations was raging; nevertheless, he eventually arrived safely in Pondicherry, then the center of French trading and missionary activities in South India. Most likely to avoid entanglement in the war, Taillandier did not sail, as his predecessors did, around the African cape to reach India. Rather, he took a safer route—he traveled westward to Mexico which he crossed on foot, then sailed across the Pacific Ocean to the Philippines, and finally to the Bay of Bengal via the Malacca Strait. By the time he arrived in India in 1710, Taillandier had navigated the two largest oceans in the world and trekked across mountain passes over 8,500 feet high in Mexico's eastern Sierra Madre Mountains.

In his letter, penned in 1711 to his correspondent Father Willard in Paris, Taillandier gave a richly detailed account of his extraordinary voyage. During the long odyssey, Taillandier likely used his knowledge of astronomy to help navigators calculate their geographic position at sea. He faithfully recorded the oceanographic as well as nautical data he might have been asked to provide the Jesuit organization that sponsored him. Certainly, King Louis XIV, through his Science Academy in Paris, would have been interested in the details of Taillandier's observations, for at the beginning of the 18th century there was still much to learn about the art of navigation. The physical and technical observations he provided could only improve the quality of the scientific documentation amassed ever since sailors first took to the sea. "I hope," he wrote to Willard, "that the details I have given would be to your satisfaction." In the age of sail and exploration, Jesuit missionaries persevered not only to introduce Christianity to the inhabitants in the far-flung missions, but also to contribute to the advancement of scientific knowledge in their field of expertise.

While traveling through the Spanish colonies, Father Taillandier profoundly acknowledged "the virtue and zeal" of the Spaniards he met, military and missionary alike, who worked and prayed together as they brought Christianity to those territories. For example, while in the Marianas which Spain had annexed as part of the Spanish East Indies, he declared he felt honored to say mass on the island of Guam that had been "bathed by the blood of many Jesuits who had baptized all these infidels."

He was fascinated by the diversity of the races he encountered in the different parts of the world, whether in Manila or in Mexico: "… Blacks from Africa, Creoles, Mestizos, and other people who are descended from a blending of these diverse nations among themselves, and with Europeans. This is the reason why there is a great range of colors from white to black, such that among a hundred faces one can hardly find two of the same color."

Father Taillandier meant to inform, even impress, the reader with his keen eye, but it seemed he clearly was shocked to witness open cohabitation among the different ethnic groups in the Spanish colonies—no doubt a condition that displeased the Catholic Church so fervently engaged in establishing a new faith based on Christian virtues and the salvation of souls. Perhaps, for the first time in his life Taillandier was confronted with the contrasting colors of humanity evolving from this era of unprecedented commerce enabled by sailing ships. But he must have understood rather quickly that despite the tint of one's skin, a man's pursuit of happiness was as robust outside of Europe as it was within it.

Once in India, Father Taillandier found he had many pressing priorities: first, to regain his health; then to finish the report of his journey that was required of him; and third to master the language of his mission. All these he had to accomplish within a year or so of his arrival. There is much to glean from Father Taillandier's letter regarding what fascinated him as he nearly circled the globe to find his fate.

* * * * *

The desire to discover new lands and wealth at the far reaches of the world's vast oceans generated fierce competition among European rulers to establish empires in Asia and the Americas. Seeking profit, explorers and merchants brought back precious metals and gems, spices, aromatics, medicinal plants, silk, and muslin—the sheerest of cotton cloth never before available to the aristocracy in Europe. We will try to illuminate those times to better understand the hurried early-modern period in which Taillandier lived, where faith played an important role in the lives of the people who traded with the Europeans.

Where there was commerce there was also conversion—a matter of great importance to Louis XIV (1638-1715), Catholic king of France, known also as the *Roi Soleil*, or Sun King. When in 1664 his *Compagnie des Indes Orientales* (French East India Company) was granted a *firman* (royal permit) by the Mughal Emperor to trade with India, the king introduced, along with his merchants, Jesuit missionaries with the zeal to bring the gospel of Christ to the people who produced the exciting products he sought for France.

In that ancient country, however, controversy arose over conversion methods first employed by Portuguese Jesuits in Madurai, the southernmost kingdom in India. The prominent feature of the polemics, which devolved into the so-called "Malabar Rites Controversy," was the egalitarian accommodation employed by the Jesuits to the manners and customs of the elite among the Hindus to achieve conversion. This tactic did not go unnoticed by the Vatican.

Despite this accommodative posture, the Jesuit rejection of Hindu religious ceremonies and festivals in Pondicherry, or at least their attempt to limit their deleterious influence among the townspeople, greatly affected the lives and fortunes of everyone—both Indian and European—who was involved with the French East India Company. This, too, got the attention of the Vatican.

Father Taillandier's letter was an extraordinary document—unexpected like a comet that remained hidden in interstellar space and then blazed a visible trail through the darkness of space and time to our modern era. His recollections stimulate our curiosity to dig deeper to understand why men such as he set out across trackless seas to confront adversity and give freely of themselves for the salvation of souls.

Beyond recounting Taillandier's epic journey, *The Devil Disguised as St. Elmo* provides insights rich with the perspective of history. It sheds light on the struggles and accomplishments of men who left their stories on foreign shores and their epitaphs woven into the substance of other men's lives. In all these, one can see the hand of Providence, for man cannot suspend his fate nor deny his will to take the fall and lay down his life for noble deeds ever unquenchable.

PART ONE –

PIERRE TAILLANDIER

Astronomy compels the soul to look upwards and leads us
from this world to another.

The Republic, VII, 529
Plato

HIS EARLY LIFE IN LYON

Born on 6 March 1676 in Lyon, a city in southeastern France and the second largest in the country, Pierre Taillandier grew up near the left bank of the Saône river. In 43 BC the Romans selected this site for an important military outpost of their Empire because of its strategic position at the confluence of the Saône and Rhône rivers. They built their town, though, atop Fourvière Hill (Map 1) above the right bank of the Saône and called it Lugdunum, capital of Gaul. Despite persecution at the hands of the Romans, Christians from Asia Minor established a church there. Christianity survived the collapse of the Empire, though. During the Middle Ages, the city, by this time known as Lyon, expanded across the Saône, opposite the heart of the Roman city, to the area now called the Presqu'ile district where the Romans had built their warehouses. For centuries, due to its strategic location, Lyon thrived but also suffered devastating sieges at the hands of its enemies.

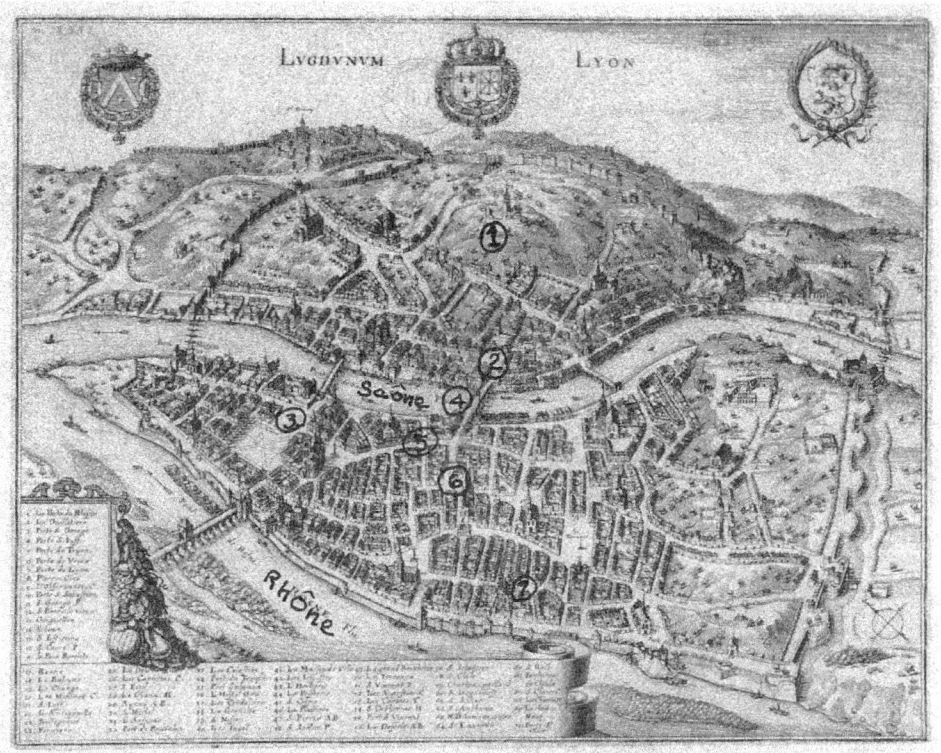

Map 1: *Lugdunum (Lyon), c 1650. (1) Fourvière Hill, (2) Vieux Lyon (Old Lyon), (3) Presqu'ile, (4) Pont du Change, (5) Rue Mercière, (6) St. Nizier church, (7) Collège de la Trinité. In Topographia Galliae, M. Merian, 1657.*

Nevertheless, the city became a market for black pepper that came in from India's Malabar Coast via caravan routes through the Levant to Europe. The French silk industry, launched by King Louis XI in the 15th century, benefitted Lyon's economy and eventually led to the city becoming the hub of the European silk trade. Also in the 15th century, the first French language book published in France was printed in Lyon. From then the city remained the second most important printing center in France after Paris. All this economic activity made Lyon a significant financial center in Europe.

Pierre Taillandier spent his youth in the city's bustling business section, along Mercière Street, Lyon's publishing quarter in the Presqu'ile district. Here his father, Robert Taillandier[4], and his grandfather, Pierre Compagnon,[5] owned small bookstores[6] and a printing company. An early mention of Pierre Compagnon[7] dated 1648 described him as a bookseller located on rue Mercière. Twenty years later in 1668 we know that Pierre Compagnon was associated with Robert Taillandier, his son-in-law, and their business address still was on rue Mercière.[8]

St. Nizier Church. By Israel Sylvestre, 1649.

At this time Lyon had become one of the most active printing centers in Europe as printers had been working there since the 1470s.[9] Robert Taillandier's main shop on rue Mercière probably occupied the building's ground floor while the family lived on the second level. A few blocks away was the ancient Church of St. Nizier where Pierre was baptized, as were his siblings. Pierre was the third of at least four children born to Robert Taillandier and Anne Compagnon.[10] Sadly, though, Pierre's father died when Pierre was only ten years old. As his father and grandfather were partners in the bookstores and printing business, it seems likely that after his father's death Pierre would have grown up under the wing of his mother's father, Pierre Compagnon.[11] Since both his father and grandfather were booksellers and therefore educated men, Pierre would have had a privileged upbringing compared to many of the children in his neighborhood. Surely, as a youth he would have assisted in the shops where he would have had the opportunity to read the books on the shelves and converse with the customers—experiences that would open his eyes to the world outside Lyon's Presqu'ile. Perhaps these encounters inspired him toward his future profession as a Jesuit missionary and astronomer. Among those books[12] were such diverse titles as works by Cyrano de Bergerac, *Fables d'Esope*, Maffei's[13] *Life of Ignatius*, Herbert's[14] *Voyage de Perse*, Schroder's *Pharmacopia*, as well as translations of various books of the Bible and other religious texts, and a globe by renowned cartographer, W. J. Blaeu.

Entrance to the Collège. It is now the home of the Collège-Lycée Ampère, 29 rue de la Bourse. Photo by the author, 2015.

Pierre attended the nearby Jesuit Collège de la Sainte Trinité.[15] Since its establishment in 1604, the college had one of the strongest traditions in teaching mathematics in France. By Taillandier's time the Jesuit colleges also had adopted geography, evolving out of the age of exploration, as an important subject. "Maps of the world were hanged on the walls …, creating emulation for missions."[16] It seems entirely likely that this important Jesuit institution would have displayed such significant French maps. Pierre no doubt would have pondered them while a student and later a novice, perhaps dreaming of evangelizing in some far-off place.

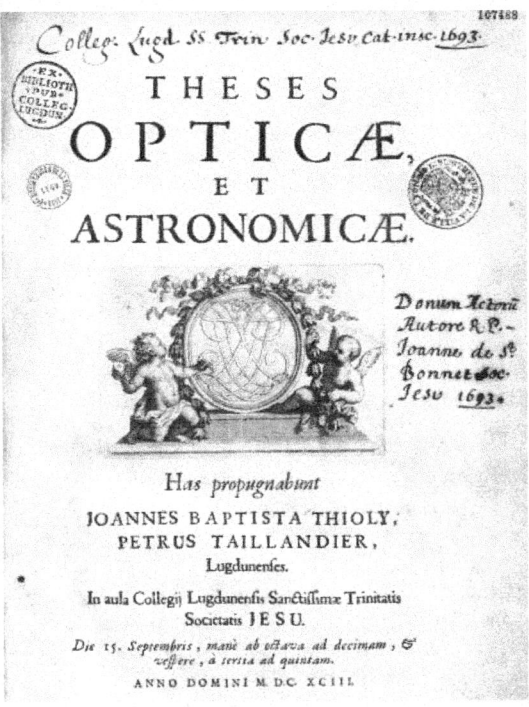

Title page of the Theses.

On 15 September 1693, as a requisite for graduation from the college, he and a classmate, Jean Baptiste Thioly,[17] submitted and defended their thesis entitled: *Theses Opticae et Astronomicae.* On the 23rd Taillandier became a Jesuit when he entered the novitiate at the college. Five years later in 1698 he was ordained. He then taught grammar, humanities, and rhetoric there. By 1702 Father Taillandier was attached to the observatory being constructed atop the college[18] and upon its completion, he became the director.[19]

A CALL TO SERVE

S ometime during the spring or summer of 1707, perhaps in June after the academic year ended, Pierre Taillandier must have received his appointment as a missionary to India. He departed that fall on his long journey by crossing the Atlantic Ocean. He walked across Mexico and then sailed the Pacific via the Philippines to his destination: Pondicherry on India's Coromandel Coast.

En route, Taillandier found real adventure in the Malacca Strait some two years after leaving France. He and his companion, Pierre Bonnet, and a hundred other passengers aboard a two-masted ship, most likely an Arabian dhow, narrowly avoided a shipwreck off North Sumatra during a howling storm that lasted for several days. He described the feeling of momentarily defying gravity as the vessel lost contact with the water's surface before gliding into the troughs of mountain-like seas. In his words: "The sea was very agitated; the waves were high and quick to break over our heads. They kept menacing us with the specter of death. One alone would have been enough to entomb us." But their prayers were answered even as the devil himself, the vessel's frightened crew believed, put up a fight by showing itself as points of St. Elmo's Fire, off the dhow's masts whose sails were made of rush and bamboo cross-battens.

Despite the travails encountered during his long and fitful crossing, Taillandier maintained a sense of irony and even humor. Though the raging waves and the creaking of the dhow's old timbers may have alarmed him, he knew God somehow would keep the ship afloat. Tempest-tossed and blown off course for days, "the wind kept its incessant howl accompanied by the pitiful laments of the Moorish crew, while we were at peace and ready to receive the fate that God had destined for us."

Providence finally stranded their vessel at the mouth of the Perlis River near Kedah, then a tributary to the kingdom of Siam, on the west coast of today's Malaysia. Unable to find a ship that would take them across to Pondicherry, another seventeen hundred miles to the west, Taillandier and Bonnet spent the next seven months sick and lost amid Kedah's Muslim population. Tongue-tied by the intricacies of the local language, they could not have hoped to convert very many through a demonstration of love and charity. They might have wished they had wine with which to celebrate mass and to spread the gospel of the Lord, but this was not granted them for they had arrived, unbidden, in a place unreceptive to Christians.

During those dark days, Taillandier wrote about the transcendent world he saw and the privileges he thought would have accrued to him as a European living in the Orient: "I do not include among our predicaments the services that could be rendered by others to maintain life. We could not find a single Moor who would go to the river to bring us some water."

Even if Taillandier had fetched water for himself, he would not have been welcome there. Not only was the river the site for communal baths and a convenient place for early morning hygiene, but it was also the place for the Muslim faithful to perform *wudu*, the required daily ablutions before prayers.

"God afflicted Father Bonnet and me with a disease common to all Europeans when they live for some length of time in a climate as hot as this one," he wrote. "However, we had the good fortune of being able to rescue from slavery a Christian from Macao who for four years had not been able to obtain his freedom. But what do I know? Perhaps, to save this zealous Christian, God delayed our trip with all the bad weather we had so that we might enter Kedah?" Divine Providence may have freed this Christian from abject slavery so he could be of service to the missionaries. In return, he would have gladly done their bidding, including fetching water for them.

* * * * *

Taillandier began his letter from Pondicherry with his sincere expression of gratitude to his sponsor in France, Father Willard:

> My Reverend Father,
> Since, after God, I owe you the happiness that I enjoy
> dedicating my remaining days to the conversion of Infidels,
> it is my obligation to inform you of what concerns me
> and to tell you truthfully and in detail what I have seen
> or learned during the long voyage that I had to take to
> reach India.

His relation of that journey is a tantalizing window through which he illuminates the struggles and achievements met by many as the West converged on the East to trade and introduce Christianity in the colonies.

We shall now open that window and take a unique journey of our own to visit those lands, especially India, which Arab merchants who sailed with the monsoon trade winds called *bilad al-filfil,* the land of pepper.

CHRISTIANITY MOVES TO THE EAST

T he early modern world began just before the close of the 15th century. The Portuguese explorer Vasco da Gama, knowing Christopher Columbus had failed to find his way to the distant East, ventured into the unknown—the sea route around the African cape to spice-laden Arabia and India. Crossing that wind-tossed sea in 1498 was a horrifying experience for the many superstitious and ignorant sailors pressed to serve aboard men-of-war. They fell to their knees on the decks of the heaving ships to thank God the ocean did not drop them into a dark and monster-filled abyss!

Others sailed in the hope of striking it rich or restarting their lives in some far away land. Dreams were all they had; literacy was uncommon among the men of the sea. In the Europe of their day, it was almost futile to evade the Impress Board set on enlisting any male it found to serve aboard warships. A boy of thirteen was for all practical purposes a man, and a man of forty was often physically wasted—crippled by wounds—but it did not matter, his duty was to obey orders or die trying. If he survived the wretchedness of his life in the airless quarters before the mast or the consumption of putrid and maggot infested sea rations, another terror called scurvy would soon swell his gums and rob him of his health and his teeth. The few who made it back home, often the very young who started out as seamen then became mid-shipmen and later officers, had nothing but praise for God and His blessings. At last, they could enjoy what remained of their lives, away from the terrifying waves and winds that flung them from the yardarms and buried many of their companions at sea.

And so, began the period when trail blazers embarked on years-long and often contentious voyages of exploration and colonization of far-flung lands. Eventually, they established regular routes to the Arabian Sea, India, and Southeast Asia. Venetian merchants[20] who, for centuries, sold the spices and exotic textiles that arrived in the Mediterranean via the Silk Roads, now had to compete with merchants bringing the same goods into other western European ports aboard English, Dutch, and Portuguese ships.

* * * * *

Like a tightly clinched left hand with thumb pointing down towards the Indian Ocean, the subcontinent of India was violently thrust against the Himalayan Mountains—their peaks the highest in the world. Formed by India's two long coasts, the tip of the thumb was the point most rounded by merchants buying and selling goods as varied and exotic as the sailors traveling aboard fluyts, brigs, dhows, and junks. The southwest monsoon,[21] predictable but often packing violent cyclonic winds, brings in the more humid ocean air that rises and condenses resulting in torrential rains. The storms irrigate the vast farmlands without which India would not be able to feed its people or produce and manufacture its much-sought fine cotton cloth.

A Dominican friar named Nicholas Pistoia, along with his Franciscan companion, John of Monte Corvino, landed in Mylapore in 1291. They were the first European missionaries to proselytize in the south of India, but they left few traces of their accomplishments. Preaching the Gospel of Jesus for a year while waiting for a ship that would take them to Cathay (China), Nicolas fell ill and died. John buried Nicholas at Mylapore before sailing away.

A second Dominican friar, Jordan of Severac,[22] arrived there in 1321 from Persia along with four Franciscan friars. However, within a year, martyrdom took the lives of his four friends. Utterly alone and abandoned in a foreign land, Jordan wrote a letter to his superiors in Persia begging them to send missionaries to India. Jordan (1280-1330) was a Catalan Dominican missionary and the first bishop of the Roman Catholic Diocese of Quilon on the Malabar Coast of India.

The first Jesuit mission in India started in Goa, the Portuguese stronghold on the Malabar Coast, with the arrival in 1542 of Francis Xavier (1506-1552).[23] Xavier's spirited quest to help the underprivileged Indian and his passion to educate the young and minister to the sick ushered a new era in zealous proselytism through the agency of the Society of Jesus.

Akbar the Great, Assembly with Jesuits, c 1605. By Nar Singh.

From the court of Emperor Akbar in Fatehpur Sikri near Agra in 1579, word came to the Jesuits in Goa that the great Mughal wanted Christianity explained to him. "Three fathers were chosen for this exciting mission:

Rodolfo Aquaviva, thirty-year-old, gentle and prayerful nephew of [General] Claudio Aquaviva, Francisco Henriquez, a Persian convert from Islam, and Antonio de Monserrate, a Catalonian."[24] They arrived in Fatehphur Sikri on 17 November that year, but by 1583, Father Aquaviva, the only Jesuit left in Fatehpur, was recalled to Goa by his superiors after it was determined that the goal of converting Akbar "had long appeared to be a hopeless task."[25]

In 1637 Urban VIII sent the Theatines[26] to Bijapur and established the Vicariate Apostolic of Idalcan (Bombay), a part of the bishopric of Goa, to which were added the kingdoms of Pegu (Bago, Burma) and Golconda in 1645. "The first titular bishops of the East were appointed in 1638."[27] Antonio de Santo Felici, titular bishop of Myra, Turkey, was put in charge of the Japan mission, and Matteo de Castro Mahalo, a converted Brahmin, was assigned as the bishop of Chrysopolis (Uskudar, east Istanbul) and as the administrator of Idalcan. However, with the Dutch victory over the Portuguese Empire in the East after the Dutch-Portuguese War (1602-1663), neither Santo Felici nor Castro Mahalo arrived at their new posts in Asia.

Thirty-one years would pass before Rome could name a titular bishop acceptable to the Dutch and English powers in India. That honor went to Costudius de Pinho of the Order of Discalced Carmelites, and, like Castro Mahalo, he was a Brahmin educated in Rome. "In practice, the Dutch allowed only Italian, Belgian, and German Catholic missionaries access to Malabar after 1663."[28]

With Lutheran influence on the rise around the world the Sacred Congregation for the Propagation of the Faith in Rome sought "political and economic support" from France which King Louis XIV, through his Finance Minister Colbert, gladly embraced, having been for a long time envious of Portuguese religious and commercial successes in the East. Beginning in the 1690's, French Jesuits arrived at the Coromandel Coast to reinforce the missions started by their Portuguese brothers in south India, and to establish a new one to the north in the Carnatic at the start of the 18th century.

On the singular theme of seeking ways to convert and baptize the poor and oppressed in India, or anywhere else, even to the point of bringing martyrdom to themselves, the Jesuits were of one voice. Their willingness to accept orders and to live in extreme poverty was inspired by Ignatius of Loyola who declared that the Society of Jesus was founded for those desiring to soldier for God: *todo el que quiera militar para Dios*. He never ordered any distinctive garb for them. The dress of a "priest in good standing" in the locale would suffice and be in keeping with the vow of poverty Loyola's organization professed. Many did so, hoping for an assignment to the remote missions in the south of India—Mysore, Madurai, and Carnate.

PART TWO –

THE EASTER EFFECT

Though I have all faith, so that I
could remove mountains,
and have not charity,
I am nothing.

1 Corinthians 13:2
St. Paul

START OF MISSIONARY WORK

Religious missions to foreign lands may have begun with the ministry of Paul, the Apostle. Richard Tarnas asserts that the spectacular achievements of St. Paul (4 BC? - 62/64 AD) in Asia Minor (Anatolia) and Greece sparked the creation of the foreign missions, the sole purpose of which was to "expand its gospel beyond the confines of Judaism."[29] Jewish by birth but a Roman citizen, Paul, then known as Saul of Tarsus, was on his way to Damascus when he was overcome by a vision of the risen Christ. Struck down from his horse, the once fervent persecutor of Christians in Jerusalem converted to become a passionate supporter of Christianity.[30]

From the beginning of his ministry Paul recognized Jesus' unique religious message: He was God's anointed one—the world's Lord and Savior. An earlier supporter of Judaic orthodoxy, Paul became the new religion's leader together with the small and fervent group of Jewish disciples who believed in the resurrected Christ.

His "Letter to the Romans," said to have been written when Paul was in Corinth, sought to justify to a minority of Christians living in Rome that the new faith was a "more perfect covenant" than what the Jewish Christians were advocating from the Old Testament. "For him, the purity of the religious understanding of Jesus as the source of salvation would be seriously impaired if Gentile [non-Jewish] Christians were obligated to amalgamate the two religious faiths."[31]

Along with the Apostle John, Paul continued preaching in Ephesus in 53 AD to gain followers for the new and evolving religion. About the same time Mark, the Evangelist, traveled to Egypt and founded the Church of Alexandria—today the Coptic Orthodox Church and the Greek Orthodox Church of Alexandria. He is honored as the founder of Christianity in Africa.

According to tradition, around this time the Apostle Thomas landed on the Malabar Coast of India having followed the trade route from the Mediterranean to the Persian Gulf. He is said to have established the first Syrian Christian mission in Kerala in southwestern India. The "Doubting Thomas of the Resurrection," who had to probe Jesus' wounds to believe, is the most revered Christian saint among the Thomas Christians in India since it was he who founded their church in 52 AD. Several unauthenticated sources relating to the Apostle's missionary journey out of Jerusalem assert that he proceeded to Mylapore on the Coromandel Coast. He spent the rest of his life there until his martyrdom in 72 AD. Today, the National Shrine of St. Thomas Cathedral in Mylapore is built over the saint's tomb in the section of the city called San Thomé.

The universal message contained in the Acts of the Apostles[32] and the successes of thousands of churchmen who spread the gospel in the early years of Christianity gave its followers reason to hope that pagan practices would cease. Indeed, after the Romans destroyed the Jewish temple in Jerusalem in 70 AD, Christianity embraced the wisdom of the Apostles to rid the world of polytheism, animal worship, and temple sacrifices. Over centuries, Tarnas wrote, "something like a spiritual crisis appears to have arisen in the culture" of the peoples in Asia Minor, Egypt, Greece, and Rome itself. This crisis of the spirit encouraged its members to reexamine their personal significance and life's meaning in the light of the salvation offered them through faith in Jesus Christ.

In Constantinople, the capital of the eastern Roman Empire, Constantine the Great accepted Christianity in 324 AD. Having reorganized the Empire and united the eastern and western divisions under his rule,

Constantine essentially converted the whole of the Holy Roman Empire to Christianity.[33] Constantinople became the largest and wealthiest city in Europe and a repository for Christianity's holiest relics: the Crown of Thorns and the True Cross.

In 325 AD Constantine convened the first meeting of Christian church representatives since the crucifixion. Called the Council of Nicea, held in what is today Iznik, Turkey, it established the universal Christian declaration of faith in the Holy Trinity first expressed by St. Peter and St. Paul more than two centuries earlier. The Council also established that Easter would be held on the first Sunday after the first full moon occurring on or after the March equinox, as it was on the Sunday that the first Christians encountered the Risen Lord.

Early Christian leaders resolved to reveal to the world their new faith—one that rejected the worship of nature, human sacrifices, and the belief in the divinity of the stars and other heavenly bodies. Almost no one in those days who spoke of the Christian faith, or even carried it in his heart, escaped ridicule and persecution. John Chrysostom, appointed Archbishop of Constantinople in 397 AD, epitomized such a man. An eloquent public speaker and defender of the spiritual and temporal needs of the poor, he became unpopular with the city's wealthy citizens and clergy against whom he spoke for their lavish lifestyles and pagan ceremonies. He railed against their abuse of wealth and personal property, reminding them of what Jesus had said: "Whatever you have done to the least of my brothers you have done it also to me."

Four hundred years would pass before Constantinople felt the fury from adherents of Islam determined to spread their faith beyond the frontiers of the Levant. By then Constantinople was at the forefront of the long struggle between Islam and Christianity for the true faith. On 29 May 1453 after waging innumerable sieges and battles against European Crusaders,[34] the Ottoman Turks finally succeeded in removing "the bone in the throat of Allah," and obliterated a millennium of Christian existence in Western Europe's most iconic city-state.[35]

Despite the threat of Islam's spread, early Roman Catholics persisted in their zeal to bring their religion to all corners of the world. Their devout faith drove missionaries, such as Pierre Taillandier, to climb the highest mountains and ford the wildest rivers, often encountering ferocious beasts, poisonous snakes, stinging insects, and the fury of heathen peoples. Frequently alone, he and missionaries like him heeded no instincts but their own. Though bent by never-ending suffering, they did not break. Their heroic examples instilled in the hearts of many converts a belief in the salvation of souls through faith.

HINDUISM AND THE CASTE SYSTEM

Conversion of a Hindu by Francis Xavier in 1542.

When the first Portuguese Jesuit missionaries led by Francis Xavier arrived in Goa, India, the Brahmins were the elites of the Hindu social order. They were easily recognized by the white cloth they wrapped around their lower torso and the thin linen cord, or *tali*, they wore over their left shoulders and across their naked chests. The *tali* signified their rank. According to Pierre Loti, a French naval officer and writer who visited India in the late 19th century, "they painted on their foreheads, between the dark grave eyes, a red disc with three white lines for the followers of Siva [Shiva], and for those of Vishnu, a red and white trident above their eyebrows, giving an almost menacing look to their expression."[36]

No one knows for sure when and how the Brahmins, who spoke Sanskrit, settled in India. A former missionary in India observed: "Strictly speaking, the Brahmin language, caste and faith are as foreign to India as Mohammedan institutions."[37] Before the Brahmins arrived, there were five vernacular languages in South India, known as the Dravidian tongues.[38]

The arrival of the Brahmins intensified the hierarchical grouping of the people in India into four ranked castes called *varnas*. One's varna determines his occupation and access to wealth, power, and privilege. The Brahmins, usually priests, intellectuals, and teachers are at the top of the rankings, then the Kshatriyas, or political leaders and soldiers. They are followed by the Vaishyas, or merchants. The fourth are the Shudras: laborers, farmers, artisans, and servants.[39]

In south India, the Tamils, many of whom are Shudras, are widespread on the Coromandel Coast of the peninsula. Among the Shudras are gardeners, carpenters, barbers, porters of money (coins), and letter carriers. "Each village in southern India has one or more families whose members have the exclusive right to practice their profession [be it gardener or carpenter, for example]," wrote the Indologist, Eugène Burnouf, professor of Sanskrit at the Collège de France. Rarely would a member of one profession marry outside of it.

Most Hindus are loath to touch a dead animal, above all beef flesh, yet some Shudra tribes did wear sandals containing cow or horse leather— wooden clogs, *padukas,* with a leather loop or a peg between the first and second toes. "Brahmins and the 'Vishnu and Shiva' cult devotees [wear these sandals and] … the Catholic missionaries adopted them."[40]

All who worked with cow leather, even though they were Shudras, were classified as pariahs for no other reason than they had handled a part of a sacred animal. Thus, they were scorned and despised as the lowest of men. Heredity played a big part in the lives of Hindus, and seldom could a lower caste person aspire to step up the ladder of success to another caste, especially if he belonged to the lowest caste.

The Europeans who ate beef prepared by a Hindu, besides committing the most egregious of sins by participating in the killing of a sacred animal, were also considered to be lower than those the Hindus called pariahs, the outcastes.[41]

A pariah could be severely punished just for looking his master in the eye. On the other hand, if a Brahmin took advantage of an outcaste woman, he would be better off retreating to the hills and living a life of renunciation as a hermit. The smell of her body on his would have polluted his dharma[42] and robbed him of his status as a power broker in his community.

Ignatius of Loyola, Martin Luther, and the Birth of the Society of Jesus

St. Ignatius of Loyola, French School, 16th century.

The Jesuit Society came into existence in 1534, long after the discovery of the New World. The founder, Ignatius of Loyola (1491-1556), the Patron Saint of all Jesuits, was born Iñigo de Oñaz y Loyola. A Basque from the province of Guipúscoa, he was the youngest of eleven children. In 1521, while zealously defending a citadel in Pamplona against the French, Ignatius was wounded by a cannon shot that broke the young officer's leg. He almost bled to death except that some French soldiers, impressed by how he conducted himself against great odds, took him to a hospital after the battle. During his long convalescence, the dashing former courtier and captain underwent a remarkable conversion to dedicate the rest of his life to the service of God.

To keep his mind occupied during his recuperation, Ignatius read the histories of martyrs that he found in his room in Manresa, near Barcelona. One of the many religious books he discovered was called the *Passion of our Lord*. On reading the story of the greatest of the martyrs, he made up his mind—he vowed his body and soul to follow closely in Jesus' footsteps. In Manresa he became a penitent, begged alms for the poor, and continued writing his *Spiritual Exercises*, a compilation of notes and meditations from his readings that eventually defined him throughout his life.

Having sufficiently recovered the strength of his shattered leg, Iñigo (he started using the name Ignatius in 1537 out of devotion to St. Ignatius of Antioch) made a pilgrimage to the nearby monastery of Santa Maria in Montserrat. There, having reached a momentous decision, he hung his arms on a pillar and pledged to forsake his past and become the man he believed God wanted him to be. The lame mendicant would later tell six of his ardent followers one early morning in a chapel in Montmartre near Paris: "We will not be the warriors of the sword, but of the word; we will preach to men; we will teach children; we will make Christians by precepts and by education."[43]

Within ten months of his injury in Pamplona, Ignatius judged that he was well enough to begin a pilgrimage to Jerusalem. On his way he stopped in Rome to humbly seek the Pope's blessing. Throughout his journey Ignatius maintained a program of great austerity—begging for his food and often sleeping at the mercy of the elements.

However, Ignatius' desire to stay in Jerusalem for the rest of his life would be unfulfilled. Relations between Christians and Muslims there were tenuous at best. So, he returned to Spain and entered the University of Barcelona in 1526 to study for the priesthood. With a firm resolve to help others, the contemplative Spaniard sought a deeper understanding of who he was and why his life had been spared in Pamplona. Over the next several years, homelessness and poverty notwithstanding, Ignatius mastered Latin while caring for the sick in nearby hospitals and teaching catechism to children in Barcelona, Alcalá, and Salamanca.

Ignatius did not fare well in the Spain of those days. His pursuit of theological and intellectual advancement at the Ximenes University in Alcalá put him at odds with Spanish Inquisitors. They saw in the long-haired and pilgrim-attired Basque leader a threat to the philosophy and theology of men such as Peter the Lombard. Peter was a leading scholastic theologian and bishop in the twelfth century. His work became the basic textbook for the education of university theologians from the 13th to the 16th century. Ignatius opposed some of Peter's controversial views contained in his seminal work, *Four Books of Sentences*,[44] which also ran counter to the more conservative doctrines of some theologians in the Vatican. For that Loyola was told to desist from teaching, publicly and privately, under pain of excommunication.

Having left Spain to avoid persecution in his own country,[45] Ignatius of Loyola and six close companions, whom he met while studying at the University of Paris,[46] put themselves at the disposal of the Pope. Fourteen years after the incident in Pamplona, the lame, but indomitable, forty-three-year-old had finally gathered around him in Paris the core of his organization—the fruit of his painful journey to discover what God intended for him to do.

They met before daybreak in the chapel of Saint Denis at the summit of Montmartre on 15 August 1534, the Feast of the Assumption of the Blessed Virgin. The men wore almost identical attire, peculiar to poor students enrolled in the University of Paris. Among them was an ordained priest, Pierre Favre, having the appearance of a French man; "all others, including the cripple, bore on their dark-complexioned countenances the impress of the Spanish race, which then shared with us the empire of the world. Francis was the first king; Charles V, emperor; Columbus had just discovered an unknown half of the earth,"[47] the Americas.

What did Ignatius know about the Spanish discovery of the Americas? Even as the treasure fleets from the New World brought to Europe, and to Spain in particular, silver and gold from the Americas, Ignatius' unfortunate accident left him with no other concern save salvaging his ruined life. It seemed his future would not amount to anything. In fact, in May of 1521, while Ignatius was delirious and near death from his wounds, Hernán Cortés was laying siege to Tenochtitlán, the seat of the last Aztec Empire.

* * * * *

Toward the 15th century new discoveries and scientific claims about the solar system began conflicting with Catholic dogma that required one to possess a much deeper faith in revelation than in reason. A spiritual malaise slowly creeped into people's certainty that the chaos on the earth and in the skies was the work of their ancient gods. The apparent motion of the sun or the moon, or the diurnal rotations of certain heavenly bodies, made better sense to them if used to plan the seasons in their lives. According to the new scientific dogma, the earth and all the other planets revolved around the sun and not the other way round! Lightning did not come down to earth hurled by an angry Jupiter or Zeus, but as an electrical discharge caused by nature.

Many now felt "compelled to transform their lives, to atone for their sins and the sins of others, and to secure eternal bliss by turning their backs on ordinary pleasures."[48] The intellectually conflicted, many of whom lived in monasteries and convents, practiced self-flagellation. Even Ignatius lashed his own back to bring pain to the flesh as a way of imitating Christ's suffering.

At the University of Pisa, young Jesuits would recite a Latin prayer every day to purge atomism—the belief that the universe was formed by the forces of ever moving atoms—and to claim that the structure and beauty of things were the work of God. "Faith must take precedence among all the other laws of philosophy," declared a Jesuit spokesman, "so that by what established authority, the word of God may not be exposed to falsity."[49]

* * * * *

In 1537 Ignatius and his six companions, all newly ordained, gathered near Venice so they might sail to the Holy Land. They had promised God that after finishing their theological course they would undertake a voyage to serve Christendom in the heart of Jerusalem, troubled by a never-ending conflict between the Cross and the Crescent. Though they waited a year, the ship did not come. Taking this disappointment as a sign from heaven, they instead went to Rome and placed themselves at the pope's feet, hoping he would send them to the Indies. "The pope gladly accepted this magnanimous offer. Pierre Favre interpreted this event as the quasi-foundation of the Society of Jesus."[50]

Another year would pass for these dedicated men to decide upon the nature and structure of their Society and to complete the rigorous requirements for papal approbation. Ignatius himself drew up the defining documents, and although brief, they "forecast the spirit of the future Jesuit *Constitutions*."[51] Notwithstanding initial opposition by some cardinals to the formation of a new religious order, letters of commendation flowed into the Vatican from persons of influence who had seen the work Ignatius and his men had accomplished. Mainly looking after the advancement and salvation of souls anywhere they were needed, the new organization professed vows of poverty, chastity, true faith, and obedience to the pope.

On 27 September 1540 Pope Paul III gave his full approbation to a canonical order in the Bull *Regimini militantis ecclesiae*. Thus, the Society of Jesus was founded, and its members became known as Jesuits.

When on 14 March 1540 Ignatius informed Francis Xavier that he was to go to Goa instead of his close associate Nicolas Bobadilla who had fallen ill, Xavier's reply was as expected: "Fine. I'm your man." Appointed as an Apostolic Nuncio in Lisbon in 1541 before his departure, Xavier, then thirty-five years old, was given authority over all the Portuguese clergy in

India. He preached and converted thousands to the faith in Goa and along India's southeastern shore above Cape Comorin. Before leaving for Amboina in the Moluccas and eventually ending his ministry in China, Xavier paid homage to the tomb of St. Thomas in Mylapore.

Of Ignatius' original six companions, Francis Xavier, a man said to possess the gift of miracles, heroically inaugurated Jesuit evangelization of remote areas in India and Asia.

⋆ ⋆ ⋆ ⋆ ⋆

Also in the first half of the 16th century, on the eve of All Saints' Day 31 October 1517, an Augustinian theologian named Martin Luther posted his Ninety-five Theses to the door of the Castle Church in Wittenberg—an act that is often cited as the beginning of the Protestant Reformation. This obscure monk, who initially wanted reform and not reformation, accused the Church of reducing a once "vibrant faith to rituals and obligations, mediated by Church authorities and performed under the threat of corporal punishment."[52] He railed against Papal power: "Spiritual law was merely an invention of the papacy, designed to frustrate laypeople from reforming the Church; the authority of Scripture must come before that of the pope; anyone can call a council when the need arises, and those most suitable to do so are the temporal authorities."[53]

A few years after Luther posted his Ninety-five Theses, the worsening religious feud coalesced in Wittenberg. Armed people began attacking priests' houses. All over Germany monks and nuns, having read Luther's declaration that faith could not be forced on anyone nor be compelled by any religious authority, ran out from their cells in monasteries and convents.

Luther's "Sermon on Indulgencies and Grace," sparked outrage as his message spread across Germany through two dozen printings between 1518 and 1520. What started out as strictly theological and procedural debate of church activities, the most egregious of which was the sale of indulgencies,[54] would become a social and political conflict that forever split European Catholic hegemony.

The Peasants' Revolt in Germany signaled the beginning of the religious wars in 1524 when the theologian Thomas Müntzer led a massive rebellion of farmers against the feudal aristocracy in southwestern Germany.[55] Martin Luther, increasingly fearful for his life, opposed the "murderous, thieving hordes of peasants." He sought and found protection from the princes of the German aristocracy, the same people who once defended the papacy but now opposed it. In the ensuing war against superior armies, 75,000 of the insurgents were slaughtered. Müntzer was captured, killed, and his head was displayed on a pikestaff.

Religion was an affair of the state and kings. Henry VIII, bedeviled by lack of a male heir, declared himself head of the newly established Church of England when Rome refused to annul his marriage to Catherine of Aragon so he could marry Anne Boleyn. Thomas More, the king's lord-chancellor, was beheaded after he refused to acknowledge Henry as head of the new Protestant church. But in 1553 when Mary, the daughter of Henry and Catherine, came to the throne, she ordered the beheadings and burning at the stake of hundreds of Protestants who refused to recognize her attempt to restore Roman Catholicism in England. The slaughter earned for Queen Mary the sobriquet of "Bloody Mary."

Though the Lutheran attack on the Papacy unleashed a torrent of destruction and abuse by disgruntled Catholics themselves, Martin Luther still believed in the real presence of Christ in the bread and wine during the sacrament of Communion. But, against his opponents who passionately believed in the Catholic Church, he declared that the pope was not only the Antichrist but also a sodomite and a transvestite. In his later years Luther also unleashed violent tirades that belied his deep anti-Semitism, asserting that the Jews were filled with the devil's excrement. "The Devil... emptied his stomach again and again, that is a true relic, which the Jews, and those who want to be a Jew, kiss, eat, drink and worship."[56]

Ignatius of Loyola represented a formidable stumbling block in the way of Luther's Reform movement.[57] He was uncompromising in his defense of the Catholic Church and of the true faith. Of Martin Luther, Ignatius said: "It is the orgy of the beast in human shape, who accuses the Blessed Virgin of impurity, and the true God of falsehood; they reject the Mass, that is to say Jesus Christ; these men who call themselves Christians, and more than Christians, since they pretend to reform Christianity, by overthrowing the altar of the insulted Christ, and his dishonored Mother."[58] And of the king of England, he asserted: "Henry VIII, the knight of the axe, between the assassinations of two queens, finds time to write pamphlets, wherein he calls Rome a harlot, because Rome refuses to whiten the nuptial bed which he has prostituted and steeped in blood."[59]

Seldom is a man's existence more than a coincidence in the times to which he belongs. Ignatius of Loyola's life exemplified the honor that only a few can claim. He lived during a period when two serious problems shook the Roman Catholic Church to its very foundations. First, the pope needed someone strong and loyal to counter Lutheran charges that the Church was being undermined by Italian aristocrats and influence peddlers. Second, the pope also wanted an organization that would stimulate and strengthen new ideas on how to expand Catholicism not only in Europe but throughout the world. He found both in the Jesuit Order and in Ignatius of Loyola, the first Jesuit General.

Ignatius' arrival in Rome could not just have been coincidental—it was downright miraculous. In 1539, upon seeing the future saint of the Catholic Church, Pope Paul III exclaimed: *Hic est Dei digitus!* ("Here is the finger of God!"), an apparent reference to Michelangelo's fresco "The Creation of Man" on the ceiling of the Sistine Chapel.

Soon new pastoral and doctrinal guidelines were transmitted all over Europe and beyond the New World via Jesuit Colleges. Whether as a reaction to the Protestant movement or the demands within the Roman

Catholic Church itself, the Counter-Reformation had gathered impetus from Loyola's organization.

* * * * *

The consequences of the religious wars and political revolution that convulsed Germany, Holland, Spain, England, and eventually France in the 16th century, slowed down Jesuit initiatives. Since the 1550s successive French monarchs fought for and defended the Jesuits, but Parliament in the time of Francis II, supported by the Huguenots (French Protestants), refused to legitimize the Society of Jesus[60] by denying it Royal letters patent.[61]

Some of the conflicts were motivated by deep religious enmity between Catholics and Protestants. Others, notably those initiated by Spanish and French monarchs, were motivated by resentment of the pope's encroachment on their sovereign territories.[62]

In 1572, with relations between French Protestants and Catholic monarchs at its lowest point, a young Charles IX ordered the marriage of his sister Margaret to a Huguenot, the future King Henry IV of France, in a final bid to keep the peace. But Charles' appeasement policy miscarried, creating an opportunity for his mother and regent, Catherine de Medici, to order the assassination of the Huguenot leaders at her daughter's wedding in Paris. The event known as the St. Bartholomew Day Massacre, crippled their movement, and as a consequence Europe would convulse into many more wars of long duration. Famine and disease took their toll in the great cities as warring nations killed thousands of men every day thereby committing women and children to a miserable existence, if not early death.

The violence of the Reformation ceased with the Treaty of Westphalia signed in the towns of Münster and Osnabruck on January 30, 1648. It also ended several wars in Europe, including the Eighty Years' War between Spain and the Netherlands and the German conflicts that raged without stop in the continent for a hundred years.

Beginning in the late 17th century, the Age of Enlightenment continued to challenge the human spirit even as intellectualism permeated the minds of the world's greatest philosophers. The battle between science and religion, for example, focused on the unyielding position the Church held against those espousing heliocentrism. But even as Jesuits and others embarked on noble endeavors to save souls in faraway lands, Europeans continued to make horrific moral choices for themselves—follow the orthodoxy of the moment or die, not by burning fagots at the stake in a public square, but by the more humane, albeit gruesome, method of execution: the guillotine.

The Jesuits would travel the world and settle in any place where the gospel of the Lord might be spread, and the conversion of infidels might be achieved. Within a short time, Jesuit Colleges all over Europe began receiving letters from their brothers who dedicated their lives to the salvation of souls. One such Lettre Édifiante was written by Father Pierre Taillandier from Pondicherry, India, on 20 February 1711.

PART THREE –

THE DECCAN, INDIA

Lives of great men all remind us
We can make our lives sublime.
And, departing, leave behind us
Footprints on the sands of time.

A Psalm of Life
Henry Wadsworth Longfellow

ISLAM ON THE MOVE

After the death of the Prophet Mohammed in Medina in 632, his successors the Caliphs Abu Bakr (reign 632-634) and Umar (r. 634-644) forced the new faith, Islam (meaning Submission), into the four corners of the Arabian Peninsula. It was the duty of the faithful to plunder and enslave all those who did not accept the Prophet.

By the middle of the 7th century the Arabian Peninsula's remaining tribes were subdued and unified to the faith. Despite religious and partisan infighting that followed the Prophet's death, Islam's expansion was unstoppable. Under Umar's successors, Uthman (r. 644-656) and Ali (r. 656-661), Islam crossed the desert to the north, into Syria and Mesopotamia (Iraq), to the east, into Persia and the Turkic cities of Bukhara and Samarkand. During the Umayyad caliphate, the first Muslim dynasty (661-750), Islamists appeared for the first time in India with the invasion of Sindh and the Punjab. "They were the first Mohammedans to descend from the western frontier into Hindustan, their abode being up to the present day between the river Indus and Kabul."[63]

Before the end of the first millennium the whole of North Africa, known as the Maghreb, was subjugated. Egypt and Hispania (Iberian Peninsula) fell one after the other. Jerusalem, the object of Muhammed's "night dream," was seized in 638. In the squares of major cities, where citizens had capitulated in the bold belief that surrender would best conserve their way of life, a muezzin led the prayers to Allah in the manner they were heard in the holy cities of Mecca and Medina.

New sectarian denominations formed during Islam's expansion as tensions broke earlier alliances over the spoils of war, political leadership, and succession. The caliphate, which Abu Bakr of the Sunni community started in Mecca, followed Muslim law based on tradition. However, in 656 the fourth Caliph, Ali ibn Abi Talib, who belonged to the Shia or Shiite faction, claimed succession based on kinship with the Prophet Mohammed as his cousin and son-in-law.

Ibn Battuta, the 14th century Moroccan who chronicled his travels in the Middle East, India, and Asia, described the great divide[64] that existed then, and to this day, between Sunni and Shia Muslims when in 1325 he visited the mosque of Ali in Basra, southern Iraq. "This mosque has seven minarets, one of them the minaret which shakes. Or so they say, when the name of Ali ibn Abi Talib … is mentioned. I climbed up to this minaret from the top of the roof of the mosque, accompanied by one of the inhabitants of al-Basra, and I found in one angle of it a wooden handgrip nailed into it, resembling the handle of a builder's trowel. The man who was with me placed his hand on that handgrip and said, 'By right of the head of the Commander of the Faithful, Ali, shake.' And he shook the handgrip, whereupon the whole minaret quivered. I, in my turn, placed my hand on the handgrip and said, 'By right of the head of Abu Bakr, the successor of the Apostle of God, shake,' and I shook the handgrip and the whole minaret quivered. They were astonished at this. The people of al-Basra are followers of the Sunna and the Community, and no one who does as I did has anything to fear from them. But if anything like this were to happen at Mashhad Ali (in Najaf) or Mashhad al-Hussain (in Karbala) or at al-Hilla or al-Bahrain or Qumm or Qushan or Sawa or Awa or Tus, whoever did it would perish, because they are fanatical Shiites."[65]

Within two centuries after Islam reached Persia, whose Gulf shores abounded with merchants from tribes around the Arabian Sea, a new Islamic philosophy began to emerge. It was called Sufism, derived from the Arabic

Sufi, the coarse woolen garment used by heretical Muslim ascetics. Their quest to acquire an inner peace and to understand what Islam was all about, distinguished them from the orthodox followers who were content with the formal observance of Islamic law and rituals.

Writing at a time when philosophy was attacked throughout the Islamic world as secularizing and godless discipline, Averroes (1126-1198), also known as Ibn Rushd, political scientist and theologian of the Arab world, boldly argued that forbidding the philosophical discussion of Islam "is to bar the door through which scripture invites men to knowledge of God—namely, the door of rational speculation."[66] It was at this time that Sufism, that almost impenetrable mystical dimension of Islam whose adherents maintain a direct and personal experience with a deity, spread throughout the Middle East and India.

In Persia, Islam's austere monotheism started to unravel in favor of drinking, mysticism and intellectual discussions, the effects of which completely modified Islamic orthodoxy. Despite the Islamic ban on alcohol, wine drinking was widespread, and in the walled Persian gardens, or *pairi-daezas,* the Farsi word for paradise, drunken bouts sharpened the pens of poets and ignited their passions. Literature reached its apogee, for example, in the works of Omar Khayyam, considered the greatest poet and philosopher Persia ever produced.

India, in her peculiar eventful history, was invaded many times by bellicose Turco-Afghani dynastic clans with Sufi mystic traditions during the 10th and 11th centuries. They came down from their abodes in the steppes to the north and west of the Indian subcontinent.[67] These clans sought to expand their territories and dominate their rivals for economic gains.

Having settled the extent of their realms amongst themselves, five dominant late medieval period kingdoms emerged and became known as the Deccan Sultanates of Ahmadnagar, Berar, Bidar, Bijapur, and Golconda.

In 1565 the combined armies of the Shia Muslim kingdoms of Bijapur, Ahmadnagar, and Golconda reached the Deccan Plateau region in South

India and defeated the forces of the Hindu Vijayanagara Empire in the Battle of Talikota. This watershed battle finished off the last great Hindu kingdom in Vijayanagara. As a result, thousands of small Hindu enclaves arose all over South India. Though independent from the Vijayanagara, they were more accommodating to the machinations of Mughal rulers, beginning with Akbar the Great when he crossed the Narmada River into the Deccan in 1605.

THE MADURAI AND

MYSORE MISSIONS

W hen they first reached the Indian subcontinent, the vanguard of Portuguese Jesuit missionaries, following in the footsteps of Francis Xavier, did not understand nor realize how deeply ingrained the hierarchical customs of the country were. But they persevered and tried to overcome the difficulties that barred them from approaching the poorest of the poor in their missions. Not long after, the Jesuits resolved to make no distinction between castes, nor between themselves and the pariahs. Consequently, the Hindus called them *Pranguis*[68] and that epithet eventually was used to refer to all Europeans.

According to the missionaries whose letters had arrived in the West, some of the happiest moments of their lives were spent overcoming the problems of the down-trodden brought about by the oppressive caste system.

Roberti de Nobili, 16 January 1656. By Alfred Hamy, 1893.

A pattern of accommodating the privileged class was soon evident when Roberto de Nobili took charge of the Madurai mission in 1606. De Nobili, a twenty-eight year old scion of Roman nobility, quickly realized that the path to a successful evangelization was to adopt the ways and social concepts of the ruling class, the Brahmins, since he judged himself an equal in stature with them.[69] By first learning Tamil and later Sanskrit, "he also acquired a social fluidity which enabled him to move not only among his own class of Rajahs but also among the Brahmins, the Vaisyas, and the Sudras, the latter a kind of intermediate stratum which embraced the greater part of the population."[70]

But de Nobili's methods were condemned by many theologians and the Provincial for Goa and Malabar[71] who, in 1613, ordered de Nobili to stop baptizing Brahmin converts. They believed that tolerating the symbols of Hindu nobility was stretching the limits of Catholic dogma.[72]

Along the southern coasts of India, the hatred of the Hindus toward Portuguese merchants came to the boiling point when they demanded that the Zamorins, the local sovereign rulers of Calicut (Kozhikode), expel the Muslim merchants from the pepper trade.[73] Not only did the Portuguese desire to monopolize that trade, but they also tried to collect taxes by erecting toll gates leading to the Hindu temples. One day in 1549, a mob of Hindus descended on the fishing village of Vedalai, southeast of Madurai, where a young Portuguese priest, Antonio Criminali, was visiting a sizeable and flourishing Christian community. The angry men murdered all the Christian converts in the community and beheaded the Jesuit missionary.[74]

From the earliest days of the Jesuit missions throughout southern India, the desire for sanctity through martyrdom was irrepressible. For fervor and zeal, few could match John de Britto, a Portuguese of noble birth, who said upon arrival in Goa and learning he was being assigned as a seminary teacher by his superiors: "I came to India not to seek the laurels of science, but martyrdom."[75] On 4 February 1693, nineteen years after his arrival, he got his wish. Accused of having insulted the king of the Maravas, de Britto was beheaded.[76] It had angered the king that his niece's husband, a prince who had several wives but had converted to Christianity with the blessing of de Britto, was forced to leave her to prove his true faith.

De Britto's letter, dated 1669, requesting assignment to India. Photo by the author in the Jesuit Archives, Shenbaganur, 2016.

François Martin (1634-1706), the first Governor of the French East India Company, recalled the sad martyrdom of his friend Father John de Britto with these words:

> *He honored us by coming to see us in Pondicherry. Although we could not keep him with us for as long as we would have liked, we did manage to detain him for a short time. His heart always led him towards his dear Maravas, a term of affection he himself would use when referring to this people. The prohibition of the Nayak or king of the Maravas, the prospect of certain death which awaited him if he chose to return, did not reduce his zeal in the least. In the course of his arguments with the Brahmins, Father John demonstrated with blinding clarity the truth of his religion. He asked one of the catechists who had followed him, to go to Pondicherry and inform Reverend Father Tachard and myself of how his life had drawn to a close.*[77]

The Jesuits already had two large missions—one in the southernmost part of India and the other in the middle of the peninsula's thumb—when, at the start of the 18th century, they created a third one. Father Pierre de la Lane, who arrived in Pondicherry in 1703, defined the boundaries of the three missions this way in his letter dated 30 January 1709: "The first is the mission of Madurai that starts at Cape Comorin and extends to the upper reaches of Pondicherry towards 12-degree north latitude. The second is that of Mysore, a great kingdom, whose people pay tribute to the Mughal. It is north of Madurai and almost in the middle of the peninsula. The third is what is called Carnate, where Providence has assigned me. It begins at the latitude of Pondicherry; its northern border has no limit but the Empire of the Mughal, and the western side by a part of Mysore."[78]

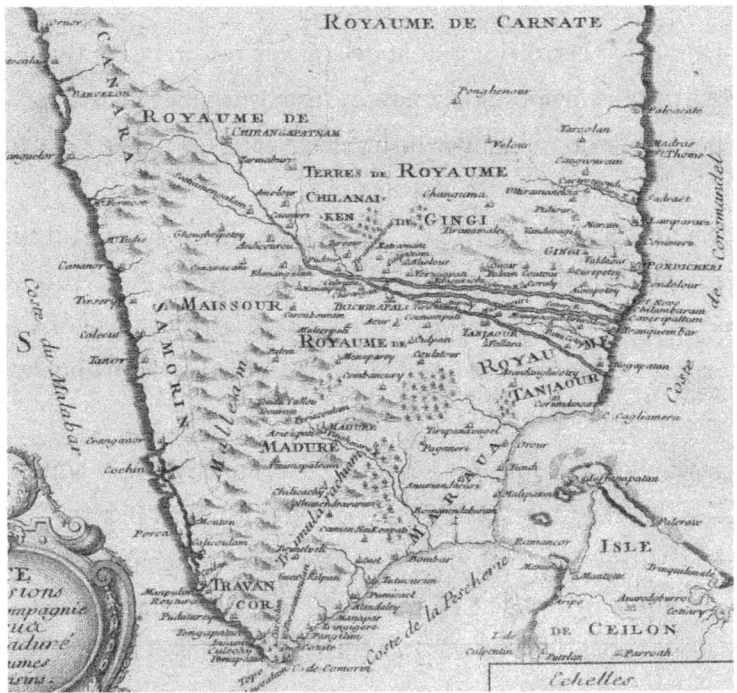

Map 2: *Carte des Missions des PP de la Compagnie de Jesus. By J V Bouchet, SJ, (1 April 1719. In LEC, Vol. 15, 1722.). Gallica.bnf.fr. (Note: Maduré = Madurai, Maissour = Mysore.)*[79]

But de la Lane's letter was also an indictment of the abuses and petty crimes of the rulers in the north and center of the Deccan.[80] "The country is greatly populated and has many cities and villages," he said. "It would have been more fruitful if the Moors [Muslims], vassals of the Mughal who has them under his control, stopped trampling the countryside with their unending aggravation. It has been almost fifty years since they conquered these lands, and they have spread out all the way to the end of the peninsula. Only a few states have conserved their old form of government: these are the kingdoms of Madurai, Marava, Trichirapali, and Gingee; all the others are governed by officials of the Mughal, except a few particular gentlemen whose provinces are left to their own governance, but they pay a large tribute and live in such dependence that their powers are taken away at the sign of a minor suspicion, thus they are better off as landlords of the Moors than kings of their lands."

* * * * *

Father Domenico Ferroli, SJ,[81] an indefatigable researcher in Rome and in India, said that the first Jesuit missionary to arrive in the kingdom of Mysore was Father Leonardo Cinnami, who had left Naples for Goa in 1643. Initially, he was assigned to the Canara Mission under the Archdiocese of Goa on the west coast of India. His early days were rough and unsuccessful since the Canarese imagined that Christianity and Portugal, which had controlled Goa since the early 1500s, were one and the same. Thus, they mistook Cinnami for a Portuguese—a name abominable to Hindus for they knew that the Portuguese eat cow flesh and drink wine.

Having worked for four years in the Canara Mission without visible success, Cinnami obtained the permission from his Provincial, Father Manuel de Mendonça, to go inland and away from Canara, where he was unknown. Imitating Roberto de Nobili in Madurai, he dressed as a Sanyasi and proceeded eastward over the ghats to the kingdoms of Bittur, Narsapura, Siringapatna (the capital of Mysore), until Satamangale on the southern border of Mysore and Madurai. It was his desire to meet with Father de Nobili there and find inspiration from the man "who had been led by God to find a new way of life, never thought of by our first Fathers, by which he opened the path of conversion for Brahmins and men of other castes, who despised the Europeans very much."

Though unable to meet de Nobili, Cinnami met Father Martinez,[82] who had come up from the mission in Madurai and had waited ten days for him. "I was so glad to see a man, who, for the love of God, had been imprisoned four times, beaten, banished, and tormented to death. I reverenced him as a living martyr," said Cinnami.

Despite suffering many hardships, Cinnami also felt great courage and confidence that God's word would be received among the many groups of Brahmins, soldiers, and peasants he met on his journey into Mysore. In 1648, with the help of Italian and Portuguese laborers, Father Cinnami erected his first church in the small town of Bassuapura (Basapura), not far from

Siringapatna. His first converts there were a peasant, his wife and children, and their extended family.

In Siringapatna, where he stopped for six weeks after his visit with Father Martinez, Cinnami said: "… I baptized 40 adults. But so many came to be instructed that I had no time even to breathe. They did not spare me even during the night. And from what I can judge of the people of the kingdom, I hope in a short time there will be thousands of new Christians. But more missionaries are needed."[83]

Before the end of the 17th century, there were eighteen missionaries (Italian and Portuguese Jesuits) and 30,000 Catholics in the kingdom of Mysore.[84]

THE MUGHAL RULE IN INDIA

For three-hundred twenty years (1206–1526) Islamic sovereign rulers, or Sultans, ruled northern India from Delhi near the foothills of the Himalayas, a region called the Delhi Sultanate. In 1398 Amir Timur,[85] the founder of the Timurid Empire in Central Asia and better known to the world as Tamerlane (1336-1405), overthrew the Sultan of Delhi and eventually conquered northern India. Thus, Tamerlane, a descendant of Turkic and Mongol tribal leaders, laid the foundation of the Mughal[86] Empire that ruled the Indian subcontinent until the 18th century.

The new Turco-Mongol rulers established the distinctive character of Indian Islam when Tamerlane's descendant Babur (r. 1501-1530) founded the Mughal Empire after overthrowing Ibrahim Khan Lodi, the last of the Delhi Sultans, at the battle of Panipat in 1526. Thus began the dynastic line of rulers[87] known as the Mughal Emperors. The Empire reached its zenith with the defeat of the Pashtuns, nomadic clannish people in southeastern Afghanistan, by Akbar the Great (r. 1556-1605), the third Mughal Emperor. India's new rulers, with their horse-borne armies, swooped down from the north and the steppes of the Levant, marched along the Silk Road, and disrupted the flow of commerce from China to the West. They massacred entire populations and left behind the message that resistance was useless. Fleeing for their lives ahead of the invaders, millions of displaced Hindus[88] crossed the Narmada River into the hinterlands of the Deccan, a transliteration of the Sanskrit *daksina*, meaning south. Emperor Akbar continued pushing his armies to the south and east until Bengal was taken and made a *subah*, or Mughal province.

By 1605 Akbar had brought most of the Deccan's Hindu population under his control by winning the loyalty of the Rajputs[89] who were awarded appointments as *subahdars* (provincial governors) through conversions and marriage alliances. This large class of feudal gentry acquired a taste for the finer things in life. Copying their rulers, they dressed themselves opulently in the finest woven cotton such as Dacca[90] muslin, considered the "web of the woven wind" with no equal in the entire world.[91]

Akbar was a patron of literature,[92] painting, and poetry, a trait he passed on to his son Jahangir, the 4th Mughal Emperor (r. 1605-1627). Jahangir was also known as Salim, in honor of the Sufi mystic Sheikh Salim Chishti whose daughter nursed him as a child. Jerònimo Xavier, the Spanish Jesuit and nephew of Francis Xavier, who had known Akbar since 1595, said that the Emperor "entertained great hopes for the conversion of Salim."[93] Jerònimo, "wrote in Persian the life of Jesus, the *Mir'at al-quds* (Mirror of Holiness) and the life of St. Peter, among other works,"[94] and presented them as gifts to Akbar.

Jahangir's son and 5th Mughal Emperor, Shah Jahan (r. 1628-1658), built Delhi's Red Fort and the Taj Mahal, long considered the crowning achievement of Mughal architecture. According to the Portuguese Jesuits, Emperor Shah Jahan was unhappy with the Islamic religion, whose Sharia law he found too restrictive. Enjoying his riches, Shah Jahan entertained himself with music, drinking, and narcotics, which his predecessors detested or forbade. He allowed the Jesuit Fathers to argue publicly with the *ulamas*, or Muslim theologians, and to convert the Hindus to Christianity. "He delighted to listen to talk about the Gospel," according to Niccolao Manucci[95] (1638-1717), the Venetian writer who spent most of his life in India.

Aurangzeb, 6th Mughal Emperor.

Shah Jahan's policy of permitting the rise of Christianity during his reign was reversed when his son, Aurangzeb Alamgir (1618-1707), succeeded him. Aurangzeb reintroduced Sharia law, banned music at his court, and abandoned his father's legacy of pluralism. When Shah Jahan fell ill in 1657, Aurangzeb quarreled with his brothers, Dara and Shuja, over succession and engaged them in battles from the northwest of India to Bengal in the east. Aurangzeb, then governor of the Deccan, put his father under house arrest at the Red Fort in Agra until his death in 1658. Shuja fled to Arakan, in present day Myanmar, where he disappeared. Having vanquished Dara in Afghanistan, Aurangzeb had him executed upon his capture. In short, the sixth Mughal Emperor, a reform-minded and devout Sunni Muslim, avoided sharing political power or mixing socially with Hindus.[96]

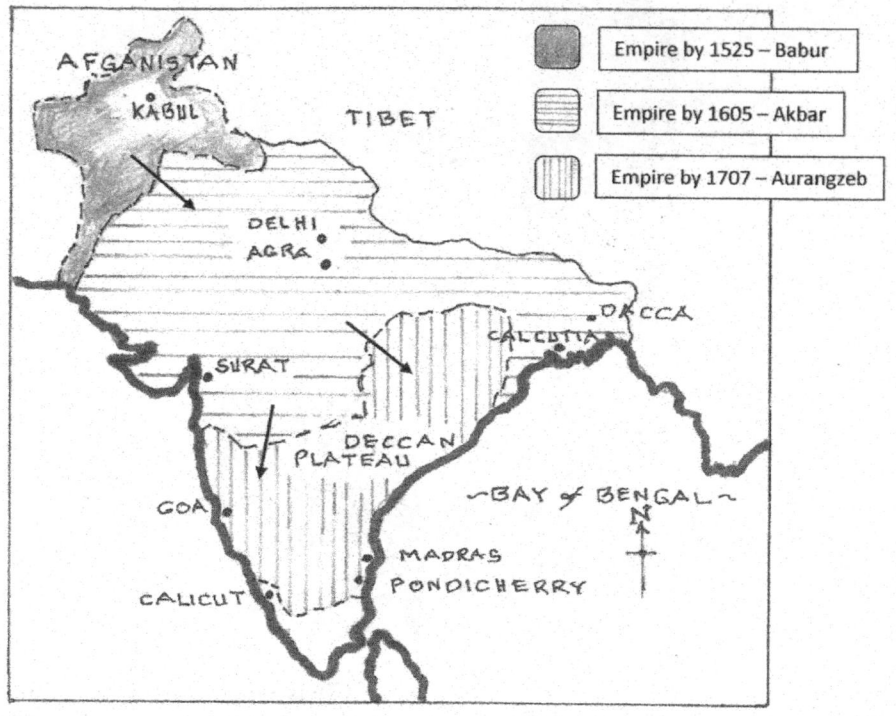

Map 3: *Expansion of the Mughal Empire in India from 1526 to 1707.*

Thereafter, the Emperor's implacable hatred for Christian converts drove him to frequently level reprisals upon the Christian "harvests," as the missionaries called their neophytes, in the Jesuit missions. Always at risk and steadfast in their beliefs and the faith that brought them to India, the missionaries tried not to provoke a confrontation. Rather, they obeyed the local *subahdars*, who were the only authorities that could keep violent Islamic retributions at bay. From his mission in Chinnabalabaram in the Carnatic, Father Le Gac wrote in 1709: "The prince ordered us to get out of the city, quickly, since it was impossible to pacify the seditious crowd who were revolting against our presence."[97]

THE MARATHA REBELLION

From the 1650s the Maratha, a Hindu rebel group from the Western Ghats[98] led by Shivaji Bhonsle (1630-1680), began crossing into central India where they posed the greatest threat to the Mughal Empire. Shivaji was the son of a Maratha officer who commanded forces under the Sultan of Ahmednagar, in western India. At the time of Shivaji's birth, power in the Deccan was held by Shia Muslim Sultanates in Ahmednagar, Bijapur, and Golconda.

Having a reputation as a skillful warrior and leader, Shivaje founded the Maratha Empire. He revived ancient Hindu political traditions by promoting the use of Marathi and Sanskrit over Farsi (a legacy of Persian domination) in all court and administration proceedings under his control. Unlike his father, he was deeply interested in religious teachings and preferred the company of Hindu and Sufi sanyasis over Muslim fundamentalists.

Shivaji's successes in battles against his enemies in the Western Ghats brought him to the attention of Aurangzeb who saw him as a threat to Mughal rule in the Deccan. Shivaji had defeated Mughal forces defending the forts in Vellore, Gingee, and Mysore. In 1677 Shivaji visited Hyderabad and signed a treaty with Abul Hasan Qtub Shah, of the Golconda Sultanate, to jointly oppose the Mughals. Until his death in 1680 Shivaji undertook aggressive campaigns to rid the Deccan of Mughal occupation.

Unable to govern by military force alone, the Mughals ruled Deccan provinces and city-states through their *subahdars*. These local governors collected the *jizya* tax (tribute) from the villagers in lieu of military service. Father Pierre de la Lane, writing from the Carnatic mission of Tarcolan[99] in 1704, made this observation: "At harvest time, the same officials order the reaping of the grains, and having them piled high, install over each pile the seal of the king. When it suits them, they come to take the grains, leaving behind but a quarter, or at times, even less for the poor farmer."[100]

Battles between Mughal forces and the Maratha rebels continued long after Shivaji died, and his son succeeded him. Between 1680 and 1707 the Maratha War of Independence against Mughal rule raged on in the Deccan, from the Narmada River, the traditional boundary between northern India and the peninsula, to Gingee (in present day Tamil Nadu) in the south. Territories repeatedly changed hands despite Aurangzeb's formidable standing army of close to a million well-equipped soldiers. Even as Aurangzeb defeated and placed the Deccan kingdoms of Bijapur (1686), Golconda (1687), and Gingee (1698) under Muslim rule, he moved his court to the Western Ghats and built a town that he named Aurangabad after himself. From there he personally led his army against the Marathas.

As a devout Sunni Muslim, Aurangzeb could not maintain the loyalty of his subjects whose temples he ordered destroyed and replaced with mosques. Though a large number converted to Islam, many reverted to worshiping the deities of their ancestors. Those who did not revert practiced Sufism, that mystical path followed by a growing community of Muslims seeking inner peace within themselves. The chaos in the Deccan, particularly in the Carnatic,[101] encouraged Jesuit missionaries based in Pondicherry to seize the moment and offer Christianity's compassionate ethos to a downtrodden people.

* * * * *

Power struggles among the rebels and would-be successors of Shivaji bedeviled the process of reconciliation within the Maratha Empire. Repeated rebel raids on British East India Company factories in Surat, a wealthy Mughal trading center on the Arabian Sea, and Madras (now Chennai) on the Bay of Bengal, provoked the English to deploy naval forces to defend their interests in these far-flung trading centers. According to Sinnapah Arasaratnam, a Sri Lankan academic, "commercial investment was increasingly supported by the deployment of military and naval force and by a more aggressive diplomatic involvement with rulers and *subahdars* of the hinterland."[102] With the decline of Portuguese power in South Asia, in particular India, and the ascendancy of the English over Dutch ambitions in the Spice Islands (Moluccas),[103] the stage was soon set for a fierce Anglo-French commercial rivalry that lasted through most of the 18th century.

THE CARNATE MISSION

Guy Tachard, 1687. By Carlo Maratta.

N o doubt every Jesuit missionary assigned to evangelize in the kingdom of Carnate, or the Carnatic, at the start of the 18th century would have met Fathers Guy Tachard (1651-1712), Superior of the French Jesuits in the East Indies, and Jean Venance Bouchet before taking on an assignment. Born in Angouleme, France, Guy Tachard taught grammar, humanities, rhetoric and, by studying math "was set for a career as a missionary."[104] He spent four years in the colonies of South America until 1685 when he departed for Siam. Father Bouchet (1655-1732), born in

Fontenay-le-Comte, joined the Society of Jesus in 1670. He, like Tachard, was sent to Siam by Louis XIV. However, Bouchet and others, including Tachard, were expelled because of a revolution in 1688. Both escaped and eventually arrived in Pondicherry the following year.

These men, pillars of the first Jesuit church in Pondicherry, began planning for the conversion of the population to the north and west of the town after they arrived[105] and sought sanctuary with the French East India Company in Pondicherry on the Coromandel Coast.[106]

In his 1703 letter from Pondicherry, Father Tachard described the new Carnate mission and the first missionaries he assigned there: "After the revolution in Siam, Father Bouchet passed through the Malabar province and was devoted to the Madurai mission, where God had given him so many blessings—of success to his zeal which he had developed at Aour, about four leagues[107] from the town of Tiruchirappalli,[108] which is today the capital of the kingdom, a church and more than 20,000 Christians whom he baptized with his own hand…. However, it was necessary for us to have a man of his experience and his ability to give the new mission of Carnate a form suitable for our purpose, I mean so that its foundations would be solid and that we would then be able to apply ourselves effectively to the salvation of souls. Father Bouchet brought with him from Aour another French missionary named Father de la Fontaine, whom he had trained himself, so that in March of 1702 there were three missionaries [Bouchet, de la Fontaine, and Mauduit] in the kingdom of Carnate." [109]

Father Pierre Mauduit, who went to the Carnate mission at the request of Tachard, came from the Madurai mission in Puliyur. Within a short time of his transfer, he laid the foundations of two churches, one in Carouvepondi and the other in Ponganour. He mastered the Telugu language, which is vastly different from the Tamil tongue spoken in the south of India, including in Pondicherry. In the face of persecution by Brahmins and Moors alike, who repeatedly stole his belongings and threw him in jail, he persevered in spreading the Gospel and baptized a great number of people in the northwest of Pondicherry. "His valor and fearlessness have made him a greater person despite these trials," according to de la Lane.[110]

After Father Bouchet was named superior of the new mission, he settled in Tarcolan, a city west of Madras that fell to the Muslims after Maratha forces could not hold the kingdom of Golconda against Aurangzeb's army. Mauduit remained in Carouvepondi while de la Fontaine was sent to Ponganour.

In 1702 Bouchet accepted two more missionaries in the new mission. The first was Father Petit,[111] who had arrived from France with Father Tachard very early that year. The other was Father de la Lane, who wrote: "I was the fifth [missionary], but poor health forced me to come to Pondicherry. I lived for three years in Tarcolan, which is a large city. I cannot repeat all the unfortunate things that I suffered there from the Indians, who, as much as I tried, always took me for a *Prangui*, and from the Moors, whose village was but a short trip from my church."[112]

Persecution of Jesuit missionaries as well as converted Christians in the missions was a daily occurrence. From the Jesuit mission in Chinnabalabaram, "a strong large Fort"[113] in the Carnate, Father Etienne le Gac wrote in 1709: "Throughout the town the gentile priests forbade giving fire or the drawing of water by anyone who came to the church: and thereby the Christians were expelled from their castes, they could no longer communicate with their relatives nor with those who engage in occupations that are the most necessary to survive. In short, by this type of excommunication they were declared infamous and were forced to leave the town. Nothing distressed us more significantly than this new development, because of the disastrous consequences it cannot fail to have for the Religion."[114]

De la Lane added in his letter: "Father le Gac, having dedicated himself for some time to the mission of Madurai, has joined Father [de la] Fontaine. He scarcely had arrived when the Moors threw him in jail, where, during a period of one month, he suffered a lot. Without any doubt he will convert many more in this mission.[115] Lastly, Father Petit is assigned to a village where he is less exposed to the fury of the pagans and the Moors. But occassionaly, he is persecuted. His church has the most congregants in all of Carnate, and he has baptized nearly all of them."

* * * * *

The five new Jesuit Fathers mentioned above successfully converted thousands to the Catholic faith despite repeated persecution by the Hindus under their Muslim rulers. In much the same way as de Nobili and de Britto did in Madurai,[116] they resolved to adopt the ways and dress of the Brahmin Sanyasi. They abstained from consuming meat, fish, and eggs. Rice, which was indispensable, was seasoned with spices like chili pepper or pimento, ginger, anise, or sprinkled with clarified butter, called *ghee*. Another plant-based spice was asafetida, or *hing*, a staple ingredient in Indian cooking,[117] used in savory dishes such as curry, or lentil dishes like *dal*. Further, "they must wash every morning in a public pond, regardless of the season and bathe again before their meal, taken once a day. They must have a Brahmin for a cook, for they could not eat food prepared by someone from a lower caste. They subjected themselves to a life of rigorous solitude because a Sanyasi never goes out unless forced by the need of others."[118]

* * * * *

The Spanish Jesuit archeologist and historian, Henry Heras,[119] wrote about the first two Jesuits who walked about 140 kilometers from Mylapore to Chandragiri in medieval Andhradesa (present Andhra Pradesh state) in the early 1600s. They went to meet the Emperor Venkatapati Raya II of the Vijayanagara Empire who was living in Chandragiri. Simon de Sa, Portuguese Rector of the College of San Thomé, and Francisco Ricio, "two western sanyasis," wore "black gowns, black sash" around the waist, "black biretta" on their heads, staffs in their right hands, and a "humble knapsack on their backs." However, according to Heras, they were advised to take off the black cassock, which made them look like *pranguis*, and put on a white one. By that time Father de Nobili had already adopted the dress of the Brahmin sanyasis in Madurai.

Eighty-eight years would pass before another Jesuit arrived in Andhradesa. He was, as mentioned above, Father Pierre Mauduit who settled in Carouvepondi (present Karuveppampoondi) in 1701 where he studied Sanskrit. Mauduit and his successors in Andhradesa adopted the white dress from the very beginning. Father Heras noted that Mauduit's host in Vellore took "Mauduit to be a sanyasi of great authority," indicating that the change from black to white dress helped the Jesuits assigned in the Carnate mission gain access to many potential converts.

* * * * *

To succeed, a missionary had to learn the language of the area he was to serve, specifically the Telugu-speaking central region north of Madurai that extended as far north as the Mughal Empire and the Tamil-speaking south-eastern region. "I have at present totally immersed myself in learning the Malabar [he meant Telugu] language," wrote Father Petit in 1702,[120] "so I can enter the new mission of the Carnate, which our French Fathers established in the model of the Portuguese Jesuits."

A new missionary also had to persevere. Father de Nobili took much care to inspire his (Brahmin) disciples to act as true Christians toward the lower classes. He insisted on making them understand that "religion was by no means dependent on caste; indeed, it must be for all, the true God being one for all; and unity of religion destroys not the civil distinction of the castes nor the lawful privileges of the nobles."[121]

While conversion of the native population throughout the world was a common endeavor of the Catholic Church, the methods by which this was accomplished by the Jesuits in India were legendary and not always sanctioned by many ecclesiastics, including the higher-ups in Rome. The *Accomodatio*, or Accommodation Method[122] of conversion in the south of India, often termed "Malabar Rites," though controversial, was the most effective way of converting the elite Brahmins who dominated the social order of the Hindus. This was the challenge faced by many Jesuits, including Roberto de Nobili and John de Britto. But, converting those in the highest-ranking caste first made it easier to approach a greater number in the lower castes, including the pariahs, whose station in life was dire and hopeless.[123]

* * * * *

As Portuguese power and presence waned toward the middle of the 17th century,[124] particularly in Goa and Madurai, France became the remaining European power capable of protecting and promoting Catholicism in India, notably Pondicherry after it became the focal point of French imperial ambitions.

The Jesuit missions were often challenged by hostile Muslim religious chiefs as well as Hindu tribal leaders who controlled large swaths of territory near where the priests established their churches and trained new Christians. Accidents, disease, and, indeed, murder often took their toll in the many inhospitable villages in the Carnatic missions. Father Mauduit, founder of a mission in Carnate and Father de Courbeville, a new member of the mission, were found dead in a hut in 1711,[125] "no doubt by enemies of the Faith who poisoned them."[126]

From Tarcolan, the capital of the kingdom of Carnate, Father Bouchet wrote: "The gentiles of the city of Tarcolan, could not tolerate the joyful birth of the Christian religion, which made new progress every day in their country. Their principals frequently met to plot our downfall and suffocate our holy religion in the cradle. The way they did it was to denounce me to the Sexsaeb [Sek Sahib], governor of the entire province, and to pique his avarice by persuading him that I knew how to make gold, that I had untold riches, and that by arresting me and putting me in a small jail cell he, together with the rest of his family, could become rich in a short time."[127] Father Bouchet, who was near death by then, was rescued by Father Pierre Martin who had come all the way from Madurai to save his close friend.

From Chinnabalabaram (now Chikkaballapur) Father le Gac, who replaced de la Lane in 1709, wrote about the difficulties of establishing a new mission in the kingdom of Carnate, which he said was modeled after those of the Portuguese Jesuits in Madurai. "We also are having the same difficulties they had to overcome, and perhaps even bigger. Just recently we had to quell one of the most violent assaults ever raised against this nascent mission. The Dasseris, who worship Vishnu, had been making vain efforts to stop the progress of evangelization for a long time. But, seeing that their occult ways were useless, they finally resolved to strike out violently, relying on their numbers and on the prince, who easily grants them everything they demand."[128]

Jesuit Scientific Endeavors

Though the primary task of the Jesuits was related to conversion, the few who were trained scientists and astronomers played an important role as the early surveyors of south India. The *LEC* (*Lettres Édifiantes et Curieuses, Écrites des Missions Étrangères*) were a source of much scientific information on the geography, botanical resources, and medical practices of India. "Jesuit interest in astronomy had to do ... with two raging Biblical themes: that of the commencement of the world and that of dating the deluge. Astronomy and the scientific interpretation of passages of the Bible would provide the hermeneutic [knowledge] to decode the precise history of these events."[129],[130]

An unfortunate event in Siam led the first French Jesuit mathematicians and astronomers to pursue their fortunes in India. In 1687 King Louis XIV had sent a team of mathematicians, which included a few astronomers, to Siam on an invitation from King Narai. Among the astronomers was Father Jean Richaud.[131] However, a palace coup the following year overthrew the king and forced the Jesuits to leave the country in a hurry. Those who reached the French colony of Pondicherry were Fathers Guy Tachard, Jean Richaud, and Jean Venance Bouchet. "We are not more than three from all [fourteen] those who arrived from Siam," wrote Richaud in 1690.[132]

Richaud (1633-1693) brought the 12-foot focus telescope he used in Siam to Pondicherry. There he made astronomical observations until his death in 1693. "Once in India, Richaud lost no time in getting down to astronomical observations. He observed the longitude and latitude of Pondicherry and the latitude of San Thomé … in Madras, where St. Thomas had stayed and died. Richaud also made observations of zodiacal light. He observed a comet in 1689. … He discovered that the bright southern star Alpha Centauri is in fact a double star. … Richaud taught astronomy at a school opened by the Jesuits at San Thomé."[133]

Louis XIV's Letters Patent (*Lettres Patentes*) to the Society of Jesus dated March 1695 laid out the king's plan that the French Jesuits "selected by their superiors to go to the Orient in the capacity of missionaries or mathematicians, had complete freedom to attend to our subjects, to urge them to start trade as well as conduct studies that can contribute to the perfection of the arts, science and navigation, and allow them to establish in the many places outlets, factories, and other establishments in the name of the Royal French Company of the Indies."[134]

On 10 January 1705 the director of the Paris Observatory, Giovanni Cassini, who was the first of the famous line of four Cassini astronomers, received a Mercator chart from the Jesuit missionary M. de May who accompanied Carlo-Tomasso Maillard de Tournon, the pope's legate to China."[135] This chart delineated "the course which the ship *Maurepas* made each day from the Canaries, which they left on the first of May 1703, to Pondicherry, where they arrived on the sixth of November, after a voyage of upwards of six months. During this voyage, they observed the variation of the needle in several places by the rising sun and setting of the sun and took care to express the same on the chart, in the proper place of their route for the day of observation."[136]

Father Jean Bouchet covered the Coromandel Coast on foot, made astronomical observations at Pondicherry, and prepared maps and plans. From this research he produced the most important map of southern India up to the 15th degree of latitude that existed in that period (Map 2). "Features are the great Indian states of the Nawabs of the Carnatic, Mysore, Madura,

Tanjore, Cannara, Marava, and Travancore. A legend at bottom left identifies 'important locations,' the residences of princes and governors, churches, and temples."[137] Bouchet sent this map to France along with his letter, dated 19 April 1719. He commented: "So far, we have only fairly confused ideas of this part of southern India located between the Coromandel and Malabar coasts: as there are only missionaries who have entered these lands, where they have been working for over one hundred years to convert the idolatrous Indians. Only they can give reliable information."[138]

The earth, as a magnetized body, absorbed Pierre Taillandier's interest throughout his voyage to India. The variation of the compass, or magnetic declination, had continued to stump the minds of early seafarers since the early 16th century when they realized that the needle did not always point to the true meridian but rather declined towards the earth's magnetic north. Taillandier made several observations in his letter, for example: "The magnetic declination of the compass, which in France is at the Northwest, slowly shifts until one arrives close to the Canary Islands and the beginning of the Americas. In this region there is no declination but approaching the Americas the needle declines towards the Northeast and keeps increasing until Vera Cruz where it measures 6 degrees."

Did Taillandier realize that the variability of declinations of the compass between two points on the earth's surface was due to the earth's asymmetrical magnetization? One cannot be sure that he did, nor that anybody else within the community of Jesuits did.[139]

The pursuit of astronomical observations in Pondicherry may well have taken a back seat after the first decade of the 18th century. Father Taillandier, who arrived there in 1710, did not report that he made any, or even that he had a telescope. Likely, he was busy, as every missionary was in the town, attending to the spiritual needs of converted parishioners and studying the Tamil or Telugu languages.

PART FOUR –

The French East India Company

It raises hope and promotes wealth.
Token, French East India Company

The Beginnings of

French Trading

L ong before the Europeans sought India's fine woven cotton cloth, rice, pepper, gems, indigo, and even copper and tin, merchants along the Coromandel Coast were already trading these commodities across the Bay of Bengal into Southeast Asia. The coastline south of Madras to Pondicherry, "was littered with a number of ports situated within a few miles of each other, all serving points of outlet for the rich textile manufacturing hinterland up to several miles deep in the interior... areas of ancient settlement and cultivation."[140]

In his book, *The History of the French in India*, George B. Malleson, an English officer during the British occupation of India in the 19th century, wrote that on 1 June 1604, during the reign of Henri IV, a Company was established under Royal letters patent to trade in the Eastern seas for fifteen years. But "disputes amongst the proprietors, and the paucity of funds, hindered the action of the Company, and the design came to nothing."[141]

French vessels leaving for the Indies to trade and found colonies, 1699.

In 1616 two merchants from Rouen, fed up with the inactivity of the Company, petitioned the King to transfer to themselves the privileges accorded the Company. In a bold quest to profit from commerce with the East they outfitted two ships that same year. This initial venture was thwarted by the Dutch in Java who captured one of the French ships but allowed the second one, commanded by Antoine Beaulieu, to sail back to France minus a considerable number of Dutch sailors who had been impressed to serve aboard it.

A second attempt to trade in the Eastern seas was made in 1619, this time with three ships under the command of newly promoted Commodore Antoine Beaulieu. His small fleet arrived at the trading port of Ache on the island of Sumatra. One ship, the 400-ton *L'Espérance* carrying a hundred and sixty-two men, disappeared on the homeward voyage. The Dutch were rumored to have sunk her off Java. Her cargo was valued at seventy to eighty thousand pounds sterling. Nevertheless, Beaulieu returned "well laden," according to Malleson, to France on 1 December 1620.

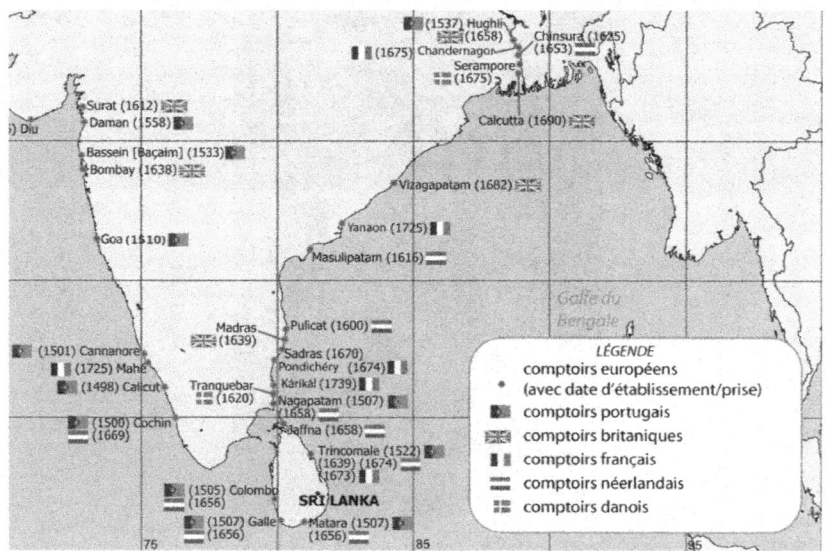

Map 4: _European Trading Posts (Comptoirs) between 1501 and 1739. By Webmaster, Association des Amis de Mahé de La Bourdonnais, 2013._

For the next forty years, the formation of a French company that could compete with the lucrative Portuguese, Dutch, and English enterprises in India (Map 4) and around the world eluded France. In the 1640's French traders reached Madagascar and established a settlement, named Fort Dauphin in honor of the young Louis XIV, on the island's southeastern coast. But the natives repeatedly resisted their presence, and though the settlers planted the crops the settlers and traders sought, the soil proved to be infertile. In the succeeding years all the island offered, at great cost to the Company, was shelter for French ships rounding the African cape on their way to trade in ports farther to the east.

Louis XIV. By Hyacinthe Rigaud, 1701.

Louis XIV was jealous of Portuguese trading dominance in the East, especially regarding the influence and advantage they wielded through their Jesuit missions in China. Eventually though, at the height of his reign, Louis XIV did position France among the world's foremost seafaring nations, as he consolidated his authority over the Church and ruled with an iron fist the aristocracy that had humiliated him as the Dauphin.

Jean-Baptiste Colbert. By Claude Lefèbvre, c 1666.

Not until the accession of Jean-Baptiste Colbert[142] as Minister and Chief Financial Officer during Louis XIV's long minority did France start to challenge its maritime rivals. Colbert transformed the French navy into an international fighting force. Aware of the potential for riches from trade with the other side of the world, he formed the *Compagnie des Indes Orientales*, or French East India Company in 1664.[143] He offered the Company a charter to trade exclusively with India for fifty years. Capitalized at 600,000 livres,[144] the new royal Company was incorporated with the assets of a St. Malo company already trading in the Arabian Sea and new investors eager to explore opportunities abroad.

That same year the Mughal Emperor Aurangzeb granted Colbert a *firman* to trade in India. This gave the French administrative and judicial rights and customs concessions. With their situation in Madagascar so dismal the Company proceeded at once to India's western coast where in 1668 it established its first textile *karkhana*,[145] *comptoir* or trading post, in Surat (Map 4).

Spices and Manufactured Cotton Cloth

French ships involved in the India trade always stopped in the Canary Islands, a Spanish colony since the late 1400s, to resupply their stores of wine, salted meats, firewood, water, and other necessities before proceeding around the African cape and taking an essential respite on Madagascar before sailing onward to India. Even with these provisions, the rough seas, hunger, and ill health often took their toll on the morale of everyone aboard.

Seeking to emulate Dutch successes in the eastern seas and assert France's naval strength, Louis XIV sent four large ships equipped for war as well as trade in March 1665. Among the passengers aboard the *Aigle Blanc* was François Martin. They reached Madagascar about four months later.[146]

Emblem of the French East India Company. "Florebo Quocumque Ferar." ("I will flourish wherever I go.")

While in Madagascar, Martin concentrated his talents on managing the French trading post.[147] Eventually, he was chosen as the first Director of the French East India Company. In that role he became the most influential personality among those attempting to establish a French empire in the East.

But the non-stop threats of the Dutch and the English to dominate the spice trade in India put France in continuous conflict with her European rivals even before she was able to secure a single trading post on Indian soil.

Having been driven away by the Dutch in their quest to establish a base for trading in Ceylon, Colbert's fledgling Company returned the favor and captured the Dutch fort in San Thomé on the Coromandel Coast in 1672.[148] Under Admiral Jacob Blanquet de la Haye French marines stormed the garrison, which was defended by Dutch marines and the forces of Golconda's Muslim king who owned San Thomé. After a brief battle the French overwhelmed the Dutch and the native defenders with only a small loss of their own men.

With the Dutch determined to retake San Thomé and conceivably scuttle French ambitions in India, the directors of the Company ordered François Martin, who had assignments as merchant and Company officer in Madagascar, Surat, Masulipatam (Machilipatnam), and Chandernagore, to communicate with Sher Khan Lodi, the governor of the possessions of the King of Bijapur and Carnate. The king had expressed willingness to open a trading center. The governor permitted Martin to purchase a plot of land for the Company on the coast of Gingee south of San Thomé.

In early 1674, just as the French had feared, San Thomé fell to the Dutch with the help of the army of the king of Golconda, a sworn enemy of Sher Khan Lodi. According to the French traveler Abbé Barthélemy Carré, who was sent to India by Louis XIV on the pretext of being a religious envoy when actually he was a clandestine agent supporting the French efforts to secure a foothold on India's Coromandel Coast: "Admiral de la Haye managed to hold out for eight months through the marvelous courage of a nation that had newly arrived from Europe and was as yet unknown in this country, namely the French, who had already slain over 20,000 men of the army sent in vain by the King of Golconda to expel them."[149] Of the French garrison's nearly six hundred defenders, sixty survived and were set free to choose their own fate.

By April of 1674 François Martin lead these sixty Frenchmen to the new outpost that he had recently obtained from Sher Khan Lodi for France's East India trade. Receiving the help of the native population, Martin put up the first palisaded defenses of the town which became known to the French as Pondichéry.

A year earlier in 1673, the French East India Company received a *firman* from Ibrahim Khan, the Muslim governor (Nawab) of Bengal, to establish a trading post on the right bank of the Hoogli (Hooghly) River in Chandernagore (Chandannagar). Several Islamic dynasties under Mughal control had ruled Bengal, that fertile north-eastern area (now comprised of West Bengal and Bangladesh) since the 13th century.

In time Pondicherry and Chandernagore became the two principal French settlements and trading posts with large warehouses that stocked an array of spices—pepper, nutmeg, mace, cinnamon, and cardamom. Silk and porcelain pieces arrived via Chinese traders despite imperial opposition at home in China.[150] Baled cotton cloth as well as rice, sugar, coffee, and tea often reached these trading counters from Nagapatam (Nagapattinam) to Baleshwar (Balasore) in the north. Because they were exquisitely made and the dyes were colorfast, painted and printed cotton cloth from Masulipatam and Pulicat were the most sought after by discriminating buyers, including worshippers adorning their divinities and nobles decorating their palaces on the Coromandel Coast.

Tisserand, or Cotton Weaver.

Over the better part of twenty years Pondicherry grew from a hamlet of a few fishermen into a bustling textile trading port. The town expanded as factories, warehouses, churches, temples, and homes were built. Almost every native house had a loom for weaving cotton thread into cloth. The fertile soil surrounding the port and into its hinterlands provided the spinners and weavers the cotton to create the finest yarn that eventually would clothe many of the feudal gentry of India, East Asia, and Europe.

Up to the middle of the 19th century India's cotton cloth would also dress the poorer classes of South and East Asia. Henri Pirenne, a Belgian writer and historian, stated: "The riches of Asia were incomparably greater than those of the European states. Her industrial techniques showed a subtlety and a tradition that the European handicrafts did not possess. And there was nothing in the more modern methods used by the traders of the western countries that the Asian trade had to envy. In matters of credit, transfer of funds, insurance, and cartels, neither India, Persia, nor China had anything to learn from Europe."[151]

However, there was always the danger of being swept up in India's internal civil wars, not to mention European rivalries, for control of the lucrative trade in spices and manufactured cotton cloth. François Martin often wrote about the battles being waged at Pondicherry's backdoor by the Marathas and the Muslims under the Mughal Emperor Aurangzeb and about his dilemma of following "a neutral course between the Moors and the Marathas."

With every passing day the Marathas were retaking lost territories near the French fort while being pursued by the forces of Aurangzeb. In August of 1692 Maratha forces attacked a group of fifty Muslims, including merchants and their assistants who had encamped on the riverbanks near the sea south of Pondicherry. During the back-and-forth skirmishes, the wounded sought medical help in the Jesuit House outside the western wall of the fortress. "The Jesuits took in all the wounded, irrespective of the side to which they belonged. Sometimes, the number of patients here went up to as many as fifty. Many of the remedies provided by the Jesuits were not available to us at the fort. The Jesuits had rich returns for their charity, for some of these unfortunate men who had been mortally wounded accepted our religion prior to their demise."[152]

François Martin, as the Governor-General of French India, was particularly concerned about the situation at Gingee, the most impregnable fort in India, since in 1698 Aurangzeb finally succeeded in taking it from the Maratha king Shivaji. Only three leagues to the northwest of Pondicherry, Gingee was by no means totally subdued and marauding rebel forces continued to fight throughout Martin's almost forty-year presence in India.

THE DUTCH CAPTURE PONDICHERRY

Pondicherry[153] was at the intersection of the main road from Gingee to the sea and the road running parallel to the coastline. The natural terrain surrounding Pondicherry made it easy to defend—to the south was the Ariankuppam River, to the north were the marshes and sand dunes, and to the east the roadstead was shallow which prevented ships from approaching in the dark of night. A prolonged naval bombardment, unopposed, would turn out to be Pondicherry's Achilles' heel, however.

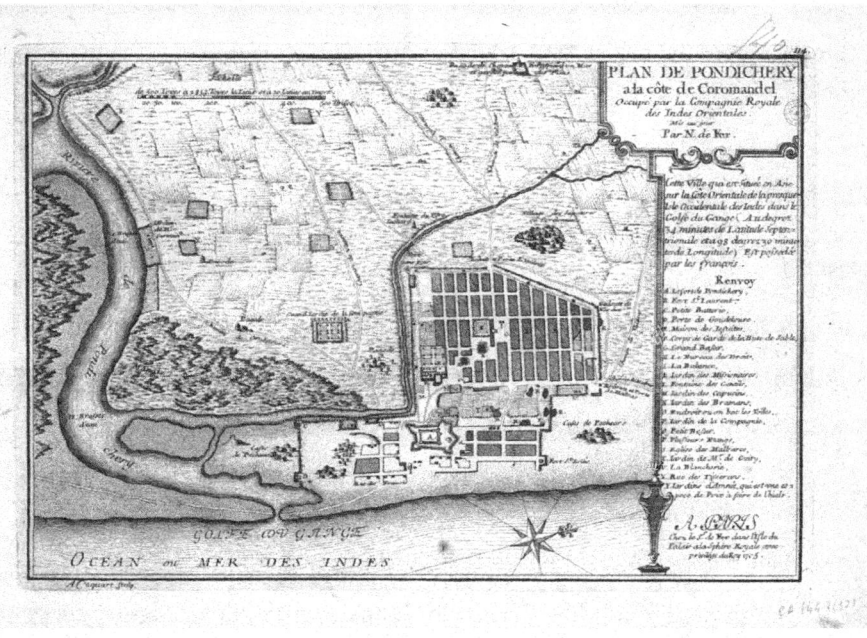

<u>Map 5</u>: *Plan de Pondichéry a la côte de Coromandel. By N. de Fer, 1705.*

The high sand dunes along the shoreline encouraged the locals to build permanent houses. The little river, the Petit Canal, passing through the town provided irrigation for growing crops and fruit trees—making it an ideal place for the different Indian communities to work and live peacefully, each according to his status in the town's hierarchical society.

As early as August of 1689 François Martin reported his premonitions about the future of the burgeoning French enterprise in the south of India. "Once again, the Dutch began to scheme against us at the Gingee court. They had managed to win over all principal Brahmins. The avarice of these men, whetted by the presents which they had already received and additional ones which they had been assured would follow, made them vigorously promote Dutch interests at the court of the Governor-General."[154]

"Our fears regarding the Dutch intentions proved only too well founded. We were reliably informed that Laurens Pit[155] had received orders from Batavia [Jakarta] to secure the eviction of our Company from Pondicherry. To ensure the success of the onslaught, five ships were being sent out charged with ammunition. Forces consisting of European, Macassar, and Bughi troops had also been embarked."[156] In the summer of 1693 Laurens Pit, Jr, commanded eleven Dutch ships that arrived off Nagapatnam, Dutch Coromandel's busiest port, located one hundred fifty kilometers south of Pondicherry.

From 23 August until 6 September 1693 Pondicherry held fast against the Dutch onslaught directed primarily at the fort. The Catholic Church was destroyed by a cannon shot on the first day of the attack. "The defense of Pondicherry became impossible—our native soldiers left their posts," wrote François Martin. "The guard at the battery on the seashore should be withdrawn. We were afraid that if we left the men there, they would desert, and the four pieces of cannon would thus be abandoned. The enemy would then be able to seize this position and deploy the cannon against us. We decided to split the cannon and blow up the large ammunition store, which was by the seashore."[157]

By 7 September 1693 all was lost; the Dutch captured Pondicherry and ordered many French East India Company and military officials, as well as

Jesuit priests, to return to Europe.[158] The mercantile and military personnel at Pondicherry were evacuated aboard six vessels: three departed for Batavia and three for the island of Ceylon.

François Martin and his wife embarked on 24 September for Batavia and temporary exile with their granddaughter, Agnes Marguerite Desprez. Accompanying them were Jesuit priests led by Father Tachard, Capuchin Father Laurent, and some soldiers and Company personnel. Tachard and other priests were eventually sent back to Europe on a ship bound for Holland, despite Martin's intercession that Tachard be allowed to proceed to China as was his wish. Martin, with his family, chose to return to Chandernagore, Bengal, on 15 February 1694, where he continued directing the affairs of the Company.

＊ ＊ ＊ ＊ ＊

The 1697 peace treaty of Ryswick, which settled the conflict begun in 1689 between France against Great Britain, the Holy Roman Empire, Spain, Italy, and the Dutch Republic, compelled the Dutch to return Pondicherry to the French with its fortifications intact. François Martin returned to Pondicherry from Chandernagore where he was renamed Director General of French affairs. He immediately began building a much larger walled town and facilities, including a new hospital by the seashore, to care for the growing European community and their dependents.[159]

But, with the outbreak of the War of the Spanish Succession in 1701, Martin realized his town needed an even more robust fortress and defensive walls to repel any future invasion by Dutch or English forces. In 1702, he began construction of Fort Louis, a star-shaped fortress conceived by Marquis de Vauban and executed by the engineer Denis de Nyon. Vauban was Louis XIV's military advisor, and a preeminent French architect known for his skill in designing fortifications and conducting sieges on enemy defenses. Save for the completion of government buildings, staff residences, and storehouses within the new walls, the fort was essentially finished[160] when Martin died on the last day of 1706.

PART FIVE –

TILTING AT WINDMILLS

We never know how high we are
Till we are called to rise
And then if we are true to plan
Our statures touch the skies.

We Never Know How High We Are
Emily Dickenson

JESUIT CONUNDRUM IN PONDICHERRY

The ten years that preceded the arrival of Fathers Taillandier and Bonnet in 1710 were the busiest and the most controversial in the history of Pondicherry and the French East India Company. With the peace treaty of Ryswick and the reoccupation of the town, François Martin resumed his former post as Governor and President of the Superior Council of Pondicherry. He gradually expanded the town's size by implementing the Dutch "grid pattern" to establish organized work areas and attract more craftsmen and merchants. By February of 1700 "there were 500 [weaving] looms in the town, and, very likely, all these artisans had set up houses in the northern part of the town designed by the Dutch," often referred to as Black Town.[161] The Dutch grid also placed the Europeans in the section closest to the fort and the seashore, the White Town. The Jesuit residence (Map 6 – B, D) was outside the western wall of the fort in the section designated Black Town where Tamil-Hindu craftsmen and their families resided.

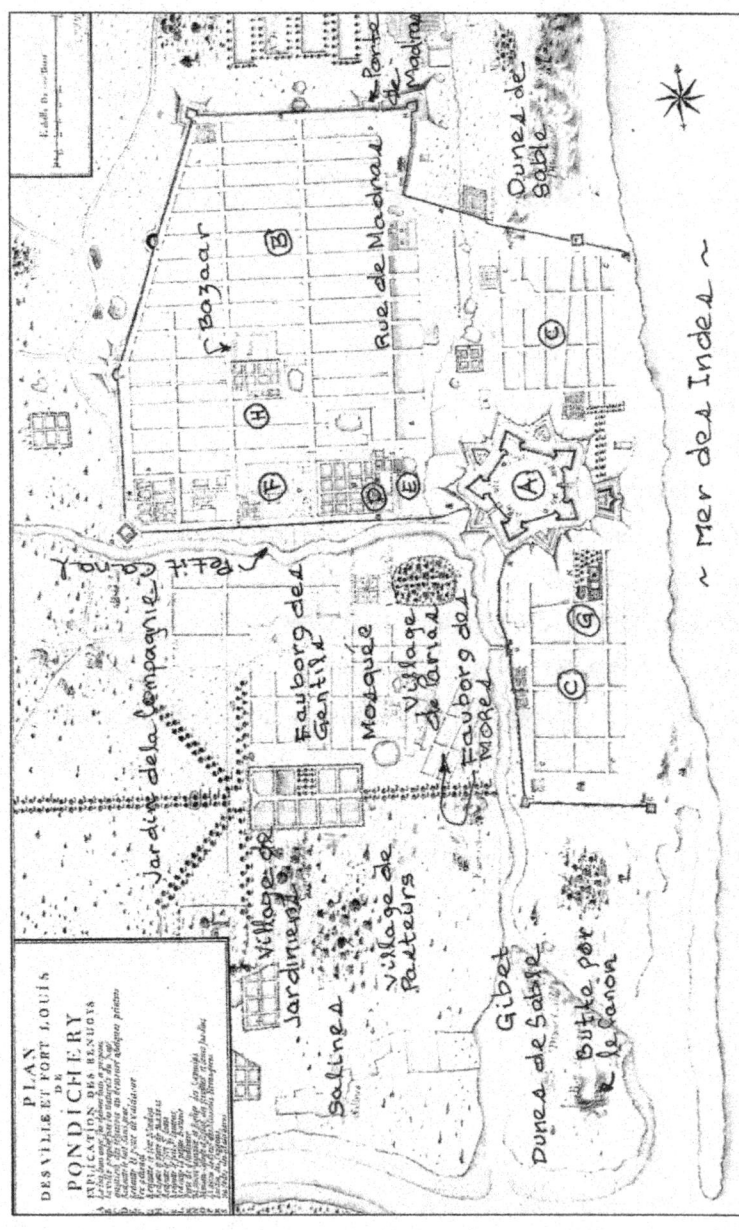

Map 6: _Plan des Ville et Fort Louis de Pondichéry._ By Denis de Nyon (Denyon), December 1716. (A) Fort, (B) Black Town, (C) White Town, (D) Jesuit House, College and Church, (E) Pagoda, (F) Jesuit Gardens, (G) Capucin House and Church, (H) Missions Étrangères House.

With King Louis XIV's aid, the Jesuits constructed their first parish church in 1692 near their residence and gardens (Map 6 - D). The Dutch destroyed it when they occupied the town in 1693.[162] After the Dutch left the Jesuits put up a second church, which is probably the one Father Taillandier knew.[163]

Immaculate Conception Cathedral. Photo by the author, 2016.

Over the years the Jesuits were vexed by the Hindu pagoda next door (Map 6 - E).[164] They demanded that it be torn down to allow for the extension of Madras Street, the main artery connecting Pondicherry with Madras to the north. The Fathers feared that worship of Hindu gods in temples such as this one next to the church would make it impossible to evangelize and convert the natives to the Catholic faith. They could not stand silent and permit the lavish ceremonies of the privileged Hindu classes in this Catholic town, nor could they endure the sight of precious food being offered to their gods while the famished lowest classes and their children, those that gathered outside the temple grounds, were dying from lack of nourishment.

Jesuit Superior Tachard demanded that only Christian feasts and processions be celebrated within the fortified walls of the town. The Jesuits were confident of the pre-eminence of the Catholic faith above all religions. After all, the greatest stories written in the Bible: of the creation of the world, of the Ten Commandments handed down to Moses from God, of the Crucifixion and Resurrection of Jesus Christ, and of baptism for the forgiveness of sins—all grandly inspirational, monumental, and universal in scope—suited conversion to the Catholic faith. A God-fearing state was what they wanted. Like St. Cyprian, the missionaries believed there was no salvation outside the Church. Therefore, all their hard work and sacrifice to convert Hindus to Christianity would have been for naught if idolatry of deities having all sorts of imputed divinity was tolerated.

* * * * *

Relations between the Jesuits and the Capuchins,[165] who were mostly French Franciscans of the Order of Friars Minor (OFM), had soured over the years in Pondicherry since the Jesuits had been assigned to minister to the natives.[166] This falling-out was particularly difficult for the many Europeans who depended on the two orders for spiritual comfort and Christian services. The Capuchin church, Notre Dame des Anges (earlier called the Malabar[167] Church or the Church of St. Lazare), catered to the French East India Company employees, their families, and many other foreigners[168] living and trading for their own benefit in Pondicherry.

The Capuchins vehemently opposed the Jesuit strategies of conversion, an accommodative method the Jesuits had used in the Madurai mission and now were implementing in the recently opened Carnate mission. The long simmering conflict between the orders, which had zealous detractors as well as sympathizers among Pondicherry's merchants, colonists, and missionaries, finally reached Rome. In January 1703 Pope Clement XI sent a delegation of ecclesiastics to India and China[169] headed by Carlo Tommaso Maillard de Tournon, whom he had appointed Patriarch of Antioch and consecrated as Bishop in 1701. His appointment as legate of the Holy See invested him with full powers to examine and arbitrate the controversy for the "East Indies, the Chinese Empire, and neighboring Islands and Kingdoms."[170]

Vaishnava Brahmin Wearing a Tali, 1855. By J. W. Dulles.

De Tournon arrived in Pondicherry on 9 November 1703 and by June of the following year had issued his famous decree which in effect disallowed the Jesuits the following conversion innovations deemed sacreligious: the baptism of a Brahmin who wore a *tali*; the mixing of the oil of sacred chrism with the ashes of cow dung; and the act of spreading it on the foreheads of the faithful during baptism and confirmation.[171] Two practices which De Tournon challenged under pain of ecclesiastical censure especially appalled the missionaries. They concerned the rite of baptism and visits to sick pariahs in their homes. Because applying saliva and breathing on a person were repugnant to the Indians, the Jesuits omitted these rituals in the baptismal ceremony. De Tournon insisted on their restoration. Since the Jesuits were considered *pandarams*, or ascetics of the Shudra class, a status that precluded contact with the pariahs, they avoided open visits with the outcasts. Nevertheless, de Tournon required that the missionaries attend to sick pariahs in their huts.[172]

The Madurai, Mysore and Carnate missions quickly became embroiled in this "sacreligious" crisis of their own making. It threatened their existence and more than a hundred years of painstaking effort and sacrifice by members of Loyola's army in India.[173]

Considering the vast number of letters and reports that reached the Jesuit governors in France,[174] it was likely Pierre Taillandier would have known of the conditions by which conversion, baptism, marriage, and other Church sacraments were administered in Indian missions even before he departed in 1707.

Though de Tournon's decree was confirmed in June of 1706 through the Holy Office, its immediate enforcement was modified and carried a caveat from Clement XI whose sentiments leaned heavily with the Jesuits, to wit: "until the Holy See has decided otherwise...."[175]

Pondicherry's Superior Council called the original decree an abuse of the legate's mandate. "The discussions then 'became *extrêmement vives* [extremely lively]; the Indian scholars gave each party... favorable testimonials to sentiments adopted on both sides, so that one found more embarrassment than ever, to recognize the truth in the midst of the darkness in which all these contradictions enveloped it."[176] The situation for the Jesuits worsened in 1708 when a "Portuguese Jesuit, the admirable Francis Laynes, became bishop of Mylapore, and when, in the following year, a former Jesuit, Claude de Visdelou, who had been secretly consecrated by [de] Tournon in Macao as vicar apostolic of Kweichow in China, arrived in Pondicherry, separated himself from his former confreres and took up his residence with the Capuchins."[177]

During the next forty years, *AMDG (Ad Majorem Dei Gloriam)*,[178] the protracted Affair de Tournon between the Jesuits in Pondicherry and the pope in Rome remained at an impasse.

In 1734 Clement XII changed de Tournon's decree and the final decisions were spelled out in the Bull "Omnium Sollicitudinum" issued in 1744. "The main points were: (1) In the administration of Baptism saliva, salt and the insufflations must not be omitted; (2) No heathen names to be given in Baptism; (3) Child marriages to be discontinued; (4) The Tali should bear sacred images; (5) Superstitious ceremonies at weddings to be dropped; (6) Public festivities on the occasion of a girl reaching maturity to be abolished; (7) Women in their menses not to be kept away from the Sacraments; (8) Sacraments to be administered to Pariahs; (9) Christians not to play any musical instruments at pagan feasts." [179]

∗ ∗ ∗ ∗ ∗

Meanwhile, in response to Louis XIV's decree that Jesuits attend to their subjects with complete freedom in their capacity as missionaries, Jesuit Superior Father Tachard put together a *memoire des demandes* of "religious and temporal issues" that had long been points of contention in Pondicherry since the turn of the century, that is after the Jesuits were appointed priests of the "Malabars," the Tamil-Hindu population. Tachard addressed his memoire to the Chancellor of France, the Comte de Pontchartrain. [180]

Of the more than a dozen demands included in Tachard's memoire, the thorniest were: the destruction of a pagoda next to the Jesuit church on rue de Madras; a ban on Hindu religious processions and superstitious ceremonies performed in the town; and the replacement of the Brahmin Nayiniyappa (or Naniapa) Pillai, the French East India Company's chief commercial broker, or *modéliar,*[181] with a Hindu Christian.

On the 14th of February 1711, with the king's approval, the Comte signed the settlement of demands contained in Father Tachard's memoire. [182] Unfortunately this *Conseil du Roi*, or Royal Counsel, did not arrive in Pondicherry until the spring or summer of 1713, further exacerbating the conflict of competing commercial and religious agendas between the Jesuits and Nayiniyappa, whose influence and authority across a broad spectrum of the trading business was incontrovertible. [183]

NAYINIYAPPA VS LAZARO

Pierre Taillandier arrived in Pondicherry just as Guillaume Hebert, who had become governor of French India after the death of François Martin, and the Jesuit Superior Guy Tachard were heavily embroiled in a dispute over the ownership of four *aldées*, or properties, in the town.[184] According to Hebert, the Nawab of Carnate, Daud Khan, had already promised him the assignment of these lots when the Jesuits "intrigued with the Governor of Gingee, a subordinate of the Nawab, to prevent the assignment."[185] Hebert wasted no time in sending the Company's broker, Nayiniyappa, to the Nawab to close the deal. He succeeded in bringing back the *firman* Hebert had requested in exchange for 5000 rupees.

The falling out between the Jesuit Superior and the Governor had started brewing a few years earlier. Father Tachard had demanded that Hebert retain the multi-lingual Hindu Christian named Lazaro,[186] who had served as the *modéliar* since François Martin's tenure began with the Company. In *Les Jésuites à Pondichéry de 1705 à 1721 et l'Affaire Naniapa* Paul Olagnier described the duties of the chief broker succinctly: "The commerce was all in the hands of a broker, called a '*modéliar*,' who served as an intermediary between the Company, the merchants, the weavers, and all other trades. He served at the same time as interpreter, contract writer, security for the local farmers, and finally as expert; his character was thus of primary importance."[187]

Lazaro was a devout Christian and had earned a reputation as the valued eyes and ears of the Jesuits. He reported to them every transaction and every business-related discussion to which he was privy. At the Superior Council of Trade in Pondicherry Lazaro represented the Church position, which at times involved business transactions affecting Jesuit interests and welfare.

On one occasion, after Governor Martin's death, Lazaro divulged to Father Tachard a negotiation which he had transacted for the Company with the governor of Gingee. On learning of Lazaro's indiscretion, Governor Hebert immediately took steps to replace him with an Indian Hindu named Nayiniyappa whom the governor judged to be very honest and very capable.

But the Jesuits continued to demand Lazaro's appointment as *modéliar*. Tachard explained that elevating Nayiniyappa to this role would generate distrust for the Christian natives of Pondicherry, halt new conversions, and render the outlying missions unsafe.

Over the next three years, Hebert and Tachard exchanged a flurry of letters. Meanwhile, presumably, the affairs of the Company languished without a broker having a firm commission. While Tachard remonstrated about Hebert's lack of respect for the Church and the king, he asked him whether in the presence of God, he could still support a pagan as *modéliar* in charge of Company negotiations. In his response dated 20 October 1708, Hebert accused the Jesuit Superior of being unduly involved with the affairs of the Company and of embarrassing previous governors by his constant threats of writing to the king, thus obliging them to acquiesce to the Jesuit Superior's demands.

The bitter and long quarrel between Governor Hebert and the Jesuit Superior (Tachard was replaced by Bouchet in the latter part of 1710) over the post of Company's chief commercial broker was eventually decided with the recall of Hebert to Paris and the reappointment of Pierre Dulivier as Governor-General. Dulivier received instructions to enforce a decision, taken at the instigation of the Jesuits, by the Conseil du Roi at Marly dated 14

February 1711 which proclaimed that the job of *modéliar* was reserved for a Christian and that the Brahmin Nayiniyappa was in no position to assume it.

News of the decision by the Conseil du Roi reached Pondicherry several months ahead of Dulivier's arrival on 24 September 1713. The governor's departure from Saint-Malo had been delayed by a fierce storm in the North Atlantic. On his arrival "Dulivier found Hebert enjoying excellent health. However, as Hebert had learned of his disgrace several months earlier, he neglected the affairs of the Company. Dulivier found the treasury notably depleted with only fourteen pagodas remaining in cash, not sufficient to pay the troops and administrative personnel at the end of the month. Fortunately, he had brought 75,000 livres with which he hoped to meet the primary needs of the town. With these funds and those generated by the Company he could meet necessary expenses until the following month of April."[188]

It was not until a meeting of the Supreme Council in Pondicherry on the 9th of November 1714 that the issues of banning Hindu processions and ceremonies, and the destruction of the pagoda, decided on 14 February 1711, were implemented. "The gentiles should be allowed only two grand pagodas in the town of Pondicherry, to wit: one called Issouren on rue de Madras, and the other called Piroumal on the rue de Tisserans [weavers], with freedom to make sacrifices there two or three times a week, except during the fifteen days of Easter, Sundays, the Feasts of the Ascension and of St. Louis, Assumption of the Virgin, All Saints' Day, and Christmas. Regarding the other public pagodas, one must little by little wall up the doors, so that they finally destroy them themselves, and forbid them to build new ones. The governor and the missionaries, together, will act with wisdom and the moderation required to execute this order."[189]

However, Jesuit Superior Bouchet could not persuade Governor Dulivier to reverse his decision to disobey one of the mandates issued by the Comte de Pontchartrain: a Christian must be installed as the Company *modéliar*. In a long letter addressed to the Comte on 18 July 1714, Dulivier justified his selection of Nayiniyappa this way: "This Brahmin, to the knowledge of everyone is one of the most skilled men to negotiate for the Company in India. His connections extend everywhere. When I arrived aboard the *Auguste*, the last of the ships leaving St. Malo in 1713, I found on my arrival here that this broker had been responsible for cargo handling of the *Deux Couronnes* and the *Lys-Brillac*, and he had in his hands most of the funds that these ships needed to make their purchases."[190] Although Dulivier agreed to appoint a Christian *co-modéliar*,[191] with the same authority to enter into all the businesses, take full knowledge of them and protect the interests of Christians, he worried that the loss of the Brahmin Nayiniyappa would be disadvantageous to Pondicherry.

Thus, Pondicherry was a colony in turmoil since the beginning of the 18th century, particularly so after the death of Governor François Martin. Jesuit Superior Bouchet had known of Martin's distrust of Brahmin government officials when legal matters pertaining to Company business often reached all the way to the Gingee court for adjudication. Despite the legitimacy of the governor's position, he was expected to provide gifts or honoraria to dignitaries and other Hindu officials at any time and on any pretext.[192]

THE TOWN AND THE COMMERCE

Vue de Pondichéry. By Jacques-Gabriel Huguier, 1750. (Note: the artist took liberty with the scene, as there is no landmass offshore.)

The French ships that were taking on cargo off Pondicherry near the end of February 1711, Father Taillandier was informed, would hoist sails and immediately depart as soon as loading was completed. He knew that just about everyone living in the French colony was writing a letter or sending packages to loved ones back home. Taillandier may have longed to write to his mother and to Genevieve, his younger sister in Lyon, but first he needed to finish the letter/report required of him before it was too late.

For a year since Taillandier arrived no Company ships had appeared on the horizon off Pondicherry. Then suddenly, there they were! This put everyone in town in a festive mood; the textile warehouses were busy baling and bundling cotton fabrics; the Company's merchants, administrators, and clerks were abuzz organizing bills of lading; and the Macouas, who belong to the fisherman and boatman caste, were joyously rowing their *masula*[193] boats loaded with the town's merchandise, toward the ships anchored in the Bay of Bengal.

Masula Boat, Madras, 19th century.

In 1710 the population of Pondicherry was over 60,000,[194] or roughly double the number of inhabitants reported by Father Tachard in 1703. However, the number converted to the Catholic faith was no more than fifteen per cent of the town's population, or 9,000. Since their arrival, Fathers Taillandier and Bonnet were likely assigned to help care for the newly baptized Christians many of whom were children of mixed race.[195] To be able to hear confessions, catechize, and read the books of the country, they dedicated themselves quickly to learning the Tamil and Telugu languages. Likely they studied the local language dictionaries prepared by missionaries who were experts in south Indian languages. Writing to Father Superior de la Chaise in Paris in 1703, Father Tachard said:

> *We are five Fathers here and two Brothers of our Company.*
> *All are busy. Father de la Bruille, who has returned from the*

Carnatic because of poor health teaches philosophy; Father Dolu is the priest of the Malabar parish; Father de la Lane, arriving by the last ships, is learning the languages of the country to enter the mission next year; Father Turpin works very successfully at converting the gentiles of this town and teaches Latin to some young French and Portuguese who are destined for the ecclesiastical way; Brother Moricet teaches reading and writing, arithmetic, piloting and other sciences to the children, so that they can subsequently earn a living.[196]

* * * * *

Well capitalized merchants and associate owners of the Saint-Malo Shipping Company, who in 1706 had taken over the French East India Company when it went into receivership, now helped Pondicherry regain its faded commercial reputation. The trade monopoly enjoyed by the state sponsored company since 1664 had gradually unraveled well before the fiftieth year of its founding. Many original investors and financiers of the king's enterprise refused to put up additional capital, preferring instead to finance a guild of their own, free from nepotism and political interference.

Along the Coromandel Coast it was not unusual to encounter traders from Basra, Ormuz, Mecca, Aden, the Maldives, the Malabar Coast, Malacca, Batavia, Manila, and Canton.[197] The goods sold by many of these foreign traders ended up in local merchants' bazaars and the Company's warehouses up and down the coast. Neither was it unusual to see itinerant salesmen from Burma, Siam, and Ceylon hail merchant ships anchored in the roadsteads and inquire if they wished to buy any or all the cargo aboard their junks or dhows: precious stones, pearls, and silk popular since the days of Vasco da Gama. Money also changed hands in the form of specie[198] for rice, coffee beans, tea, and all sort of spices, especially Indian pepper, whose price in Genoa or Venice once approached that of gold.

Driven by the Indian Ocean's monsoon winds,[199] this network of intrepid seafaring merchants had been trading their exotic products centuries before Marco Polo set out along the Silk Road to reach China.[200] The course of humanity in these roadsteads made its impress on the countenances of the different races. Sailors from around the world, when not fighting for their lives aboard their creaking and leaking vessels, vied for who could first descend the gangplanks to take pleasure in the Orient's brothels.

In his book describing the manufacture of cotton textiles along the Coromandel Coast of India in the 17th century, Sunil S. Amrith writes: "Words convey the reach of India's Empire of cotton: into every language and lingua franca across the Bay passed detailed descriptions of Indian cloth. Ships' cargo lists have a mesmerizing quality that comes from the endless terms for textiles—*longcloth, salemporis, moris, gingham, dungarees, guinea cloth and kaingulong.*"[201]

TAILLANDIER'S SOLILOQUY

Following their arrival on 2 February 1710, Fathers Pierre Taillandier and Pierre Bonnet probably resided at the Jesuit House adjacent to their church (Map 6 - D). It was located along rue de Madras (now rue de la Cathedrale), less than a hundred yards to the west of Fort Louis' ramparts.

Whenever he left the Jesuit House for a walk to the seashore, Father Taillandier no doubt felt comforted by the sight of the French flag prominently flying above the star-shaped red ramparts. Surrounded by a moat, Fort Louis' brick and mortar battlements contrasted, like an apparition, with the dense and curvy shapes of the coconut palms growing on either side of the walled fortress[202] and the white sand dunes near the shore. The palm trees, Taillandier wrote, reminded him of the ones he had seen in Mexico, along the sandy trail near Cuernavaca, when he trekked down to Acapulco.

Now in his first winter in Pondicherry, the balmy and fresh breeze from the bay may also have reminded Taillandier of the summer air in France—dry and invigorating. It assuaged the awful and often stale and pungent smell coming from the Uppar River and Petit Canal that flowed through the center of town.

It would be immediately apparent to him why all the ships anchored far offshore. Even at high tide, the long expanse of the bay in front of the town was hardly more than two feet deep. Looking southward, Taillandier would have seen the fleet of *masula* boats forming a long, zigzag course from the mouth of the river[203] as they rowed to the frigates anchored two or more miles offshore. Silhouetted against the endless bluish gray horizon of the Bay of Bengal, the setting sun gilded the spars of furled sails. For days now the Macouas, who lived along the marshy shores of the winding river, had been loading their vessels with baled textiles and then rowing them out to the ships. Pondicherry, like the rest of the trading posts along the Coromandel Coast, possessed no harbor, and relied on these ubiquitous boats to ferry cargo and personnel to and from the ships. A much smaller vessel, called a *kattamaram*,[204] was often used to transport mail and light packages.

The lean but muscular Macouas were almost naked except for the white cotton cloth that girdled their loins and another that encircled their heads to protect them from the hot sun and the rough bales they carried. Typically, a masula boat was manned by four rowers, two on each side of the craft. Each held an oar inserted in a davit while a coxswain, facing the rowers, controlled the boat's direction with its long tiller. The boats slipped out of the river's narrow mouth, one by one, into the oncoming sea which tossed them every which way. The boats' high sides allowed them to ride the swells while taking on less than a bucketful of seawater. Stashed astern and in the small hold under the prow were the bales of export textiles woven in Pondicherry's handloom factories.

After his walk to the beach, Taillandier would have returned to the Jesuit House via the path leading to the fort's seaside Royal Gate, and then through a short tunnel underneath its watchtower. Inside the fort's rotunda carpenters, laborers, and brick layers, were still finishing various buildings including the Government headquarters, a grand two-story structure with a flat terraced roof that offered a view of the fort's five bastions and the Bay of Bengal. Taillandier would have exited the fort via the Dauphin Gate, between a large cotton cloth warehouse to his left, and to his right, the Capuchin's unfinished Saint Louis church and the two-story barracks occupied by the French Expeditionary Force.

The original Jesuit House was built in 1689 soon after the French "Jesuit mathematicians" unexpectedly arrived in Pondicherry from Siam. The new arrivals managed to obtain a large garden to the west of the French settlement, which was "apart from the Portuguese and the Italian Jesuits."[205] In 1692, they constructed a small church that within a year was destroyed along with the House when the Dutch captured the town. Another church and residence were erected in 1699 after the French reoccupied Pondicherry.

This second Jesuit House likely would have been designed in the Tamil style prevalent throughout south India. The house and its terraced roof were made of mud, cow dung and hay supported by wooden posts and beams and covered with white lime plaster. The front of the house facing the street would be sheltered from sun and rain by the *thalvaram* with its characteristic sloped roof. The thalvaram is the "most essential and mandatory feature of the Tamil houses … to provide shade and protection for the passers-by …."[206] Between the thalvaram and the interior of the house is the *thinnai* veranda, another common feature of Tamil homes. It would be furnished with chairs or benches to accommodate visitors: friends, government officials, catechists, new Christians, and their families. At the back of the house there would be a garden and an outhouse.

* * * * *

Between writing his letter[207] to Father Willard and taking a rest in the evening, Taillandier would have found time to pace the grounds between the church and the Jesuit House. Along the Coromandel Coast early in February, countless stars would have sparkled above him. As an astronomer, he might have imagined the excitement his predecessor, Jean Richaud, must have experienced when he discovered the binary nature of Alpha Centauri less than twenty-five years earlier.

The houses of the factory workers on other side of the Petit Canal were tinged pale blue from the light of tiny oil lamps that burned in niches throughout their homes. Now and then, he would hear the braying of thirsty donkeys and the bleat of sleepless goats. Sacred cows wandered the streets freely. He could tell from the condition of the fields, including the grazed ground behind the church, that these animals had not had much to munch on lately but dry grass and lifeless shrubbery.

The glittering nighttime sky would have reminded him of his long trip across the Pacific when he witnessed the most spectacular sunsets he could have imagined on land or at sea. What was it that he perceived as the sun, a glowing and pulsating orb, slowly disappeared in the horizon, and the clouds above it burst into brilliant hues of orange and red? What thoughts could have possibly raced through his mind when the rising Milky Way—the most beautiful and dense band of lights he had ever seen—glowed and appeared even more majestic against the blackness of the restless sea? Did he imagine life existed on one of those countless creations of God, just as on Earth? Did he long for the truth and meaning of man's existence while gazing at the soundless splendor of the cosmos whirling above him?

"I have observed the nature and the material of the Milky Way," Taillandier's hero, Galileo, declared in 1610. "The galaxy is, in fact, nothing but a congress of innumerable stars grouped together in clusters." He successfully demonstrated the importance of the telescope to precisely determine the local time of a place relative to another's known meridian or longitude. Yet, the means for determining longitude aboard a ship at sea, an unstable platform from which to make meticulous observations of the stars or the sun, eluded the best minds well into the middle of the 18th century. "Eclipses of the moons of Jupiter," Galileo claimed, "occurred 1000 times annually and so predictably that one could set a watch by them." Since the 17th century Galileo's ephemeris table, based on the "dance of its planetary moons,"[208] allowed land surveyors and cartographers to redraw the world. In fact, the new boundaries of France derived this way led Louis XIV of France to complain that he had lost more territory due to his astronomers than to his enemies!

Like every astronomer and every Jesuit mathematician of his time, Taillandier must have read a copy of Galileo's pamphlet called *Sidereus*

Nuncius, or *Messenger of the Stars*. In his remarkable treatise, the great astronomer, perhaps the most influential astronomer and physicist of the 17th century, revealed the astonishing sights he discovered on the surface of the moon, as well as nebulae, fixed stars, and the four moons of Jupiter whose orbits proved to be of great significance to navigation and cartography.

Taillandier could only have hoped for the time and the opportunity in India to apply himself again to astronomy.[209] Watching the heavens, no doubt, brought back memories of the newly constructed observatory above the college church he left behind in Lyon and of his mentor Father Jean de Saint-Bonnet.[210] Saint-Bonnet died in a terrible accident in 1702 before construction could be completed. It was Taillandier who saw the project realized.[211] The observatory floor was 80 feet above ground, and it measured 34 feet long by 30 feet wide with four rooms having large windows.[212] Finished on 26 March 1703, the observatory cost 13,832 livres.[213]

The Old Observatory (top two floors of the towers) in 1832. By Théodore de Jolimont.
(Reconstructed after the original was destroyed in the siege of Lyon in 1793).

A line of inlaid stones on the floor with astrological symbols is all that remains of the observatory, now a storage room next to the art classroom on the top floor of the college. As the observatory's director, it is possible that Father Taillandier established Lyon's first meridian, or line of longitude, whose arc is a segment of an imaginary great circle on the Earth's surface running from pole to pole through Lyon. He had accomplished what Saint-Bonnet must have intended before his untimely death—determine the observatory's geographic coordinates in relation to Paris.

The long-lost Lyon Observatory Meridian was discovered in a storage room on the top floor of the present-day right tower by Gilles Adam and the authors, 2015.

* * * * *

Back in his room at the Jesuit House in Pondicherry, Father Taillandier would have lit a couple of simple clay oil lamps, *diyas*, like those used in home shrines all over south India, some placed in the niches of the walls to frighten malevolent spirits that lurk in the night. His lamps would have been less than four inches long and an inch or so deep, oval shaped with a protruding beak, where a cotton wick laid in ghee or coconut oil.

He would have placed one lamp on the ledge of the south-facing window, and the other in the middle of the desk beside his bed—a straw mat supported by a frame made of hand-hewn wooden slats and boards. From a small drawer he removed one of his water-stained travel journals along with a few blank sheets of paper and put them on top of the desk. He opened it to the page with the marker he had inserted the previous night. Some of the pages stuck together; a few were torn and stained, making it almost impossible for Taillandier to read some of his work of more than two years. Next to the lamp was his quill pen and a tiny clay bowl filled with ink. He would have been seated in an old, caned chair by the window when he began his letter with these poignant and fateful first words:

Since, after God, I owe Your Reverend the happiness that I enjoy dedicating my remaining days to the conversion of Infidels....[214]

* * * * *

When Taillandier and Bonnet arrived in India in 1710, Father Jean Venance Bouchet, the head of the Jesuit missions in the Carnatic, would have been recovering from his long and painful captivity in Tarcolan, northwest of Pondicherry.[215] Evangelizing the natives, poor and cruelly ruled by the appointed governors of the Mughal Emperor, was a delicate matter. Too often the missionaries suffered at the slightest provocation. But the Mughal's henchmen were no match for the Fathers. Steeped in the Ignatian tradition, they relied on the righteousness of their cause with hope, faith, and charity. Despite martyrdoms and sufferings, and often controversies, they were encouraged by the growth of Christendom in the missions of Madurai and Mysore.[216] Jesuit Superior Tachard himself declared that he wished to follow the same techniques of conversion the Portuguese Fathers' successfully applied in Madurai to the new Carnatic missions north of Pondicherry.[217]

Pierre Taillandier knew that in his mission at Tarcolan, Father Bouchet had renounced a worldly and materialistic lifestyle to adopt the habit and way of life of a Sanyasi Brahmin. Bouchet together with Mauduit in Carouvepondi and de la Fontaine in Ponganour were the first Jesuit missionaries in the Carnatic. In the words of Father Tachard they inaugurated: "a very difficult undertaking, and it was but for the zeal of the apostolic mercifulness and charity that they could withstand the rigor and the austerities; because besides abstinence from all that has lived, that is of flesh, fish, and eggs, the Sanyasi Brahmin practiced extremely troublesome customs ... washed himself before the meal, ate but once a day, and had a Brahmin do his cooking since it would have rendered him odious and unworthy of his status to have eaten that which had been prepared by people of a lower caste."[218] Describing the life of a Sanyasi, the historian Ferroli said, "the life of a Sanyasi is certainly a life of the greatest mortification and extreme penance. He must ... turn or close his eyes when a woman passes by; show no sign of passion, of anger, of pain, of pleasure. Two words, according to the Indians, comprise this life: *Succaila, Duccaila*, i.e., neither pleasure nor pain. For he must renounce all pleasures and possess such exalted virtues, that no tribulation will give him pain."[219]

Thus isolated, and living alone in a cave or hermitage, and fluent in the Telugu language, the Jesuit Sanyasis in the Carnate missions attracted the natural curiosity of the people, including the lower castes, to come to them and be instructed about an inspiring concept—salvation of souls.

In this time, and in that place, no one could have done more to inspire Father Taillandier to do God's work than Father Superior Bouchet and Father Mauduit. He must have understood that to convert the many of the poorer castes, he would first have to convert the few of the higher caste—the Brahmins, who under the Mughals were privileged and often de facto rulers of the kingdoms in south India. He believed he could teach them how to live and, even harder, how to die for the Christian God.

* * * * *

While he composed his letter, Father Taillandier no doubt could hear the piercing, shrill sounds of the *kombus*[220] coming from the temple[221] nearby as the night wore on. He could only pray and try to support his brothers as they assumed the Church's enormous responsibility to shield the Christian town from the display of Hindu religious customs. Not only was it important to keep the new converts in Pondicherry from reverting to their old beliefs, but it was also necessary to calm the feelings of dread those in the European community, especially the women and children, felt as festival processions moved raucously through the streets.[222]

Manakula Vinayagar Temple in Pondicherry's French quarter was built before the Jesuits arrived.

Taillandier had learned that since the time of François Martin, the Jesuits had been adamant that the Catholic town remain peaceful and free from the resounding noise of kombus, tambourines, and the ear-splitting cacophony of tom-tom drums. Twice, before Martin's demise, thousands of Hindu factory workers, including weavers, dyers and laborers, and their families had gathered at the Madras Gate and threatened to abandon the town if they were not allowed to practice their religion freely. Twice an accommodation had been reached with Martin, who was concerned that a walk-out would destroy the Company's business and create a vacuum, ripe for a take-over by the Dutch or the English who were still at war with the French.

He would have struggled to understand the purpose of Hinduism and its many deities in the life of the poorest of the poor, since the religion offered no hope whatsoever of saving souls from the fires of hell. To the gods went the treasure and food the Brahmins lavishly offered, while the crowd of famished beggars, pushing and risking a caning by temple guards, were sequestered behind a frail rope barrier.

Pierre Taillandier no doubt firmly believed, as did all the Jesuit missionaries in south India, that the profound difference between themselves and the Hindus, as well as their Muslim oppressors, could only be overcome by converting the youth of the land, thus saving their souls for the greater glory of Jesus Christ. In the words of St. Ignatius, "… teach the children, we will make Christians by precepts and by education."

PART SIX –

THE LONG VOYAGE

… man is a little world, in which we may discern a body
mingled of earthly elements, and ethereal breath, and the
vegetable life of plants, and the senses of lower animals, and
reason, and the intelligence of angels, and a likeness to God.

Oration on the Dignity of Man
Giovanni Pico della Mirandola

LYON TO SAINT-MALO, FRANCE

S ometime during the spring or summer of 1707, perhaps in June after the academic year ended at the Collège de la Trinité where he was a professor and director of the observatory, Pierre Taillandier would have received his assignment as a missionary and begun his journey to India. He probably traveled the first leg from Lyon to Saint-Malo by stagecoach and riverboat.[223] Leaving the Collège and his family behind in Presqu'ile, Taillandier would cross the Saône on the city's oldest bridge, the Pont du Change. Perhaps he paused at the chapel in the middle of the bridge to bid a final "Adieu" to his beloved birthplace and then walked on to the Place du Change in Vieux Lyon. From there he would choose his transport headed north. The journey to Paris was long, and the hazards en route were numerous.

Lyon's Pont du Change, c 1720. Presqu'ile (on the right bank) to Vieux Lyon. By François Cléric and François Poilly.

In his letter Taillandier did not mention his trip from Lyon to Saint-Malo. But the route was well established—through ancient villages and towns, many guarded by medieval chateaux standing mute on their rocky promontories. Since the 16th century there were two types of transport: the *coche de terre* and *coche d'eau*, a land carriage and a water carriage. If heading upstream, the coche d'eau would be pulled by a team of horses on the riverbank. The road system in France would have been no better than anywhere else in Europe.[224] "There were numerous complaints from contemporary road travelers and road users about the extensive gaps, roads that were impassable for coaches, the high cost of travelling, potholes that could snap the axles of wagons and the many bridges in ruins," according to one French historian.[225]

It is likely that Taillandier took the Lyon-Paris-Saint-Malo *grande route*, a popular road that connected Paris to the ports, borders, and provincial capitals.[226] In those days travel time from Lyon to Paris was between 5 1/2 days in summer to 6 1/2 days in winter.[227] The route closely followed the ancient Roman road from Lugdunum (Lyon) to Lutecia or Lutéce (Paris) through Moulins. A *diligence,* the closed carriage preferred for long distance travel, would have offered the fastest transport, up to six to seven miles per hour, since the horses could be made to gallop along the bare ground in between the stone-paved lanes of the highway.

Along the way, Taillandier could have found board and lodging at Jesuit Colleges in Nevers, or Roanne, for example. Other than in the Jesuit enclaves, he could have stayed at one of the many *auberges*, or inns, on his route—a convenience that was not available when he traveled by foot to Acapulco from Mexico City, as he pointed out in his letter, "The miserable hostels where we stay all over Mexico have accustomed us to doing without a bed and all the other conveniences we have while travelling in France." He also recalled he had to climb mountains, traverse sand dunes, and cross rivers on flimsy rafts made of reeds kept afloat by a few gourds in the same way people did before the Spanish conquest.

Before departing for missions around the world, every Jesuit missionary during the reign of Louis XIV, probably would have had an audience with the king himself or with François de La Chaise, the king's Jesuit spiritual counselor and confessor in Versailles. On his way to St. Malo Taillandier likely met La Chaise, with whom he had something in common. Having entered the novitiate in Roanne, La Chaise taught humanities, rhetoric, and philosophy at the Collège de la Trinité in Lyon. He later became its rector, and then he was promoted to Provincial of Lyon before his appointment in 1675 as the king's spiritual counselor.[228]

Taillandier may also have called on Giovanni Cassini, the Director of the Paris Observatory. Cassini was another famous personality associated with the Collège de la Trinité. It was Cassini, a collegue of Jean de Saint-Bonnet, who encouraged the construction of the Lyon Observatory at the Collège de la Trinité.[229]

* * * * *

Declared by Charles X in 1493 to be the "handsomest port in our kingdom," Saint-Malo was founded by fishermen upon a large rock outcrop the ancients called *Rocher d'Aaron*. Tradition has it that in the 6th century a chapel was constructed here in honor Saint Aaron d'Aleth, a monk who lived and died in his hermitage.[230] By the 12th century Saint-Malo supported a cathedral, and its first lord bishop, Jean de Châtillon, began enclosing the town of sixteen acres with rubble-filled walls that followed the natural contours of the livable space.[231]

Saint-Malo, the walled city (above at the center in this aerial view), probably 19ᵗʰc. Print displayed at the Archives of Saint-Malo, 2016.

Historically, Saint-Malo had long been a sanctuary for *corsairs*, or privateers, a privilege granted them since the 12th century by Bishop Châtillon to attack ships belonging to enemy countries. Towards the end of the 16th century Saint-Malo had a population of 13,500[232] and by the next century it had increased to more than 20,000. Following a long tradition, many Malouins found it lucrative to engage in piracy or to hire on as privateers for the prized silk, gold, silver, tea, and spices aboard English, Spanish, and Dutch ships travelling the North Atlantic highway.

The golden age of Saint-Malo began in the early 17th century with the power the city derived from its successful maritime activities. Saint-Malo's good relations with the Baltic countries allowed access to lumber for the construction of ships as well as hemp rope, pitch, and iron. Malouins traded at ports in England and Holland. Cádiz, Genoa, Marseille, and Lisbon also became regular ports of call.

In Peru, Malouins traded with the captains of the so-called "Lima ships," which transshipped Asiatic goods from the Manila Galleons by way of Acapulco. These transactions contravened royal decrees, which limited the sale of these goods only in New Spain (Mexico). "Peru early promised to be an even more lucrative market for Oriental goods than was New Spain. Here was a population wealthy, inordinately given to luxury and display, and recklessly extravagant," wrote William Lytle Schurz.[233] These contraband goods thus provided Malouins with porcelain, silks, spices, iron, wax, *mantas* (blankets) from Ilocos,[234] and other knick-knacks from China and the Philippines.

By the late 17th century industries and trading activities started to move out of the tight confines of the walls of Saint-Malo into the nearby areas surrounding the tidal basin. There the entrepreneurial Malouins put up windmills, shipyards, and rope factories—all essential industries during the age of sail. Soon these wealthy ship owners and merchants managed to build their second homes, known as *malouinieres*, outside of the cramped city. Their ships, picking up the slack that occurred when the French East India Company went into receivership and started liquidating assets early in the 18th century, could be found in the Arabian Sea, the Indian Ocean, and the Bay of Bengal where they traded specie for spices and manufactured goods of cotton and silk from Surat on the Malabar coast to Masulipatnam on the Coromandel coast. On the way back to Europe they would load up on coffee beans from the Red Sea port of Moka.

The bay of Saint-Malo with its rocky coastline has one of the world's largest tidal ranges, often exceeding ten meters. Merchants and pirates amassed wealth but often paid for it with their lives when their ships foundered during a storm or ran afoul of the little islands dotting the channels to the port. It is no wonder that Saint-Malo's coastal waters formed one of the largest graveyards for ships during the era of sailing ships.

Two large corsairs, *La Dauphine*, a 300 tonne warship and the *l'Aimable Grenot*, a 400 tonne frigate, set out from Saint-Malo in 1704 on "a voyage to Cádiz, laden with linens and other merchandise from the area." They foundered just outside the port. Recently discovered on board the wrecks were two navigational instruments—a fragment of a Jacob's staff (cross-staff) and a fragment of a Davis quadrant (backstaff),[235] both used for determining the ship's latitude. Jacob's staff consisted of two parts—the first a square rod, about three feet in length, with gradations on all four of its faces. The second element, the moveable hammer, was still visible on the fragment salvaged from the wreck. The Davis quadrant was invented in the 16th century to measure altitude of the sun using its shadow. Taillandier probably saw these instruments being used aboard the ships he sailed on his journey to India.

* * * * *

Pierre Taillandier arrived in Saint-Malo a year before King Louis XIV authorized the first phase of the *agrandissement* (expansion) of the city's ramparts in 1708. Approaching the citadel along the long causeway to the northeast, his carriage could only have entered through the *poterne* (gate) called Porte St. Thomas, an entryway under the massive walls of the Chateau. The St. Thomas Porte and the Grande Porte that opened on to the harbor constituted the two oldest entryways into the citadel in the early 1700s. Near the Chateau was a square called *La Croix du Fief* with the cross that marked the city limits at that time and the statue *Notre Dame de la Croix du Fief,* "greatly venerated" by Malouins.[236]

Inside the ancient ramparts life among the inhabitants was hectic and difficult. They had not fully recovered from the great fire of 1661 nor the combined Anglo-Dutch fleet bombardment of the city in 1693 that caused more destruction to their homes, churches, and businesses. The English[237] attempted to blow up the walls with a *machine infernal,* a ship loaded with dynamite. Fortunately for the city, the device exploded prematurely. To this day a street called *rue de Chat qui Danse* (Dancing Cat Street) still exists, perhaps in memory of someone's frisky feline, the only casualty caused by that infernal machine. A Benedictine monk, inspired by God's intervention, clearly livid at the attempted murder of thousands of people inside the fort, penned these short poetic lines:

The Englishmen who, like the proverbial mountain

Only brought forth one poor rat,

In their Saint-Malo campaign

Only managed to kill one poor cat.

Lasting scars of ruin included the loss of the large rose window, *la grande rose du chevet*, of the St. Vincent of Saragossa Cathedral whose foundation stones were laid down in 1145 by Jean de Chatillon, Saint-Malo's first bishop.

The siege-like atmosphere that persisted within the citadel even as Taillandier awaited departure of the ship that would take him to the Canary Islands would be aggravated by "*les hostilités*," or the War of the Spanish Succession (1701-1714). This conflict arose following the death of the childless Charles II, the last of the Spanish Habsburgs, and aligned Spanish interests with those of France against England, Germany, and the Dutch Republic.

Malouin privateering activities in the English Channel on English and Dutch ships laden with spices, coffee, and Indian textiles made Saint-Malo vulnerable to retaliation by these two nations. The city was also the home port of many boats that fished for cod on the banks of Newfoundland, Iceland, and Nova Scotia.[238] This activity, together with sail cloth fabrication, and the expeditions to the *Mer du Sud*, or South Pacific Ocean, were the pillars of commerce during the economic heyday of Saint-Malo between 1680 and 1720.[239]

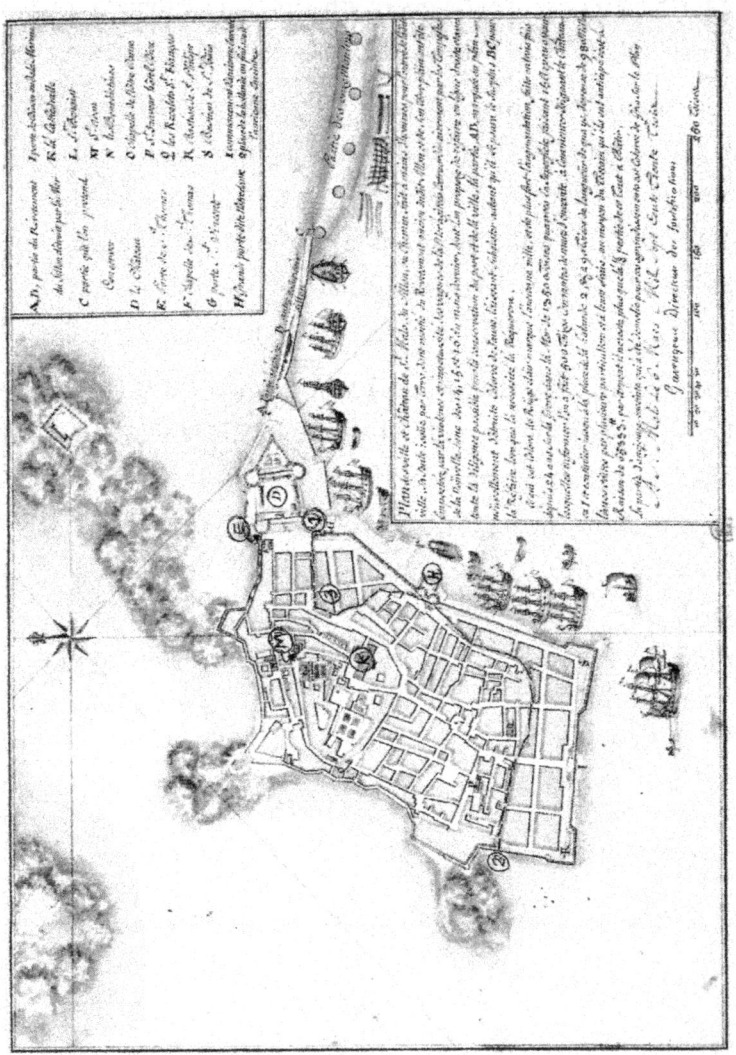

Map 7: Plan des Ville et Château de St Malo, du Sillon, ou Chemin fait à mains d''hommes. By Siméon Garangeau, 1733. (D) Château, (E) Porte de St Thomas (through which Taillandier would have entered), (H) Grande Porte (through which he would have departed) and Le Ravelin, (K) Cathedral, (M) St Aaron chapel and Jesuit residence next door (where he would have stayed). Original city wall (#1 > #3 > #2) prior to 1708. (#3) Mer Bonne cove in 1707 when Taillandier arrived but filled after 1708 to enlarge the city as shown in this plan.

* * * * *

Arriving late in summer of 1707, Fathers Taillandier and Bonnet most likely stayed in the Jesuit house next door to Saint Aaron's chapel (Map 7 - M). Since 1631 the chapel belonged to the Jesuits at the College of Thomas à Becket in Rennes.[240] Often called to Saint-Malo by the Ursulines of Ste. Anne, the Jesuits of Rennes did not always find convenient lodgings for themselves in the early years until they were permitted to use this house for their ministry.[241] The relationship between the Ursulines and the Jesuits in Saint-Malo dated from 1613 when the Jesuit Father Girard from Rennes noticed the pitiful ignorance of impoverished girls in the citadel. To improve the level of education of the children and counter the rising influence of Protestants in Saint-Malo, the Jesuits of Rennes built a convent-school and a chapel (1619-1622) on the nearby street that became known as rue Ste. Anne.

Saint-Malo's magnificent stone mansions were built by rich privateers and businessmen-ship builders who made their fortunes not only in the lucrative trade they made with the Lima ships in the South Pacific Ocean, but also with the profits they earned selling coffee called *café de Moka*.[242] Moka was a bustling emporium and coffee exporting port frequented by English, Dutch, French and Danish East India ships. By the mid-1700s the major cities of England, Austria, France, Germany, and Holland were becoming centers of social activity and communication, it can be argued, because of their coffee houses. If the atmosphere was raucous and lively in these coffee establishments, it was likely due to what the Arabs called *marqaha*, a feeling of unbridled euphoria new to European palates, brought on by the brew.

* * * * *

To be readied for her voyage to the Canary Islands, Taillandier's ship, the *Saint Esprit*, would have been anchored along the quay of the Mer Bonne cove[243] near the Ravelin (Map 7 - H). Erected in 1644, the Ravelin was composed of two half-moon shaped rampart towers that flanked the massive entry door known as the Grande Porte.[244] Erected as a military defensive installation, the structure survived until it was demolished in 1840. Vessels in the cove were sheltered from the often harse prevailing west wind and the relentless pull of the tides, among the highest in Europe. It was through the Grande Porte that everyone who went in or out of Saint-Malo passed, and so this quarter of the city became "nothing but a gigantic warehouse." Since 1656, above the exterior arch of the Porte stood a "magnificent bronze Christ with arms spread,"[245] which bid welcome and bon voyage to all travelers.

Behind the guarded entry of the Ravelin one could see a small structure—the "*bourse aux négociants*," the local traders' market where cargo and vessels seized by corsairs were sold at auction. Along the Grand Rue that began at the Porte and its side streets, sailors from around the world and victorious corsairs just returned from their campaigns "dropped their anchors in taverns where pleasant hostesses tried to help them forget months of solitude while fighting the stormy Atlantic, or the miserable life of a journeyman, or their missing comrades. They would tell tales, embellished as time passed, in taverns with picturesque names: *La Malice, La Licorne, Le Pot d'étain* and others that opened up in the vicinity."[246]

Saint-Malo's Grande Porte flanked by the iconic Ravelin, c 1900.

A "*meridienne*" that tracked the moon's phases, a very important adjunct to this tidal port that depended so much on the ebb and flow of the sea, could also be seen against the wall next to the Ravelin.[247] Above the Ravelin's interior vault in a tiny chapel stood the venerated statue erected in 1663 of the *Notre Dame de Bon-Secours* (Our Lady of Safe Harbor) among flowers and candles.[248] After the "Great Fire" of 1661 Jesuit Father Vincent Huby was said to have placed the town under her "powerful" protection. Near this statue was a small niche that housed Saint Christopher's statue—the patron saint of the port workers.[249]

A few blocks west of the Grande Porte towered the slate covered spire of St. Vincent Cathedral. While waiting for the *Saint Esprit* to sail, Taillandier and Bonnet most likely had occasion to worship in this Romanesque-Gothic style Catholic Church. Its large rose window, destroyed in 1693, was being restored at the time of their departure for India. Certainly, the cathedral's statue of St. Ignatius of Loyola, canonized in 1622 and the most venerated Jesuit saint, would have been of great interest to them.

* * * * *

The scene at the quay along the Mer Bonne cove on that day would have been joyous, for it was in the service of God that passengers such as Fathers Taillandier and Bonnet were departing. It was also a sad day, for this was the time for family and friends to bid farewell to the travelers and wish them "fair winds and following seas." In those bygone days, sending loved ones off on long voyages across the globe was heart-wrenching. Though time might ease all things that burdened the mind, the memory of the tearful, anxious goodbyes would never die completely.

The first leg of Taillandier's journey began aboard the Malouin ship, the *Saint Esprit*:

> *I left Saint-Malo with Father Bonnet on the 5th of September 1707 aboard the "Saint Esprit," a ship with thirty cannons and one hundred-forty crewmen.*

She was a privately owned 17th century frigate embarking on a prowling mission to the South Atlantic and then sailing on to ports in Peru and Chile.

Privateers preferred a frigate for its speed, size, and maneuverability. Her captain, Jacques Avice, had "pressing business in the South Pacific."[250] But first, he had to lay over for much-needed maintenance and victualing at Santa Cruz de Tenerife.

The 280 tonne Malouin corsair, square-rigged on three masts, had a lateen spar fitted to the mizzen for better maneuverability. She was armed with 30 guns, most likely of lighter caliber demi-culverins, and, according to Taillandier, manned by a crew of 140. A crew this large would about equal the number of men aboard 5th ranked frigates with a single gun deck in the French Navy of the 18th century.

With that many sailors and gunners aboard, the *Saint Esprit* would have been ready whenever a "prize" came in sight on the high seas. Still, but for the grace of God, the corsair could very well have fallen to the English, whose warships came within a week or two of sighting her along the Atlantic highway off Portugal, early in the month of October 1707.

While the *Saint Esprit* was headed south, arriving at Tenerife on the 8th of October, the English fleet, commanded by Admiral Clowdishley Shovell, fresh from engaging the French navy in the Mediterranean, was homeward bound. Instead of a one-sided naval engagement, a maritime disaster of unimaginable proportions occurred. Early on the foggy morning of October 22nd, bad luck struck Shovell's fleet of warships. All but one foundered on the coastal rocks of Scilly Isle southwest of England.

Two-thousand crew and soldiers lost their lives, including Admiral Shovell himself, who reportedly was stripped of an expensive jeweled ring soon after expiring on the rocky shoreline. Such was the sad state of navigation even into the early 18th century.[251] A shipwreck on the morning after a disaster became a sporting event for the ever-watchful inhabitants living on nearby shores. They called it a "wrecking"—searching coves and rocky shorelines for other men's treasures.

* * * * *

Though Taillandier did not mention it, there must have been other passengers aboard the *Saint Esprit*—priests, colonists, government officials, as well as wives and children—who were embarking on a fateful journey to the Americas. Despite the dangers, migration to the new colonies continued unabated in those days. There was no shortage of men from the unlettered classes as well as fortune hunters, all of whom were seeking better opportunities in the New World.

But for Taillandier and Bonnet, whose destination was India, the journey would last longer than anyone would have anticipated. A terraqueous globe, if they had had an opportunity to glance at one, would have revealed that even when they reached the New World, their journey was but one-third accomplished!

THE CANARY ISLANDS

A fter about a month of sailing when nothing extraordinary happened, we sighted Cape Finisterre in Galicia, and on the 8th of October we anchored in the harbor of Santa Cruz on the island of Tenerife.

Port of Santa Cruz de Tenerife and the Pico De Tenerife. Artist unknown, 19th c.

As they approached Tenerife, the largest of the Canary Islands and a Spanish territory since the 15th century, Taillandier and Bonnet would have seen their port of call off the starboard bow of the *Saint Esprit*. Looming above the town of Santa Cruz was a majestic mountain, the Pico de Tenerife, rising to more than 12,000 feet and appearing to gently nestle on the shoulders of its massive conical base. An English watercolor painter described the view the two Jesuits witnessed: "In unspeakable grandeur it rises far above the clouds … while the atmosphere through which you gaze upon it is of that matchlessly beautiful ethereal tint which defies all the skill of art, and all the means that art can employ, to imitate."[252] When approaching the Bay of Santa Cruz, sailors would recognize the ubiquitous dense clumps of spurge, *Euphorbia canariensis,* spread across the irregular dark bronze volcanic hills above the bay.

Aloft, the *Saint Esprit's* topmen began furling the shortened sails, while deckhands ran fore and aft securing halyards and braces as the Malouin frigate maneuvered for an anchorage spot in the bay near the rugged rocks of the Paso Alto fort.[253] Only then did the weary passengers come up one by one and stand on the gangways of the weather deck to gaze joyfully at the bay brimming with sailing ships[254] rocking at their moorings alongside smaller fishing boats of all types, colors, and sizes.

The riches of this island, its considerable commerce, and excellent wine of Malvasía[255] make it the most important of the Canary Islands. It is eighteen leagues long and five wide. In the middle of the island stands the famous mountain called Pico de Tenerife that can be seen, I have been told, from fifty leagues out. It has a conical shape, and the base is very large.

The stories about its height, the coldness of its peak, and the time it takes to climb to the top seem exaggerated. I have spoken with some people who have been curious enough to climb it, and I have concluded that the trek up would take seven hours.

It is true that at a glance it seems higher than the clouds. It snowed at the top, and at the same time the heat was oppressive down in the lowlands.

The small village of Santa Cruz is located on the northeastern end of the island. We left this place on the 10th via a rough trail and across a barren mountain until we arrived at the island's capital, a small industrial city called Ciudad de la Laguna. On the other side of the city is a plain, about two leagues in length, where the sea can be seen to the west. From here begin the beautiful vineyards that grow on the sides of the hills, inter-planted with oranges, lemons, and trees from the Americas.

For two hours we walked over hills without losing sight of the sea. Passing through the villages of Matanza and Santa Victoria, we arrived in Arotave [La Orotava], the second most important town on the island where the Jesuits from the province of Andalucía have a college. The birth of the Prince of Asturias was being celebrated then, and everything else that day was about merriment and festivities.

While in La Orotava, Taillandier and Bonnet must have visited that Jesuit school. The first stone was laid for the school, called *Colegio de San Luis Gonzaga,* and the church in 1700, only seven years before they arrived.[256] From the sloping street on the hillside next to the school, the two missionaries would have enjoyed the magnificent vista of the Atlantic Ocean and smelled the perfumed air emanating from the fruit trees and gardens in the valley directly below them. During another celebratory feast, held a century and a half after Taillandier's visit, the English artist Elizabeth Heaphy Murray described her impressions of the beauty of the valley and the homes in La Orotava: "The houses, the trees, the balconies, are covered with garlands of flowers of unrivalled beauty and brilliancy of color. The sight is so enchanting that I could almost imagine myself in some happy valley, where the ills and sorrows of mankind can never intrude."[257]

Fathers Taillandier and Bonnet arrived just in time for the *"vendange,"* or harvest, of the Malvasía grapes and the pressing that followed. Believed to have originated in Greece before the time of Christ, this popular variety of grape found its way to the Canaries as trading intensified among European and North African merchants.[258] Taillandier explained the vendange this way:

> The harvest of the Malvasía, a particular variety of grape, was also being celebrated. The grape clusters are handled very carefully and only the very ripe are harvested. Having extracted the grape juice, the workers add dry lime to preserve the liquid for shipment to all parts of the world. They also make red and white wine from another grape variety, and they drink water that is first filtered through porous rocks.

The Jesuits arrived in the Canaries during the 16th century as the islands became a stopover place for ships on their way to the Americas and the West Indies. Their presence was especially notable in Las Palmas on Gran Canaria and La Laguna and La Orotava on Tenerife. There they left traces of their artistic endeavors in the colleges and churches they founded, enriching the culture of the islands, with the use of local and as well as European works of art.[259]

* * * * *

Taillandier wrote that he calculated the height of the world-famous volcano of Tenerife, a feat only someone acquainted with mathematics would have attempted. Now called Mount Teide, the volcano is the highest mountain of Spain's insular possessions, and the third largest active volcano in the world.[260] The then unknown height of Teide probably presented a delightful challenge to Taillandier, an astronomer and one familiar with the use of trigonometric tables (a Euclidian geometry table would have been used aboard the *Saint Esprit*). He may have received simple navigational instruments as a parting gift, courtesy of Louis XIV.[261] However, he doubted the results of his observations right away:

The instruments I used to measure its height were not very accurate; however, I think it is over thirteen hundred toesas.[262]

On Sunday, the 30th of October, just as night was falling, we sailed from "la rade de Sainte Croix" [the bay of Santa Cruz], and the following day we sighted Isla de la Palma and Isla del Hierro. The water on the latter island is not potable. The story is pure fantasy about a tree whose leaves are also water fountains and that water drips from them continuously.[263] The natives of Hierro said they never have heard of such a phenomenon.

Fathers Taillandier and Bonnet probably departed from the Puerto de la Cruz in La Orotava, rather than from the port of Santa Cruz where they had arrived. Taillandier may have confused the similar sounding port names, one on the western side of the island and the other on the eastern side. They could not have continued sailing to the Caribbean aboard the *Saint Esprit* since the Malouin corsair was undergoing "repairs and provisioning [at the port of Santa Cruz] until the 14th of November 1707 when she sailed for the coast of Brazil."[264]

Puerto de la Cruz became an international port, complete with a *Casa de la Real Aduana* (Royal Customs Building) when Garachico, the principal port in western Tenerife and gateway to the Americas, was destroyed in 1706 by a lava flow from the nearby *Montaña Negra* volcano just west of El Teide. Even before this cataclysm, the port was reported to have had commercial relationships with Europe and the Indies in the 17th century, which brought a significant number of foreigners to the town.

Saint Domingue (Hispaniola or Santo Domingo)

Having left the Canary Islands more than two weeks earlier and now more than halfway across the Atlantic, en route to the island of Saint Domingue, Taillandier recalled this incident:

At eight in the evening of the 19th of November [1707] we saw a flash, like a cannon shot, fall from the sky and light up the ship. To me it looked like the flash was a foot in diameter. It broke apart and dissipated a few toesas above the surface of the sea.

On the 25th we were becalmed, and we saw a lot of "souffleurs" ["blowers," probably small whales, such as orcas]. These monstrous fish swam very close to the ship, and we calculated they were at least thirty feet long. No one seemed surprised by what I said for according to them in the north huge whales have been caught measuring more than sixty feet long.

Being entertained by *souffleurs* and witnessing falling meteors while the ship was becalmed between the northern and southern trade winds must have been a fascinating experience. A meteor exploding above the surface of the sea would have startled everyone and might have provoked anxiety, as some would believe it to be a harbinger of danger. No doubt many of the passengers recorded these surprising events in their travel journals as Pierre Taillandier did.

By the end of November 1707, Taillandier's ship would be sailing along the northeast coast of the island of Santo Domingo, close to Samaná Bay, where whales abound during the winter season.[265]

Undoubtedly Taillandier, a scientifically minded Jesuit, reflected upon the state of the art of navigation as his ship made the Atlantic crossing, and he may have experienced misgivings not unlike those that Christopher Columbus felt during his first crossing. He would have come to the realization that not even the most experienced pilot of the early 18th century could tell him, with confidence, the precise position of his ship when at sea.[266]

Though Taillandier did not write about the conditions aboard his ship, crossing the Atlantic in November with favorable winds would have been a delight. But, being caught in the doldrums, as he reported, would have raised everyone's eyes toward heaven.

Most likely the Jesuits led everyone aboard in prayer for a full restoration of the westerly trade winds that would fill the sails and send their ship on its way. Could there have been anything more frustrating for the captain of a man-o'-war than to see his ship—a tableaux of shrouded masts, drooping sails, and limp braces in the glare of a faceless sun—adrift at sea? To keep boredom at bay, he must have ordered all the men to busy themselves with maintenance work. While some may have tarred the ropes or stitched and mended torn sails, others likely were sent below decks to caulk the planks and bulkheads below the waterline.

What great jubilation and thanksgiving there was aboard when, finally, a steady breeze arose to fill the sails and put all hands to work again. A holy mass would have been celebrated on the quarter deck *tout de suite*, followed by a *Te Deum* lauding the work of God and all the saints, after which plenary indulgencies were surely granted to all hands as the ship resumed its westward course.

A little over a month of sailing had passed when, finally, Taillandier's ship arrived at Saint Domingue, or Ayiti (Haiti) the indigenous Taíno name referring to the entire island.

On the evening of the 4th of December, we entered the port of Cap François [now Cap-Haitien], on the island of Saint Domingue. We had sailed for eighty leagues along the northern coast of this beautiful island. Two rocky promontories guard the entrance to the bay making the passage difficult and dangerous.

The French own more than one hundred leagues of shoreline in the north, west, and south. The Spaniards own part of the southern coast that extends to the east.

Our joy was great upon arriving at the French zone and joining the company of other priests who assist and take care of the parishes that are scattered on the north end of this large island. Father Breton, an expert botanist, showed me some plants that grew near the house where we stayed, and he assured me that they looked exactly like the tea leaves of China. I took some of the leaves with me and let them dry naturally. Later, during my stay in Manila, I compared Chinese tea leaves[267] with those I had collected. A French surgeon who had lived in China for five years, *and whom I invited to taste the two types of tea I prepared, agreed with me that my sample was like real Chinese tea and that it was as good as what they bring from the Empire. Later, I received news that similar plants have been discovered in Peru and their tea sipped in Lima.*

The first Jesuits to arrive in Cap François in 1704 were Fathers Jean-Baptiste Girard and Jean-Baptiste Le Pers. Four others—Adrien Le Breton, Olivier, Laval and Boutin—joined them in 1705, roughly two years before Taillandier reached these shores. Their work in Cap François began with the restoration of the churches and the parishes abandoned by the Capuchins who had succumbed to fevers. "The French monarchy admitted the Jesuits to Haiti … to replace the departing Capuchins as ministers to the souls of (white) colonists."[268] Although the French were present in Haiti years before, as planters of tobacco,[269] indigo and sugar, Spain finally ceded this western third of Hispaniola to France in 1697 with the Treaty of Ryswick.

Many French colonists arrived soon thereafter and established profitable sugar and tobacco plantations in their new territory. Less than a hundred years after Columbus brought sugarcane stalks from the Canaries to Hispaniola, the production of sugar increased throughout the Caribbean Islands and into Brazil.[270] Raw sugar, or *muscovado*,[271] quickly transformed it into a premier sugar plantation island.

Indigo production was also profitable, mainly due to the labor and knowledge of thousands of enslaved Africans with cloth dyeing skills learned in Africa.[272] By 1700 Saint Domingue had "4,560 whites and 9,082 slaves."[273] Thus, it became the richest French colony.

* * * * *

Father Girard, who later became the first Jesuit superior in Haiti, "attached himself to the *Misericorde Cofraternity*. It was from the charity of the same confraternity that the Jesuits bought two houses near the *Place d'armes* where they erected a hospital for all those who were sick or poor."[274]

Cap François and the Jesuit House and Gardens above the town, 1728.

A later arrival was Adrien Le Breton who sailed to the West Indies in 1693 where he had become known as a "priest of the Negroes" in Martinique.[275] It was Le Breton, a noted botanist, who showed Father Taillandier the plants having leaves that looked exactly like Chinese tea leaves. Taillandier and Bonnet would have stayed in the Jesuit residence with its gardens overlooking the town until they left on the 10th of December 1707.

Taillandier probably encountered slavery for the first time here. He would have praised the Jesuits in Saint Domingue for giving the slaves sanctuary and protection. Overall, the benevolence of the missionaries resulted in great animosity between the Jesuits and the plantation owners who depended on slave labor in their fields and domiciles. Taillandier would also have been aware of the so-called "Code Noir,"[276] which was in force in all French colonies. It entitled the indigenous population to attend church on feast days thus relieving them of the obligation to work. Jean-Baptiste Colbert, France's powerful Minister of Finances and state administrator, was instrumental in the issuance of the Code Noir signed by Louis XIV in March of 1685. It established rigid rules for the treatment, purchase, and conversion of slaves to the Catholic faith in Saint Domingue.

* * * * *

Columbus greeted by Taínos, 1492. By T. de Bry, 1592.

Upon his arrival in 1492, Christopher Columbus took possession of this island for Spain and called it *Insula Hispana*, which became Anglicized as Hispaniola. The site of his landing was named La Navidad, the first European settlement in the New World. During the colonial era, the entire island was shown on maps as Saint Domingue or Santo Domingo. The city of the same name, on the southern coast of what is today the Dominican Republic, was the first seat of Spanish colonial rule in the New World.

Unconvinced that he had not found Cipango (Japan), Columbus died fourteen years after his momentous voyage. So did the indigenous population; it succumbed not to natural causes but to European cruelty and diseases to which the natives had no immunity. Hispaniola was the gateway to the New World and the center of imperial trade carried out by the Spanish treasure fleet prior to the Spanish conquest of Cuba.

Back in Spain, those who frequented the bars and lodgings by the docks in the burgeoning port of Seville heard rumors spinning wildly about the exploits of the vanguard of Andalucian adventurers, gamblers, and *hidalgos* (gentlemen) in the Americas. Having been granted e*ncomiendas*,[277] the new settlers speculated on the existence of precious metals on their lands. As *encomenderos* they were able to force the natives to mine gold, silver, and precious stones from the earth, and pearls from the bottom of the sea. They considered it their given right to exact labor or tribute from the indigenous population and, lacking female companionship, appropriate native women as concubines and household helpers.

* * * * *

The Spanish monarchs used the clergy to pacify, civilize, and convert the indigenous peoples of the New World, and later the Philippines. Rome had granted Spain's Catholic kings full rights to rule over newly discovered lands in return for a commitment to evangelize them. But, even as the clergy managed affairs in the areas the colonists controlled and tried to temper their abuses, the search for gold and the cruel treatment inflicted upon the native people in the Indies never completely stopped.

On the island of Hispaniola, the first salvo for justice in the face of rapidly deteriorating relations between the indigenous population and new colonists was delivered by Fray Antonio de Montesinos. On the last Sunday of Advent, December 21, 1511, in the presence of high government and ecclesiastical officials, the relatively unknown Dominican priest walked up to the chapel pulpit and delivered a sermon of great pith and moment:

> *In order to make your sins against the Indians known to you, I have come up on this pulpit, I who am a voice of Christ crying in the wilderness of this island, and therefore it behooves you to listen, not with careless attention, but with all your heart and senses, so that you may hear it; for this is going to be the strangest voice that ever you heard, the harshest and hardest and most awful and most dangerous that ever you expected to hear. This voice says that you are in mortal sin, that you live and die in it, for the cruelty and tyranny you use in dealing with these innocent people. For with the excessive work you demand of them they fall ill and die, or rather you kill them with your desire to extract and acquire gold every day. And what care do*

you take that they should be instructed in religion? Are these not men? Have they not rational souls? Be certain that, in such a state as this, you can no more be saved than the Moors or Turks.[278]

Bartolomé de Las Casas, a historian and later a Dominican friar, was one of the most well-known personalities of the early Spanish colonial era in the New World. Las Casas drew a horrifying picture of the cruelty and frequent massacre of the natives by the new settlers. This Dominican, with the support of a few soldiers, ecclesiastics, and concerned Spanish citizens, undertook aggressive and articulate measures, including a complaint to the king, to ensure the Spanish conquest followed Christian and just principles. His voice, added to that of de Montesino's, would "lead him to far places and very many times across the Ocean Sea to enrage and astonish generations of his countrymen."[279]

Doubtless the published material about Las Casas, that spawned half a century of debate arguing for the benign treatment of poor and ignorant natives, was closely studied in the missionary colleges all over Europe. Pierre Taillandier and his generation of Jesuits would have known about these issues and probably read the *History of the Indies* by Las Casas, who, more than anyone else, forced the Spanish Crown in 1542 to reaffirm its authority over the conquistadores.

CUBA

As there was always danger on the high seas, a prudent captain would be wise not to ignore it. During the Golden age of piracy, lasting a hundred years between the 17th and 18th centuries, Port Royal, Jamaica was one of the ports most frequented by pirates. It was a haven for would-be "gentlemen on the make"—Spanish renegades, Huguenot refugees, and privateers of all races. English privateers commissioned by the Crown to disrupt Spanish shipping in the Caribbean and the Atlantic used Port Royal as a base of operations.

A Spanish-flagged vessel, such as Taillandier's, passing between Hispaniola and Cuba would have attracted the attention of any pirate who spotted such a prize. Thus, Taillandier noted, the ship's captain chose the safer route to Havana—sail across the Windward Passage between the two islands, then west to the Straits of Florida.

Our ship made sail [from Cap-Haitien] on the 10th of December. We passed to the north side of Cuba to avoid the naval warships of Jamaica.

In 1707, two hundred fifteen years after Columbus arrived in the New World, Pierre Taillandier witnessed for himself that the conquistadores' frenzy to extract gold from the ground and pearls from the sea had practically eliminated a race of people—the Tainos. He observed:

There are no more native peoples on the islands of Saint Domingue and Cuba. Cuba is now populated by Spaniards who have many villages there.

When Taillandier arrived in Cuba, the "new" native population, made up of African slaves and their descendants, continued to work the sugar, tobacco, and cotton plantations of the *caciques* (local chiefs engaged by the Spanish). At this time in history slave trading was rarely carried out by the Spaniards. That business was mainly in the hands of Portuguese, Dutch, and English ship captains.

* * * * *

The island of Cuba is two hundred and fifty leagues wide. It is almost impossible to sail through its channels in winter because to the south the island is rock-strewn along its length, and to the north is the Pracel,[280] made up of many low-lying islands. In some places the channel is not even four leagues wide.

Tobacco, an excellent and principal crop of Cuba, is taken to Spain in the form of snuff and leaves. It is sold all over Europe as Spanish tobacco.

Havana from the Sea. https://www.sjsu.edu/faculty/watkins/havana.htm.

On the 16th of December, we entered the port of Havana, passing about half a pistol's shot from the Fort du More [El Morro].[281] This castle has more than sixty forged cannons. The ... channel is located ... between it and another fort [Castillo San Salvador de la Punta] that is defended with thirty-six pieces of heavy forged artillery. The cannon shots of one fort can reach the other.[282] On approaching the town, the ship comes within range of cannon shots from another much smaller fort.

Rocks have been placed up to the water's surface of the entrance, so only one ship at a time can pass through either [of the channels]. This port or, better said, this bay extends one league to the south and forms other channels to the east and west. Its anchorage is good, and here one can find refuge from the most violent winds.

The city is well fortified; the land side is protected by many bastions along the fortress walls. The fort is semi-circular, and it would take a ship at least an hour to turn around. There are three parishes, six different religious orders, and three convents.

Cuba has one bishop who lives in Havana, [283] *the capital of the island [since 1592]. He is the suffragan of the archbishop of Saint Domingue.*

A Spanish pilot, whom we took aboard in Tenerife, made us wait many days at port so we might be safe from the north winds that blow during the winter in the Gulf of Mexico. Sometimes, he said, the winds are more violent during certain lunar quarters than in others. Finally, we hoisted sails on the 23rd of December, but we hardly had left the bay when the pilot decided to turn around, fearing that we would be engulfed by the tempestuous north wind. However, his prediction turned out to be false.

By 4 January, Taillandier reported that his ship was sailing about thirty leagues north-northwest of Cap de Catoche, Yucatán.

THE YUCATÁN

During the Age of Sail, Spanish navigators knew the waters of the western Caribbean better than other European seamen. After all they had been at it—the business of looking up to the heavens for help in navigating to the next port when everything around them was a menacing sea and land was nowhere to be seen—since the end of the 15th century.

Those intrepid first pilots and cartographers, discoverers of the New World, plotted their courses and descriptions of harbors and coastlines on ancient parchment called portolans. At best these ancient nautical charts, copied and improved upon repeatedly, showed distances and courses to follow toward many ports. They were the earliest guides for sailors. At worst, the portolans that guided Columbus and Magellan burdened the mind more than helped it, and "in terms of technical accuracy, [they] were more like medieval harbor charts."[284]

Concern for a safe sailing was everyone's worry. Taillandier mentioned that a Spanish navigator boarded his ship in the Canaries to help navigate to the Antilles and into the Gulf of Mexico. Like all respected pilots and navigators, he would have been familiar with the latest portolan charts.

The astronomer, Taillandier, no doubt took an interest in the navigation of the vessels on which he sailed. He had every opportunity not only to talk to the captain and the pilot but also to copy the ship's log entries. His letter contained actual data of soundings, land masses, local times, and wind directions, as well as the ship's estimated position at sea.

Taillandier most likely marvelled at the complexity of it all—the art of navigation and the skill of the pilot standing beside him when the ship had to lower all her sails to let the "raging tempest" and a mean sea rock them endlessly.

* * * * *

From Havana they entered the Gulf of Mexico near the Yucatán peninsula.

> On the evening of 4 January 1708, we sounded the bottom and from the readings obtained realized we were thirty leagues NNW of the Cape of Catoche. This cape, which is at the east end of the province of Yucatán, was named this way because Don Fernando de Córdova, having disembarked here in March of 1517, was welcomed by the natives who repeatedly said, "con escatoch," which meant "come to our houses" in their language.[285]

Map 8: _Seno Mexicano (Golfo de México), 1762. A portolan map by A. D. Francisco Ygnacio Alarcon y Ocaña. (A) Cuba, (B) Cape of Catoche, (C) Alacranos, (D) Arenas, (E) Triangulo, (F) Arcas, (G) Campeche, (H) Vera Cruz._

The Spanish pilot directed us to take the route through the Bay of Campeche, leaving to the north the small islands of Arcas, Triangolo, and Alacranos. We suffered three northers in three days, blowing between the Northeast and the North. They are not, ordinarily, very violent, and the Spaniards call them "norte chocolatero," because they do not impede them from whisking their chocolate drinks.[286] These winds don't last longer than twenty-four hours.

According to our calculations, on the 10th, at eight o'clock in the morning, we had passed between the isle of Triangolo and those of Arenas. At four-thirty in the afternoon, from the sounding we took, we found ourselves in waters of 69 fathoms, and by six o'clock we could no longer find the bottom.

On the 11th we noticed a large school of bonitos [tuna or mackerel] swimming on the surface, jumping, and following the ship. In the afternoon the south wind becalmed the waters, but by evening a furious north wind suddenly began to blow. We maintained a course headed into the wind throughout the night and the morning of the next day. In the evening the wind abated momentarily, but the sea continued to be agitated, rocking us mercilessly all night long.

On the 13th we saw two ships that approached to inspect us: one was the King's frigate, named "Diane," constructed in Havre de Grace and belonging to M. du Casse's squadron and the other was "La Paix," constructed in Port-Louis.[287] They said that the ships' rolling during the previous night almost dismasted them.

On the 14th our small squadron was joined by a Spanish ship that had departed Campeche for Vera Cruz. That night the skies became overcast and the horizon all around turned very dark. At the same time, toward the North and close to the water's surface, we saw very low greenish clouds. These warnings, along with the becalmed sea, made us think that within a few minutes we were going to be struck by a raging tempest.

It did not take long for the north wind to arrive; it came through with a fury. Each ship took to her own devices. The Spanish ship, after struggling for a few hours, let herself go with the wind; we last saw her sailing with just the mizzen mast. The two French ships also disappeared.

The following day, the 15th, the sea was even rougher. When our ship sank between two waves, it seemed as though we were inside an endless valley, between two mountains of water that hid from view the tops of the masts of the "Saint Jean-Baptiste,"[188] which was no more than three pistol shots distant. In the evening during supper a huge wave, much bigger than the others, threw the ship to one side causing all the plates and food on the table to fly away. Although we tried to grab anything fixed, we finally fell one on top of the other. A bird, similar to and of the same size as a snipe, was blown against the ship's side from the wind's force.

On the 19th we again saw the two French ships that the tempest had separated from us, and together we arrived at Vera Cruz. There our voyage of 2,200 leagues by ship ended.

PART SEVEN –

THE TREK TO MEXICO CITY

…it seemed to me that the most fitting name for this land would be to call it New Spain—and so, in Your Majesty's honor, it has been named so.

Hernán Cortés
Letter to Emperor Charles V, 30 October 1520

Vera Cruz

F ather Taillandier wrote in his journal that he arrived in Vera Cruz on 19 January 1708. More than likely, even if just to confirm the hours separating Vera Cruz and Paris, the ship's navigator performed lunar observations or observed the phases of the Jovian moons to calculate the port's longitude.

An Original View of the Castle of San Juan de Ulúa and City of Veracruz. By M. Clairac, no date.

Vera Cruz is at 19 deg. 10 min. [north latitude], and seven hours difference from the meridian of Paris, according to the observations and calculations of our pilots.

I don't know if the bay of Vera Cruz deserves to be called a port. Ships drop their anchors on the lee side of fort Saint-Jean d'Ulloa [San Juan de Ulúa],[289] which is located on a small island that becomes totally inundated by the sea during high tide.

* * * * *

Hernán Cortés, attributed to M. Saltana, 19th c.

In the annals of historical events that paved the way toward the birth of the Spanish Empire, one of the most daring began sometime during the first week of February 1519 in Santiago de Cuba on that island's southeastern coast. There, amid street dancing and the general tumult of the large crowd of Spanish settlers, Hernán Cortés prepared for his departure to the mainland of the Americas. Did he secretly plan to establish a Spanish colony upon arrival there or did he intend to barter for gold with the natives, as Governor Diego Velázquez[290] commissioned him to do? Such was the controversy surrounding Cortés' rebellious personality that surfaced as soon as his ships disappeared from view.

Pierre Taillandier most likely read Bernal Díaz del Castillo's memoires since he referred to New Spain's history in his letter. In his celebrated memoire of the conquest of New Spain, *"La Verdadera Historia de la Conquista de la Nueva España,"*[291] first published in 1632, Díaz del Castillo said Cortés' fleet consisted of eleven caravels, with 508 soldiers and officers, 100 seamen-including pilots and artillery assemblers, 16 horses, 10 cannons, 4 culverins, 13 harquebuses, and 32 crossbows. Aboard the caravels were baskets of cassava flour bread, salted pork, dried fish, rum, fresh water, and live pigs and chickens. They brought green, red, and white glass beads to barter for gold with the *indios* or to use as bribes for favors. A priest or two accompanied them to celebrate mass on Sundays and take care of their spiritual needs, as was the practice during the colonization period.

They set out, joyous and fearless, for unknown shores. But Cortés, a married man with an *encomienda* in Cuba, not only longed for the day he would command a fleet of his own as a conquistador, but he also intended to become the governor of a new western frontier. His ambition was matched only by his unshakeable belief that once on the mainland he could fulfil a dream valued more highly than anything else and granted to only a few Spaniards: receive a family coat of arms along with a title.

Upon his arrival on the mainland of the New World, Cortés relinquished the commission Velásquez had conferred on him, thereby allowing his troops to vote him Captain-General in the elections held at the newly founded Villa Rica de la Vera Cruz.

* * * * *

On Good Friday [22 April] in 1519, Fernando [Hernán] Cortés disembarked near Saint-Jean d'Ulloa, and in honor of the holy day named the city he founded Vera Cruz, which at the time was about five leagues to the north[292] *Now it is called the Old Vera Cruz to distinguish it from the*

New Vera Cruz, where the port is located. It is the only port found on the Gulf of Mexico, a third the size of Havana, and not significant except for the merchant ships that arrive from Cádiz and return there loaded with silver, cocoa, indigo, and cochineal.[293]

Earlier, as Cortés had made his way west from Vera Cruz in late March, he won his first battle in the New World near a village they called Santa Maria de la Victoria in today's state of Tabasco. Though outnumbered by Mayans who lived close to coastal sources of fresh water, the Spaniards were victorious because they were better armed and because the horses they used in the fight frightened and confused the enemy. The Mayans had never seen such enormous animals.

The Mayans who confronted the Spaniards were descended from the Mesoamerican civilization that nearly died out from an unprecedented drought sometime before the year 1000.[294] Theirs was a story of unbearable hunger, anguish, and murder perpetrated on them by their own high priests who sought favors from the gods to provide rain to maintain and cultivate the farms. But the rains did not come—not for a long time.

Unable to live without fresh water and unable to placate the ire of their *teules* (gods) to whom they offered the best of their harvests and the fairest of their maidens, the few survivors fled to coastal areas of the peninsula, where they could fare better. There they lived in isolation and in small groups until their numbers increased. And then they resumed their ancestors' horrific practices.

Now, five or six hundred years later, the Mayans came face to face with another form of *teule*—the white men who rode horses and who would kill them with cannon shots, if they did not make peace with them.

In the peace treaty signing ceremonies that he always organized-after winning battles, Cortés ordered the celebration of the most Holy Sacrifice of the Mass in his desire to stop the natives' gruesome human sacrifices on their high stone altars. He had a simple altar constructed with a timber cross erected behind it. The first converts to Christianity were the twenty women given as gifts to Cortés and his men in Tabasco. One, whom the Spaniards called Doña Marina,[295] a Mayan princess, who would later give birth to Cortés' son, played a pivotal role in the conquest of Mexico City, then known as Tenochtitlán.

✶ ✶ ✶ ✶ ✶

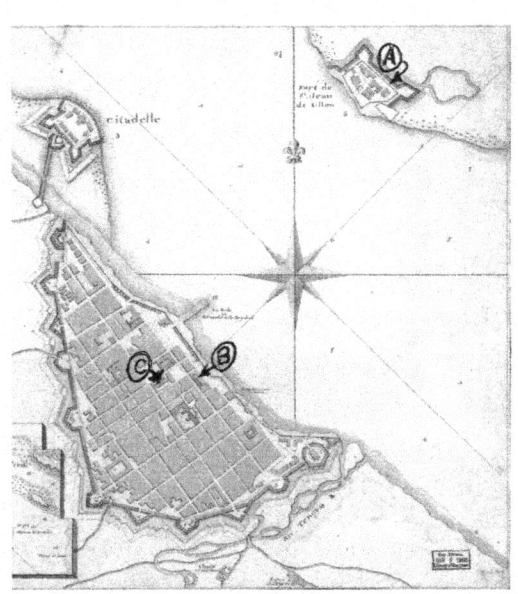

Map 9: Plan de la Ville de la Veracruz & Plan du Port de la Veracruz, 1798. By G. de Bois. (A) Fort San Juan de Ulúa, (B) Jesuit House, (C) Cathedral.

Taillandier and Bonnet spent two weeks in Vera Cruz before departing for Mexico City. Presumably, they passed the time recuperating from their Atlantic crossing and gathering their guides and provisions for the trek they would make overland. The Jesuit complex was near the shore (Map 9 - B) within view of their ship. They probably spent most of the time with their Jesuit brothers who would help them plan their journey. Nearby was the parish church which several years later was reconstructed and became the Cathedral of our Lady of the Assumption (Map 9 - C).

In those days there were two important overland routes from Vera Cruz to Mexico City. The "Camino Real" was the more important commercial trail which passed through Xalapa. The terrain was flatter this way and there were more towns to welcome travelers. The other, more westerly one that passed through Orizaba, though more difficult with many rivers to cross, was the route Taillandier and Bonnet took.[296]

CÓRDOBA AND ORIZABA

I n the middle of his life's journey, it seemed Taillandier was called upon by souls yet unsettled to make known what for centuries had been neglected in the fog of the Spanish conquest of the last Mesoamerican Empire. Between his descriptions of the rich and lush Mexican landscape with its fast-flowing rivers and spectacular views of snow-capped mountains, one can almost hear the thunder of musketry, the bedlam of war, and the neighing of massive Spanish horses as Hernán Cortés pursued his quest to capture the biggest prize in New Spain—Tenochtitlán—the capital of the Aztec Empire and today the heart of Mexico City.

Pierre Taillandier and Pierre Bonnet made the long slog to reach Mexico City, the largest and most spectacular city in the Americas in those days, eighty leagues west northwest of Vera Cruz.[297] They passed through a countryside that had been the scene of many treacherous, as well as daring, battles fought nearly two hundred years earlier by the allied armies of Cortés and Xicontecal of Tlaxcala, against the Aztec Confederation led by Montezuma[298] of Tenochtitlán.[299]

We departed from here [Vera Cruz] on the 3rd of February [1708]. We lost view of the sea as we continued our trip by land. Since it was very dry, we took the new road, which was a lot easier than the old one, especially during the

rainy season. More than a league from Vera Cruz one finds
a small place called Buena Vista. Three leagues farther one
crosses the Xamaca [Jamapa] River, which flows to the sea
eight leagues from Vera Cruz.

Map 10: *Taillandier's Route from Vera Cruz to Mexico City and then to Acapulco. From:*
Carte du Mexique ou de la (Nouvelle) Espagne. By Rigobert Bonne, 1771.

The next phase of the journey is ten leagues long and passes
through many pleasant but uncultivated places and ends
in a village called Cotasta [Cotaxtla], situated near the
Xamaca River. The next day we walked over hills for five
leagues until we saw some native huts and we entered a
plain where the Village of Saint Jean is, about eight leagues
distant from Cotasta.

On the 5th of February we arrived in a more temperate and
prettier place. We walked through fertile valleys planted
with fruit trees and cultivated with corn. We saw flying
all over an infinite number of birds of different species,

completely different from the birds in Europe. Mostly, we saw blue parakeets, much smaller than thrushes, but with very vibrant coloration.

Two leagues from here is a place called Saint Laurent [Yanga], populated by Negroes. They are descended from families of African blacks, who escaped from their masters and found their freedom on the condition they would settle in this region.[300]

Three leagues farther on is the city of Cordua [Córdoba], populated by many Spanish families. Their houses are constructed like the ones in Europe and can be compared to some of the old villages in France. The overall journey of around nine long leagues ends up in the city of Orissava [Orizaba], which is a bit bigger than Córdoba. Nearby here is the famous mountain[301] of Orizaba, which we had seen from the sea as far away as twenty-five leagues. Its summit is always covered with snow even though it is in the Torrid Zone and is much higher than the Pico de Tenerife.

That same night we were called on, with much courtesy, by two Spanish businessmen. One of them, upon learning we were French, was overcome with joy and privately visited with us to tell us he was born, as we were, a subject of the greatest king in the world, but that he had been raised in Cádiz since he was ten years old. Although now a stranger *to his native language, he reminded us in no uncertain terms that his heart was still as French as his birth.*

On the 6th of February, having walked two leagues on the plains of Orizaba, all covered in barley ready to be harvested, we climbed a mountain, or better said, a forest thick with oak trees.

Father Taillandier and his companions traveled through one of the two most frequented passes across the Sierra Madre Oriental mountains to reach Mexico City. The Orizaba pass is at about 8,530 feet and opens to the Central Mexican Plateau. The other pass at an elevation of about 4,265 feet, would have taken him via Xalapa farther north along the Camino Real. By comparison, their destination, Mexico City, is at a height of about 7,350 feet. Interestingly, Taillandier never mentioned that he experienced altitude sickness.

We then descended into a valley surrounded by very high mountains. In the middle of this valley, which was about a league in diameter, is Maltrata, a village populated by Indians. We walked for two and a half hours that afternoon before arriving at the base of a mountain covered by two species of pine trees. We ended the ten-league phase of our trip passing through a sandy stretch where there were many palm trees of the kind that grow in the sands of Pondichéry.

On the 7th, we discovered one of the most fertile places in America. I do not think there is, under Heaven, a more delightful and temperate climate. All the fruits from Europe and America grow well here. If the harvest of the vineyards and olive groves is not plentiful, it can only be attributed to the laziness of the people around here or to the clever laws of the Spanish monarchy that seeks to conserve this place in the New World as a dependent of Spain. Beautiful plains filled with villages can be seen all around, and the houses are made of brick baked in the sun. Wheat is planted every year, and the earth is irrigated by man-made canals or by spring water that flows from the nearby hills.

PUEBLA AND CHOLULA

W e arrived on the 8th in Puebla de los Angeles,[302] which is, other than the capital, the largest city in the kingdom. It is almost as big as Orleans: the streets are rectilinear, and the houses are quite attractive. Puebla is divided into four parishes, and it has nine convents for women and a greater number of Communities of men. Its churches are magnificent, especially the cathedral.

Royal Caroline College of the Holy Spirit and the Iglesia de la Compañía de Jesús. By BUAP.

Jesuit missionaries who passed through Puebla after 1578 stayed at the *Colegio del Espiritu Santo* (Royal Caroline College of the Holy Spirit) constructed by

Melchor de Covarrubias, a rich cochineal merchant. The college was erected over the ruins of an earlier home that Hernándo Gutierrez Pacheco donated to the first Jesuits—dirty, starving, and in rags—who arrived from Vera Cruz in 1572. It is possible, therefore, that Fathers Taillandier and Bonnet also stopped at the Caroline College, a block from the cathedral. Above the college entrance, a lintel bears this engraving: *Los justos entrarán por ella* ("The righteous shall pass through it").[303]

Leaving Puebla de los Angeles, we walked eight leagues through a beautiful valley, well populated and very fertile. A league from the trail to the right is a place called Cholala [Cholula], where Fernando Cortés thought he would die because of the treachery of the inhabitants.

Four leagues to the left[304] is the city and the Republic of Tlaxcala, which served Cortés in his conquest of Mexico City. Here, one can see three mountains covered with snow. One of these is a volcano[305] that has been calm for nine years but, during the last three months, has been spewing very thick smoke, which also can be seen from Mexico City.

MEXICO CITY

The next day we entered a pine forest where pheasants, turkeys, and all sorts of game abound. Upon descending from here, we discovered the lake of Mexico, and on the third day after we left Puebla de los Angeles, we arrived at noon in Mexico City, which is about twenty-two leagues from Puebla, and eighty from Vera Cruz.

This famous city, the most beautiful and the largest in the New World, is located on a vast plain surrounded by a circle of mountains for over forty leagues. During the rainy season that starts around May, the city can be approached via only three roads, the shortest of which is a good half league in length. The other two are about a league and a league and a half; but during the dry season, the lake level goes down considerably.

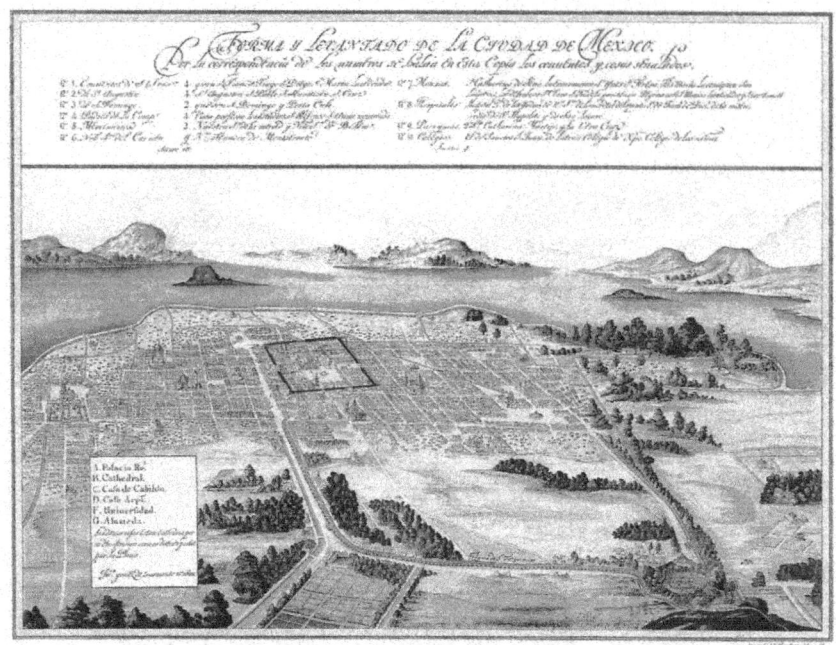

Map 11: Forma y Levantado de la Ciudad de Mexico [Mexico City]. By Juan Gómez de Trasmonte, 1628, (before the great flood of 1629). Gallica.bnf.fr.

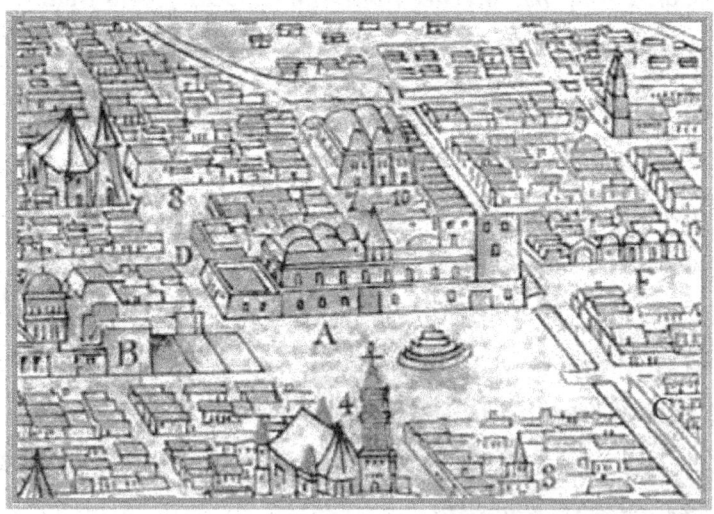

Map 12: Detail of the Plaza Mayor [facing east] taken from the Forma above. (4) Padres de La Compañia - Jesuits, (A) Royal Palace, (B) Cathedral, (F) University [beside the Acequia Real - canal], (10) Colegio [school], (8) Hospitals.

The Spaniards tried to drain the lake through channels in the mountain passes encircling this immense plain; but after a lot of expense and hard work, they only partly succeeded in their intent. However, they have solved the problem of the heaviest flooding that often threatens the city.

* * * * *

With fame preceding him, Hernán Cortés led his small army inexorably toward the Aztec capital, Tenochtitlán. He had known that his arrival in Vera Cruz coincided with an important Aztec prophecy—the Aztec god Quetzalcoatl, the white god and messiah of the Aztecs, would return from the east. Upon hearing of Cortés' arrival in Vera Cruz, Emperor Montezuma believed the prophecy had come to pass and told his people: "Our lord Quetzalcoatl has arrived."

But Montezuma was not a popular ruler, and Cortés, listening to the wise advice of Doña Marina, cobbled together peace treaties and alliances with the various caciques of the villages between Vera Cruz and Mexico. The caciques were angry with Montezuma who regularly ordered his tribute collectors to plunder their villages and enslave their men to maintain the causeways in the lake. Montezuma's soldiers also captured young women and children who were sacrificed daily in a ghastly ritual high up on the Great Temple.[306]

There were three principal causeways to the city, as Taillandier pointed out, interconnected with a maze of footpaths and wooden bridges. The wooden bridges, when removed, offered security from enemy attacks. The residents moved about in pirogues (log canoes), and lived-in dwellings constructed on floating islands called *chinampas*, made from gigantic wicker baskets filled with mud, that rose and fell with the level of the water on the plateau. Hernán Cortés and his troops marched into the Aztec city via one of the causeways from the south.

In spite of the Spaniards' profligate lives—they lived with women offered as gifts to them and had insatiable appetites for gold and silver—Father Taillandier was unabashed in his praise for Hernán Cortés whom he called a "hero in his conquest of Mexico." He also commended Cortés' devotion to the Virgin Mary, whose likeness the conquistador had ordered carved from wood and installed on the altars in the many villages he had befriended.

The Captain-General was confident that he could convert the natives to the true religion. He harangued all the caciques he met, including Montezuma himself, arguing that the gods they worshipped were nothing but devils. The ritual, Cortés asserted, of offering the still beating hearts of their children or of their enemies to appease these deities, and then partaking of their flesh, was abominable and barbaric and would surely offend his God and his Emperor.

In his first letter from Vera Cruz dated 10 July 1519 to Queen Juana "La Loca," and her son Holy Roman Emperor Charles V, Cortés wrote eloquently: "It seems most credible that our Lord God has purposely allowed these lands to be discovered... so that your Majesties may be fruitful and deserving in his sight by causing these barbaric tribes to be enlightened and brought to the faith by Your hand."

Ironically, it was Cortés' demand that Montezuma rid the sacrificial stone platforms of the vestiges of cannibalism and the stench of death that almost dimmed his bright star in history. Accompanied by the Aztec monarch, the Spaniard climbed one hundred fourteen steps to the top of the Great Temple's bloody and macabre platform from which he saw the full extent of the Aztec realm. The sight made Cortés more concerned about the chaos and madness happening all around him.

Not knowing what the future held for him or the more than five-hundred men who accompanied him, Cortés set out to achieve fame and wealth by ruining the Montezuma. He ended the wretched practice of sacrifice and cannibalism that he loathed. Cortés also demanded "that all the caciques and villages around give tribute to His Majesty Charles V and that he

[Montezuma] being a great leader, also give of his treasures." Believing that his "Lord Quetzalcoatl" had spoken, Montezuma handed over to Cortés the tribute his caciques brought to him and said, "Take all the gold that has been collected; there is nothing more I can give you. What I have prepared for your emperor is all the treasure I have from my father [Atzayácatl], which is already in your power and inside your residence."[307]

Clearly there was anger, and ultimately confrontation, between the Spaniards and their allies against Montezuma and his loyalists in Tenochtitlán. On the dark and rainy night of 1 July 1520, aptly called "*Noche Triste*" (Night of Sorrow) by Díaz del Castillo, fighting broke out. Cortés was lucky to escape along with his trusted lieutenants, Doña Marina, and the vanguard of soldiers including Díaz del Castillo. Surrounded by thousands of Montezuma´s loyal troops beating their drums unceasingly and blowing their trumpets into the night, the energized Aztecs launched a frenzy of killing and chased their erstwhile guests out of Tenochtitlán.

Montezuma's secretly stashed wealth, now seized by by Cortés' men— gold bars and chains, jewelry, figurines, and precious stones—slowed down the Spanish soldiers who carried these treasures in their sacks or war vests. The men ran and stumbled while some drowned in the lagoons as the Aztecs closed. But, in the grand scheme of things, it was of little consequence if those men were left behind, drowning and screaming obscenities—the Royal Fifth[308] was already safe with the vanguard of troops on horseback.

For the hundreds in the rearguard who were running for their lives, it was soon too late. They were overtaken by enraged Aztecs lying in wait along the causeways. Crying for their mothers and imploring the Virgin Mary to help them, they either were hacked to death or had their Achilles heel tendons cut to stop them from fleeing.

Silhouetted by sputtering torches in the darkness and pouring rain, those who survived were dragged up to the high temple by their captors who stumbled and slid in the rivulets of blood and water flowing down the Great Temple's steps made of lime and stone. Thrown one after another on the sacrificial slab, the soldiers could hear the infernal sound of drums and trumpets from the square below. The last thing each felt before total darkness descended upon him was the searing pain of a razor-sharp obsidian knife piercing his chest as the executioner wrenched his heart out of his heaving chest.

Despite one of the most spectacular and brutal retreats for an army in the history of medieval warfare, Tenochtitlán was doomed when Cortés returned less than a year later and laid siege to the city.[309] Tenochtitlán and the Aztec Empire fell because of the Spaniard's valiant and strategic moves, including manipulating local tribesmen seeking revenge on the Aztecs. It was one of the largest victories ever won by the smallest force.

With New Spain and the discovery of the Philippines on the other side of the Pacific Ocean, Spain would rule a vast empire where the sun never set. Over the ruins and unstable ground of Tenochtitlán, Cortés built a new city that guaranteed his own immortality and brought him the long-sought title of Governor and a coat of arms.

* * * * *

Less than 200 years after the fall of the Aztec Empire, Pierre Taillandier penned his description of Mexico City and its people with nostalgia and quaint curiosity. Because Cortés had razed Tenochtitlán and buried everything beneath its muddy waterways, Taillandier never saw remnants of that ancient city other than the Plaza Mayor [Map 12], later called the Zócalo, that had once been the center of the Aztec life.

The city naturally flooded during rainy seasons even though the Spaniards built it up by gradually filling in the surrounding Lake Texcoco. Since the conquest, manmade canals helped conduct the flood waters away from the the city. The main canal, the *Acequia Real* (Royal Canal), was located on the southern edge of the central Plaza Mayor (Maps 11 - 12). It seems probable that Taillandier would have passed his month-long stay in the city at the Jesuit complex near the western edge of the Plaza, the heart of this vibrant and colorful city.

The Cathedral, Mexico City, c 1870s. By Abel Briquet. In Vistas Mexicanas. Getty Museum.

On the north side the Spaniards erected a magnificent Cathedral where, on Sundays and holidays, European and Creole gentry showed off their wealth from aboard their carriages. Others promenaded the wide avenues of the plaza with their silk garments from China or their colorful cotton dresses from India's Coromandel Coast. Silk, calico, and muslin fabrics along with porcelain, precious stones, spices, perfumes arrived yearly in Mexico City aboard the galleons of the Manila-Acapulco trade. Merchants sold these wares in the Parián,[310] the bustling marketplace of stone shops built in the Plaza Mayor. As the Jesuit residence was nearby, Taillandier must have explored the Parián with all its exotic displays. But, too, he would have noted the wretched population of Aztecs and mestizos of many races who made their living selling trinkets and handicrafts or their harvests of corn, vegetables, and flowers on the very plaza where their ancestors celebrated their festivals and official ceremonies.

El Mercado del Parián. By Cristóbal de Villalpando, 1695. (Note: The Cathedral is on the north side (left), the Palace on the east, and the Acequia Real (Royal Canal) on the south.)

Mexico City is built very regularly. It is crossed by canals that are filled with water from the lake: One could dig them in all the streets. The city is much bigger than Puebla. Some Spaniards calculate the population to be about 200,000 but, looking at things realistically, one would not find more than 60,000 souls in the city.

There are 10,000 white people in Mexico City; the rest of the inhabitants include Indians, Blacks from Africa, Creoles, Mestizos, and other people who are descended from a blending of these diverse nations among themselves and with Europeans. This is the reason why there is a great diversity of colors from white to black, such that among a hundred faces one can hardly find two of the same color.

The houses there are beautiful and the churches magnificent. The city has a great number of religious societies. Other than Paris, there would not be a city in France with so many carriages. The climate is delightful. One can walk all year long dressed only in "drap d'Espagne" [Spanish cloth], although the city is at 20 degrees North latitude. During the warmest part of the summer one has only to find a shady spot to protect himself from the discomfort caused by the heat.

This gave rise to the response that a Spaniard newly arrived gave to Charles V. The prince had asked him how long was the time interval between summer and winter in Mexico, and he answered: "As much time, Sire, as it takes to pass from the sun to the shade." The rains that start in the beginning of May, and which do not end until summer is over, contribute greatly to moderate the heat.

Finally, if one considers the quantity of silver that comes in daily to the city from the mines, the magnificence of the churches and other buildings, the large number of carriages that roll along the streets non-stop, and the immense wealth of many Spaniards, then he will have an idea of one of the finest and most opulent cities in the world.[341]

After the conquest of Tenochtitlán and the total collapse of the Aztec Empire, Hernán Cortés asked Charles V to send missionaries to convert the people of this expanding colony, now dubbed *La Nueva España*, to Christianity. Cortés preferred the Mendicant Orders since in his opinion they "had in principle renounced all worldly goods and were less likely to compete with Spanish conquerors for land and resources. The three Mendicant Orders, the Franciscans, Dominicans, and Augustinians, arrived in Mexico in 1524, 1526, and 1533."[312]

Templo y Colegio Máximo de San Pedro y San Pablo.

Much later, in September of 1572, the first Jesuits headed by Father Pedro Sánchez, doctor and professor at the University of Alcalá and rector at the College of Salamanca, arrived in San Juan de Ulúa, Vera Cruz. The group consisted of fifteen Jesuits: eight priests, four co-adjutors, and three students. After passing through Puebla, they reached Mexico City on the 28th of September. By 1574 plans were underway to construct the first Jesuit institutions for Creole and indigenous boys near the west side of the cathedral—the Colegio San Ildefonso, a boarding school, and Colegio Máximo de San Pedro y San Pablo, a seminary offering university level courses in the humanities, Latin and Greek, theology, and philosophy. By the early 1700s the colleges had merged and were prospering.[313] No doubt Father Taillandier would have felt at home there among the priests and students as they probably reminded him of the Colège de la Trinité he had left behind only five months earlier. One can imagine him enjoying a pleasant conversation with the students and professors in the college's Patio Chico.

When Fathers Taillandier and Bonnet arrived in New Spain the evangelization, pacification, and assimilation initiatives by Jesuits and others had progressed well beyond the old Aztec Empire. Thousands of churches and colleges had been constructed in the mission centers to the north and south. The education of Creole and native youths and the improvement of the secular clergy was of paramount importance to bring enlightenment and new ideas for economic development to these far-flung parishes.[314]

Taillandier saw the opulence and magnificence of the churches and buildings and observed the lavish lifestyles displayed by the privileged Europeans and Creoles living in Mexico City, such as the rich landowners and businessmen. Yet, he could not hide the sorrow he felt for the marginalized native Mexican:

> But, on the other hand, when one looks at the Indians, who form the largest group of inhabitants of the city, niggardly dressed, without shirts and barefoot, it is difficult to persuade anyone that this city is indeed so rich.

PART EIGHT –

The Trek Down to Acapulco

Sunset and evening star,
And one clear call for me!
And may there be no moaning of the bar,
When I put out to sea.

Crossing the Bar
Alfred, Lord Tennyson

CUERNAVACA AND PALULA

T aillandier and Bonnet rested in Mexico City for one month. During that time, they would have arranged for their passage to Manila.

On the 11th of March we started on a new trip to reach the Mer du Sud. Taking the route to Acapulco, we walked four leagues over a well cultivated plain, and afterwards spent another hour climbing a mountain that the Spaniards call Subida del Arenal, for the great amount of sand deposits one finds there. For another five leagues, we passed through a pine forest; then we descended for three leagues to arrive at Cuernavaca, a small village situated on fertile land, but a lot more humid than the environs of Mexico City.

Known as the "China Road," it was a well-traveled trail of one hundred ten leagues that crossed high mountain passes, dense forests, rivers, and sand dunes. Initially, the travelers probably walked along the slopes of the now extinct Ajusco volcano as they progressed toward Cuernavaca. At almost 5,000 feet, the town was a popular summer refuge not only for the Aztec Emperors, but also for the Spanish and Mexican elites. In 1521 Hernán Cortés built a palace there overlooking the valley cultivated with sugar dates.

The countryside that one sees next is full of native villages;
it is crisscrossed by rivers and streams, which can be forded
during the dry season. One finds nothing but plains, hills,
and valleys until the Subida del Passarito. Afterwards
you walk down for more than a league on a very bad
road. About half a league more and you stop in Pueblo
Nuevo [New Town], a native village, located by the shore
of a lake that is a league long by about three-quarters of
a league wide.[315] This place is about twenty-one leagues
from Cuernavaca. We departed around four o'clock in
the afternoon to avoid the heat, and after a march of six
leagues we arrived at a place called Palula.

At the time Palula was a resting place for people traveling between Mexico City and Acapulco. More importantly, it was a center for business involving merchandise arriving from or destined for Asia via Acapulco.[316]

The following day we made another six leagues between
hills full of plants that the Spaniards call "organum"
[Mexican fence post cactus] and the French "cierges
épineux" [columnar or spiny candle cactus].[317] From afar
one could say they are a collection of an infinite number of
large candles made of green wax.

Las Balsas River

Taillandier's descent to Acapulco continued as he crossed the Las Balsas River (also known as the Atoyac or Mezcala River) near the small town of Mezcala, presently located along the major artery that connects Mexico City and Acapulco.

We crossed the Las Balsas River in the same way people did before the conquest of Mexico on a raft—a square framework of weak reeds, about ten feet long under which gourds are tied. One sits on a mule saddle, or on a bundle, which is placed in the middle of this "machine" to prevent it from turning over. A native, grasping one corner of the raft with one hand, and swimming with the other, guides you to the other shore. The Spaniards call this type of raft "balsas," and the river has taken this name. But it would have been apt to call it the Mosquito River because of the infinite number of these insects that, like a thick cloud, envelop the passengers. These mosquitoes, which are not larger than our smallest ones, bite them and leave marks that last around an entire month.[318] To escape their torment

*we walked the last nine leagues at night to reach a village
called Soumpango [Zumpango del Río].*

The Spanish discovered silver in the vicinity of Zumpango del Río in the
1530s. Among the owners of the mines established there was Hernán Cortés.
Toward the end of the 16th century, though, many of these mines were abandoned as the supply of cheap *encomienda* labor dwindled.[319]

*This entire area is a desert. There is nothing but a miserable
hut, erected along the road, for the use of travelers. Since
it was not occupied, we decided not to go inside fearing
we would be bitten by snakes or scorpions. We preferred to
spend the remaining two or three hours before daybreak
resting on the hard ground. The miserable hostels of Mexico
where one lodges have accustomed us to going without a
bed and all the other comforts we have when travelling
in France.*

*Two leagues past Soumpango is a community of four
hundred families, the majority of whom are Spaniards. The
town, called Cilpacingo [Chilpancingo], is located on fertile
plain about two leagues long and surrounded by hills. This
plain ends at a large native village. A league beyond
is another village. Past this last village we walked eight
leagues over very steep and rocky mountains [the Sierra
Madre del Sur].[320] We climbed up and down continuously.
In some sections two horses side by side could not negotiate
the trail that passed between two huge boulders. We stopped
and rested in a small village called Los Dos Caminos.*

Chilpancingo ("Hornets Nest") was founded by Spanish conquistadores in 1591. Today it is the sister city of Cavite City in the Philippines, so designated in recognition of the many runaway Filipino sailors and servants who settled there during the era of the Manila-Acapulco galleon trade. Los Dos Caminos, now known as Julian Blanco, is a small town 70 km from Acapulco.

The following day, Sunday, we celebrated the Holy Mass, and these good natives came to hear it. They had not heard mass in a month because the priest assigned to them lives twelve leagues away and must visit many hamlets that are far apart. In appreciation for what we did they brought us oranges and garlands of flowers. From Los Dos Caminos to Acapulco, we walked twenty-one leagues without finding a single village. Every three leagues or so there were inhospitable huts that served as hostels for travelers.

Four leagues from Los Dos Caminos we crossed the river Los Papagaios, that is to say, The Parrots. After Las Balsas, it is the largest river between Mexico City and the sea. Later, it took us an hour and a half to climb a very steep mountain, which, like the river, is called Los Papagaios, apparently because of the large birds that one sees there.[321] They are the size of a chicken; the top of the head is yellow, and the rest of the body is green. They can easily learn to talk.

Among the different species of trees that grow on this mountain there is one, called Campeche wood, which is *used in Europe to make dyes. It is not very tall; the leaves are small, like the three-leaf clover.*

In 1540 at the Mayan port of Ah Kin Pech (Campeche), the Spaniards discovered the red-orange dye which the natives extracted from the heartwood of the small leguminous Campeche tree. The dye was inexpensive to prepare by simply boiling the heartwood. In Europe the dye quickly became popular as even the poor could afford cloth colored with it. Only the logs were exported to Europe, thus the tree was also called "logwood." Ships carrying this valuable cargo were targets for pirates up to the 19th century.

ACAPULCO

Following the colonization of the Philippines, Spain launched its most ambitious seaborne enterprise known as the Manila-Acapulco Trade, or the Galleon Trade, lasting from 1565 to 1815. In addition to carrying valuable cargo, the galleons departing from Acapulco also transported many missionaries traveling to the Philippines and Asia via Manila. From Manila those bound for countries farther west—Japan, China, Siam, Dutch East Indies, and India—could find passage aboard foreign merchant vessels.

Acapulco, 1683. By Peter Schenk. (Fort San Diego is on the hill, center.)

On the tenth day of our journey, we arrived in Acapulco.[322]
The town is about eighty-seven leagues from Mexico City at
latitude 16°45' North, according to the observations of the
pilots. The merchants from Mexico City have warehouses
here where they store the merchandise brought from Manila.
Many traders converge on this port when the ship from the
Philippines arrives, but as soon as it departs, the merchants
withdraw. The residents, even the richest ones, spend the
summer inland to escape the excessive heat and unhealthy
air of Acapulco.

The world traveller and chronicler Gemelli Careri, who was in Acapulco in January 1697, asserted that the town should "more properly be called a poor village of fishermen than the chief market of the South Sea and port for the voyage to China; so mean and wretched are the houses being made of nothing but wood, mud, and straw."[323]

The port is good and safe, but the castle [Fort San Diego] is
not very strong although it is armed with handsome forged
artillery. The galleons from Manila usually arrive here
in the months of December or January, and they depart
from here in early March to at least the beginning of April.
If they sail much later, they won't encounter winds with
sufficient strength to push their heavily laden galleons; and
from the Mariana Islands, undoubtedly, they will have to
fight the contrary winds from the west that start to blow by
the end of June. The town of Acapulco suffers greatly from
frequent earthquakes. During our stay here, we felt two
tremors that were not very powerful.

Likely, Taillandier and Bonnet delayed their trek down to Acapulco to avoid meeting the long caravans of mules laden with merchandise headed up to Mexico City since "the conditions of travel were always very primitive" on this trail, according to William Lytle Shurz in his book "The Manila Galleon."

The cargo of Oriental goods arriving in Acapulco from Asia aboard the *nao de China*, as the Mexicans referred to the Manila galleon, being of "infinite variety and quality" according to Schurz, was packed in containers of all sizes and descriptions. Thus, it took at least a month to unpack the merchandise, inventory it, and complete its sale at the *Feria* (Fair), the most important event of the year in Acapulco.[324] Of equally infinite diversity was the influx of "soldiers and king's officials, begging friars and cursing muleteers and porters, and the fringe of followers who went to minister to the pleasures of the rest."

Traders of every sort, from native hawkers to Mexican and Peruvian merchants, came to bid for the Asiatic merchandise. The Peruvians, sailing to Acapulco aboard the annual ship from Lima whose arrival coincided with the appearance of the Manila galleon, brought with them as much as two million pieces of eight to purchase Chinese goods according to Careri.

However, when the two Jesuits arrived on the 21st of March, the raucous fair was over. The galleon would have been cleared to receive passengers and cargo for the return trip to Manila.

PART NINE –

Across the Pacific

For we are all like swimmers in the sea,
poised on top of a huge wave of fate,
which hangs uncertain to which side to fall.
And whether it will heave us up to land,
or whether it will roll us out to sea,
back out to sea, to the deep waves of death,
we know not, and no search will make us know;
only the event will teach us in its hour.

Sohrab and Rustum
Mathew Arnold

DISCOVERY OF THE PACIFIC OCEAN

B eyond the sandy shores of Acapulco's picturesque semicircular harbor, where the galleons from Manila sought safety and disembarked
weary passengers and exotic cargo, lay the Pacific Ocean on the
western shores of the New World. Christopher Columbus never saw its deep
and dark blue waters for he did not find a route to reach Japan and the Spice
Islands. That feat awaited another man—another conquistador—whose
sighting of that new ocean expanded the earth's size beyond the imagination
of any explorer in his day.

"Prayer indeed is good, but while calling on the gods, a man should
himself lend a hand," Hippocrates once said. The discovery of the Pacific
Ocean happened because Vasco Núñez de Balboa prayed to God while
trusting his instincts that his sacrifices in the service of His Majesty Charles
V would make him a famous and rich man.

Born in Badajoz in Extremadura, Spain, in 1475, Balboa came from
the ranks of lower nobility whose sons, according to a Spanish chronicler,
were "men of good family who were not reared behind the plow." Moved by
the faith that distinguished many Extremeños in feudal Spain, he sought his
fortune in the Indies.

Having survived his first attempt to settle in San Sebastián on the Gulf
of Urabá, in present day Colombia, Balboa led the survivors of that expedition
towards a less hostile place across the gulf on the Isthmus of Panama. Here

in 1510, as their elected leader, he named the new settlement Santa María de la Antigua del Darién. He continued bartering for gold and slave-hunting, but his ambition for greatness drove him to lead another expedition across the isthmus in search of the mother lode, which the natives said came from a place farther south in the land of the Incas on the other side of the imposing cordilleras.

Balboa Claims the Mar del Sur for Spain. By T. de Bry, 1594.

Looking southward from a mountain peak in Darién one September day in 1513, Balboa saw a vast body of water. Excited by his discovery, he practically ran down the mountain to wade into it and taste its saltiness. This new expanse of water, which the Spanish explorers at first called *Mar del Sur*, or South Sea, instantly doubled the size of the Earth. It placed the location of Japan and the Spice Islands beyond the unknown expanse of this new ocean. "In this respect, Vasco Núñez de Balboa's discovery of the new sea was a milestone in the history of navigation."[325]

Aboard the Manila Galleon

Having missed the fair in Acapulco, Taillandier and Bonnet, along with twenty one other Jesuits,[326] awaited their departure for Manila from a shaded lean-to on the northern end of the bay. The galleon *Nuestra Señora del Rosario y San Vicente Ferrer (SVF)* was being refitted and resupplied with arms and provisions for the voyage. She would sail as the *capitana,* or flagship, with the *Nuestra Señora de la Encarnación* as *almiranta,* or vice-flagship and escort.[327] Due to the depredations of English pirates, among them the notorious Woodes Rogers who flew the skull and crossbones symbol on a black flag during the early 18th century, the Mexican viceroy authorized armed escorts to protect Manila bound galleons.

Manila Galleon. https://www-labs.iro.umontreal.ca/~vaucher/History/Ships_Discovery/.

On the 30th of March [1708] we set our sails; the ship had two-hundred crew men composed of all nationalities. The majority of the mariners were from the Philippines. The viceroy of Mexico, His Excellency Sr. Duque de Albuquerque,[328] had appointed Father Bonnet as the ship's chaplain.

As on all Manila sailings, the *NS del Rosario y SVF* carried the yearly Mexican subsidy, or *situado*,[329] needed to ensure the security and governance of the fledgling colony. The galleons generally returned to Manila with up to 2,000,000 pesos, including the silver that the shippers in Manila earned from the proceeds of the fair in Acapulco. With the peso being equal to a piece of eight, or one Spanish silver dollar, the value of the Mexican remittance would have equaled about $100 million today.

A good number of passengers appointed to serve in the Philippines— soldiers, priests of the various religious orders, and civil service personnel, alone or with their families, sailed with the galleons on the westward voyage. For example, in 1671 the new governor of the colony, Don Fausto de Cruzat y Gongora of Navarra, sailed aboard the *Santo Niño* with his wife, Doña Beatriz de Arostegui y Aguirre, their five children, and Doña Beatriz´s sister, Teresa, who later married the galleon´s commander.

However, sometimes pirates attacked the ships along the galleon routes. On its return trip to Acapulco, for example, the *NS de la Encarnación* was captured by Rogers on the 22nd of December 1709, off Cape San Lucas, California. Rogers' log entry reads: "We were now something dubious seeing the Manila Ship, because it's near a month after the time they generally fall in with this coast. ... we gave her several broadsides…which they returned as thickly a while…we shot a little ahead of them, lay thwart her Hause close aboard, and plied them so warmly that she soon struck her colours two-thirds down."[330]

* * * * *

Usually, two galleons plied yearly between the two ports, one in the Orient and the other in Mexico. At first Manila served as an *entrepot* between New Spain and China, but later it participated substantially in this trans-Pacific commerce with products and produce of its own. "Above all, save for a few years, these were silk ships. Silk in every stage of manufacture and of every variety of weave and pattern formed the most valuable part of their cargoes."[331]

The sea claimed dozens of ships and hundreds of sailors during this marathon shuttle that lasted for two and a half centuries. The seabeds between Manila and Acapulco and between Vera Cruz and Cádiz could literally surrender thousands of pounds of gold bullion; untold quantities of gold and silver specie of Asian, Mexican, and Peruvian origin; and gold jewelry, including crucifixes set with diamonds, jade, and rubies.

The voyages of the galleons were the longest trade routes sponsored by any nation in the 16th century. While the route to Manila using the prevailing tradewinds was relatively straightforward, the "*tornaviaje*," or return route to Acapulco, was not. This was of great concern to Philip II. In his letter of 24 September 1559 to Luis de Velasco, Viceroy of New Spain, Philip II said: "... the most important part of this journey to our mind is to know the return route because we already know the way there[332] and it doesn't take very long. You will tell us what of this is done."

The establishment of the return route to New Spain was of paramount importance as well to Miguel López de Legazpi, the founder of Manila and the first governor general of the islands. He arrived in April of 1565 with Andrés de Urdaneta, an Augustinian friar and explorer, as his chief pilot. Without regular supplies and reinforcements from New Spain colonization of the Philippines would have been doomed.

Urdaneta, who years prior had sketched a theoretical route of the *tornaviaje* as a member of the ill-fated Loaysa[333] expedition, did not waste time in carrying out what Philip II demanded. With Legazpi's permission he took command of the *San Pablo* in Cebu, and by the 1st of June 1565 he had cleared the Philippines. Urdaneta then proceeded north towards Japan until reaching 39° N. latitude where he fell in with the prevailing easterlies known as the Kuro Siwo oceanic currents. Asia's seamen have known of the Kuro Siwo oceanic phenomena since ancient times, something Urdaneta would have remembered well, having sailed as a younger man aboard Magellan's and Loaysa's expeditions to the Moluccas.

As to what it was like to make an eastward crossing of the Pacific Ocean, Schurz narrated this harrowing incident that Antonio de Morga (1559-1666), author of *Sucesos de las Islas Filipinas*, endured: "Morga himself experienced the vicissitudes of weather in the north Pacific. In 1604 he crossed to New Spain in the *Espiritu Santo* with its consort, the *Jesus Maria*, under the command of Lope de Ulloa. The galleon left Cavite on the 11th of July but ran into rough weather on the way out of the bay ... and was left stranded three miles from deep water. Chinese junks were hurriedly brought out from Manila, cables were lashed to the galleon, and at high tide she was pulled across.... On the 10th of November she was struck by a SSW gale within sight of Cape Mendocino on the California coast. The storm lasted for twelve days.... She lost nearly all her rigging and on the 22nd was twice struck by lightning. The first bolt killed three men and injured eight others, and sixteen were severely stunned by the second. The ship reached Acapulco nearly two months later with her upper works badly damaged and her crew worn out by their sufferings."[334]

Taillandier described his experience aboard the *NS del Rosario* on the way to Manila and about the dreadful event that occurred during the galleon's previous voyage to Acapulco, a story no doubt related to him by one of the ship's officers:

Our knowledge of Spanish served us well to hear confessions and to teach all the crew. In the beginning we only had a little wind and had to endure twelve days of calm until we were about 100 leagues out to sea. The ship's course was southwest until 13 degrees north latitude, after which we encountered very strong winds that took us all the way to the Marianas. The sailing was very pleasant. We were not at all afraid of contrary winds, and the wind that blew was always fresh and cooled the warm days.

But, as easy as the voyage from Acapulco to Manila is, the return voyage to Acapulco is disagreeable and dangerous. The ships must go all the way past 30 degrees and even up to 39 degrees north latitude to avoid the ocean breezes that prevail near the tropics.

Since it is during the winter months that this trip is made, great storms are often encountered along the way with hardly a safe port in which to seek shelter. The ship that took us to the Philippines had sailed seven months to make the return crossing. Near the entry point to the Philippines, the Captain was forced to drop anchor after huge waves hit the ship, inundating her completely. Some of the ship's provisions were ruined and seven of her crew were tossed into the ocean, two of whom were tossed back into the ship by yet another wave.

Every day we saw birds that we did not see during our voyage from the Canaries to Saint Domingue, though that trip was a lot shorter.

THE MARIANAS

We dropped anchor on the 13th of June on the island of Guhan [Guam], the largest island in the Marianas, after navigating for seventy-five days a distance of two-thousand one hundred seventy-five leagues from Acapulco. This island lies along a line from the southwest to the northeast between 13 degrees 5 minutes to 13 degrees 35 minutes.

Reception of the Manila Galleon by the Chamorro in the Ladrones [Marianas] Islands. Boxer Codex, c 1590.

The next day I had the pleasure of saying mass on this island, bathed with the blood of many Jesuits[335] who had baptized all these infidels [Chamorros]. They now live on the principal islands of Guhan, Sarigan, and Saipan.

I visited Don Jose de Quiroga,[336] Sergeant Major of the islands, whose virtue and zeal contributed much to the conversion of all these idolaters. The same fervor led him to establish strong discipline among the soldiers: they all live in one place and say their prayers, day and night, with regularity. They also often avail of the sacraments of Penitence and the Eucharist. Among the soldiers here I met a Frenchman from Oléron.

The Governor, as is the custom, sent us some refreshments. I took a native canoe to go to land and return to the ship. I have not seen a vessel as light as this nor one that sails better so close to the wind. I saw some that tacked two quarters into the wind. They are less maneuverable with a following wind than one across the beam.[337]

THE PHILIPPINE ISLANDS

Taillandier described the trip westward from the Marianas to the Philippines:

We put out to sea on the 14th [June 1708] and on the first day of July we saw the Philippines, which is three hundred thirty-six leagues distant from the Marianas. We were buffeted by very strong winds, but it was only once that we were taken by surprise. We always stood guard in order to adjust the sails.

The strait between the islands up to Manila is about one hundred leagues long. Navigation there is difficult because of the rapid currents and because there are few places to drop anchor. To the north is the big island of Luçou [Luzon] where Manila is located, and to the south are many islands of different sizes.

At last, after an uneventful trip across the Pacific, the *NS del Rosario y SVF* reached the dreaded *embocadero*[338] of the San Bernardino Strait,[339] where the galleons from Acapulco usually passed to sail to Manila (Map 13). Blowing since June, the monsoon winds drew warm air from the southwest that collided with the northern equatorial air currents and erupted into cloud bursts over the islands. Now, in July, the *NS del Rosario* had to negotiate that strait, not only against the westerly breeze but also the rip tides, treacherous waves, and swift currents that crossed the deepest seabed along the east coast of the Philippines.

Map 13: *Carta hydrographica y chorographica de las yslas Filipinas [Showing the route of the galleon through the Philippine islands en route from New Spain to Manila], 1734. By Pedro Murillo Velarde, SJ and Nicolas Bagay. (1) San Bernardino Strait, (2) Manila Bay, (3) Cavite, (4) Manila.*

Had he been standing on the galleon's quarterdeck, Taillandier would have barely made out the northern tip of Samar Island—its craggy headland beaten by relentless waves. He would have heard the unmistakable roar of the ocean as the heavy combers ran on and crashed into a wall of jagged rocks forcing the intruding sea to break out into a mist over its fissures.

The Jesuit from Lyon might have marveled at the difference in conditions from the previous weeks when the sailing was so pleasant. Now the sea and the wind had gone up. He, no doubt, watched anxiously as the *gavieros*, or top men, swarmed aloft in a race to furl the galleon's giant square sails or lower topsails. Still, he must have been thrilled to experience the real-life drama aboard one of Spain's argosies, a leviathan of the spice and silk trade.

Perhaps, too, he realized that these ships were the most important means by which East Asia and India could be Christianized.

We entered the [San Bernardino] strait on the 1st of July [1708]. Although a fresh breeze allowed us to navigate a league and a half per hour, we had a lot of trouble overcoming the tide that ran the other way. Later, as the seas calmed, we took advantage of the tide that now shifted in our favor. We put the longboat in front to guide the ship, and in the span of five or six hours we managed to move eight leagues without any wind. This maneuver was almost disastrous; the current had taken us into the middle of a group of islets that the Spaniards call Los Naranjos because of the orange groves that cover them.

The ship's bowsprit and sail struck a sharp rock on the escarpment of one islet, but, luckily, we were in deep enough water that we did not run aground there. The currents turned the ship around and tossed us into the middle of a sort of harbor where we dropped anchor and waited for a favorable wind that finally came and pulled us out of a bad predicament.

It took us fifteen days to clear the strait. We were always afraid a westerly wind would push the ship back to the open sea.[340] On the 17th we arrived at Cavite, a port inside the Bay of Manila and about three leagues from the city. Two days later the west wind started blowing for twelve days and during the next eighteen we had continuous rains except for short intervals. The rainy season starts about this time and lasts until the month of November or even December.

Manila

In a little over two weeks after entering the treacherous San Bernardino Strait, the *NS del Rosario y SVF* sailed into Manila Bay. She dropped anchor on 17 July 1708 at Cavite, southwest of the walled city of Manila. Cavite was the terminus for westbound galleons. To this day it remains the port of entry for foreign vessels. Cavite was also home port for the Spanish Armada and the construction site for galleons and other vessels intended for commerce and the defense of the islands.

View of Manila from the Sea. By Fernando Brambila, during the Malaspina Expedition, c 1792.

It must have been an exciting experience for Father Taillandier to finally arrive in the Philippines less than a year after leaving Europe. "Cavite can be described as a parish town of many nations," according to the 18th century historian Pedro Murillo-Velarde, SJ, "for the many from the four corners of the world that congregate there, especially since the commerce was the most opulent, attractive, and universally vibrant…." He went on to explain that

"Cavite" is derived from the word *cavit,* or *cawit,* meaning "hook." Its land mass is shaped like a hook protruding into the bay.[341]

During his "pleasant voyage," Taillandier must have marveled at the vastness of the Pacific Ocean and been soothed by the sibilate splash and swoosh of the ship's bow slashing the dark sea. While the galleon's huge sails tightly seized the breeze, the sun's long rays peeked through the jungle of shrouds and dropped fleeting shadows across its quarter deck and massive poop deck. Later, the glowing sun, having dipped into the sea, would light up the ship's towering square sails like gilded wings.

The scenery would be even more beautiful at night with phosphorescent plankton glimmering on the sea's surface. Overhead, the starry firmament slowly whirled, displaying the zodiac of animals familiar to every astronomer. When a full moon appeared, it bathed the galleon with a soft, yellow light, and on setting, it seemed to joyously point the way westward.

As the wind freshened with the rising sun and the horizon looked the same as it did on all the previous days, what could Father Taillandier have felt or imagined as he inexorably neared his destination? Did he ask why God put him aboard this galleon to cross this vast ocean so far from home? Like his friend, Pierre Bonnet, with whom he had formed a "special bond," Taillandier must have prayed for God's blessing and that He would guide them, through example and suffering, to plant the Christian faith in the hearts of the young and old, the oppressed and the oppressors, in the Jesuit missions of India.

* * * * *

During his seven months in the Philippines, Taillandier would have been pleased to witness how Spain governed and encouraged the evangelizing efforts of the various religious orders that arrived there. Just as he was surprised at the multi-ethnicity of the population in Mexico, what he saw in Manila astounded him no less. According to Murillo-Velarde, "There are Ternates, Borneans, Timorese, Bengalese, Blacks from Asia, Malabars, Coromandels and Canarians. There are many Sangleyes, or Chinese, and quite a number of Armenians, Persians, Tartars, Macedonians, Turks and Greeks. There are people from all the nations of Europe—French, Germans, Dutch, Genevans, Venetians, Irish, English, Polish and Swiss." [342]

The Spaniards and natives from the various islands also added to the cacophony of tongues in the city that could not be replicated anywhere else in the world. Taillandier must have marveled at the congress of nations represented by these people as they walked clothed in their best Sunday garments along Manila's main promenade.

Having visited Jesuit Mission residences not only in Luzon but also in the Visayas, [343] Taillandier likely would have been introduced to the historical works of the early Jesuits, notably Pedro Chirino (1557-1635), one of the founders of the Jesuit Society in the Philippines. Published in Rome in 1604, Chirino's "Relacíon de las Islas Filipinas y de lo que han trabajado en ellas los PP. de la Compañía de Jesús," detailed the Jesuits' spiritual conquests in the Philippines during the first twenty years of their presence in the islands. [344] He went on to produce a second work, "La Primera Parte de la Historia de la Provincia de Filipinas de la Compañía de Jesus, 1581-1606." The remainder of his copious notes were left unedited until Pedro Murillo-Velarde published them as *Segunda Parte*, which covered the years that followed up to 1716. [345]

The earliest Jesuit history began with Domingo de Salazar, a Dominican of considerable experience in the Mexican missions, who was the first missionary appointed Bishop and head of the episcopal see at Manila. He brought four Jesuits with him from Mexico. The men—Antonio Sedeño and Alonzo Sanchez, priests; Gaspar Suárez de Toledo, a scholastic; and Nicolás Gallardo a lay brother—were designated to establish the first Jesuit mission in the Philippines. "In January 1581 the little band took the road that dipped down from Mexico City to the little seaport of Acapulco, where the galleon *San Martín*, 400 tons, with Captain Luis de Sahagosa waited to take them across the Pacific. ...carrying besides her compliment of 96 officers and men, a little over 100 passengers, and a subsidy for the Philippine government of 153,376 silver pesos. Aside from the illness and death of Gaspar Suárez and several other passengers, the voyage was uneventful."[346]

The Jesuits also produced regional histories that Taillandier might have read. Francisco Combés wrote the first history of Mindanao and the Sulu Islands (1667), while Francisco Ignacio Alzina described the ancient traditions of the Visayan people of central Philippines (Samar and Leyte) in "Historia de las Islas e Indios de Bisayas" (1668).[347] Alzina, who was twenty-two years old when he arrived from Spain, spent the most productive years of his life as a missionary in the Visayas. He described the "daily life and labors" the missionaries endured in the central Philippine islands. Lacking sufficient replacements, each one of them had to do the work of two. In his letter to the Jesuit General's assistant, he explained: "Each Father has under his care at least two towns; some have three, others four or even five. I myself, this Lent of 1660, visited and heard confessions in four. Thus, we are always on the move, carrying our houses on our backs like the tortoise, for wherever the missionary goes he must bring with him his domestic effects, and in many places his church equipment too. What he accomplishes by a sojourn of 19 or 20 days, he finds when he returns one or two months later to be altogether undone and forgotten. Thus, we are continually starting all over again."[348]

Nonetheless, what Taillandier saw and experienced in the countryside must have lifted his spirits for he described the Philippines as "the most beautiful of countries." After his arrival in India, he alluded to the profound difference between the receptiveness of the Filipinos to evangelization by the Jesuits and other Orders compared to the hostility of the Hindus toward the new religion.

* * * * *

At the time of Taillandier's arrival, the walled city of Manila (Map 14) was an important enclave for the Jesuits. It was the home of two Jesuit colleges: the College of San José and the College of Manila (later San Ignacio), founded in 1595.[349] The two colleges awarded doctorate and master's degrees to high achieving students. Many graduated as priests, curates, or chaplains. Some lay graduates went on to hold government jobs such as *alcaldes mayores*, or town mayors.[350]

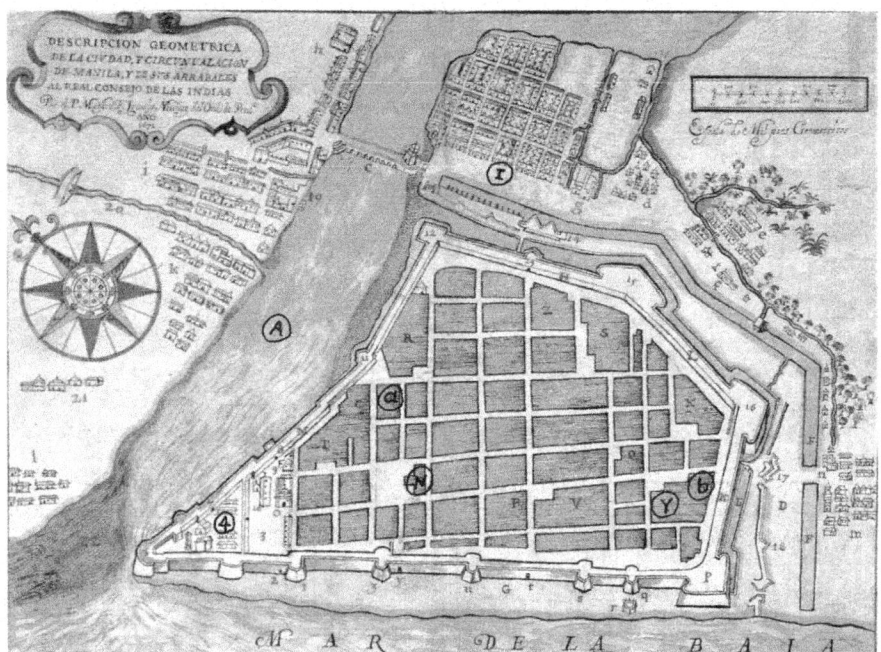

Map 14: Manila, 1671. By Friar Ignatio Muñoz, OP. (4) Fort Santiago, (A) Pasig River, (N) Metropolitan Church, (Y) Jesuit College [of San José], (a) Sto. Tomás College, Royal University, (b) Jesuit Seminary [of San Ignacio], (I) Parián. Pares.mcu.es.

Most likely, Fathers Taillandier and Bonnet were accommodated at the College of San José seminary attached to the College of Manila (Map 14 - Y). They would have experienced stimulating camaraderie among the Jesuit residents as they were the most highly educated men in the colony, including the sons of Spanish elites and Jesuits from other parts of Europe. From the window of their room and from the city's ramparts the two Jesuits bound for the Coromandel Coast would have enjoyed the view of Manila Bay. Various types of sailing ships were at anchor; many were arriving from or setting sail for Japan, China, Siam, Malacca, Batavia, and the other islands of the Philippine archipelago. The main building of the College of Manila was built around a central patio. Part of this patio was planted with medicinal herbs.[351] Taillandier would have found these herbs and other exotic Asian flora interesting, for, as the observations in his letter reveal, he was an amateur naturalist.

While travelling in the Philippines, it seems likely that Fathers Taillandier and Bonnet stayed in Jesuit residences or farms outside of Manila. The first Jesuit farms, built in the early part of the 17th century, were in the areas of Tondo, Mayhaligi, and Taytay, a village twelve miles southeast of Manila that borders Laguna de Bay, the largest lake in the islands.

Pierre Taillandier remembered his sojourn in the Philippines:

When the lowlands flood, canoes are utilized to get around in the fields planted with rice that from a distance look like very nice meadows. The heavy rains ease the heat, but being brought over by the west winds, the rains make the climate in Manila very humid. The most burnished steel will oxidize in only one night here.

The forests of these islands are full of wild buffalos, deer, and an unusual species of wild boars. The Spaniards brought cattle, horses, and sheep from America, but these animals cannot survive here because of the high humidity and flooding.

Crocodile, nipa (palm leaf) hut, farmer plowing with a carabao (water buffalo). From Carta hydrographica y chorographica de las Yslas Filipinas, 1734.

Wax is very plentiful as are different varieties of cotton. The rice here is excellent and "froment," or bread wheat, grows in some areas. One also finds ebony, Campeche wood, indigo, a variety of wild cinnamon, nutmeg, fig trees, and bananas of different species not found in America. In the end one can see many kinds of trees whose fruits are unique. Above all there are a great number of trees that are useful for construction and ship masts.[352]

The rivers are full of crocodiles that eat many animals, including people. One caught near our mission's farm had eaten thirteen people; it was eighteen feet long and its snout measured five feet.

These islands are located between 19 and 5 degrees of latitude north. Besides the big island of Luzon, the Spaniards own nine other large islands and many other smaller ones, including a part of Mindanao. The government is composed of twenty provincial governorships of which twelve alone are in Luzon. The archbishop of Manila has three bishoprics under his jurisdiction: one in Cagayan, north of Luzon; one in Camarines, east of the same island; and one in Cebu, on the island of the same name. Other neighboring islands depend upon these bishoprics. Magellan was killed on the island of Cebu.

Within the four bishoprics there are seven hundred parishes consisting of more than a million Christians, better indoctrinated than many of those commonly attending church in Europe. The Augustinian, Franciscan, and Jesuit orders manage and educate the parishioners, all of whom have converted to Jesus Christ and sworn allegiance to the Spanish monarch.

There still are found in the mountains and forests barbarous individuals, black, and of small stature, who little by little are brought to the fold to know the true God.[353] Other than the language spoken by these blacks, who are considered ancient inhabitants of the islands,[354] the people who are converted, and their number is very large, speak three principal languages: Tagalog, Pampango, and Visayan. Tagalog, which is the most sophisticated, is spoken in Manila and its environs.

These languages have a lot in common with each other, and with the Malay that is spoken in Borneo, Java, Sumatra, and the Malacca peninsula, which leads one to believe that the Malays conquered these islands and forced the ancient inhabitants to seek refuge in the mountains.

On the other hand, all those other attributes, that distinguish them [the Filipinos] from the Europeans, make them very similar to the Malays. They have the same facial features, small nose, large eyes, and the yellow-olive color like the Malays. Lastly, they dress in the same manner and construct their bamboo huts beside the river as they do. They have a gentle nature, and it is precisely this trait that distinguishes them from the Malays, who are cruel and ferocious.[355]

Village on Stilts. By E Hildebrandt, c 1895. Pasig River, Manila.

All the islanders are very fond of the Spaniards, and gladly offer them their children as servants, in contrast to the Americans who up to now have not gotten accustomed to the domination of their conquerors. It is true that the Filipinos accepted the gospel and the Spanish government; the force of arms had very little part in the conquest of the islands.

Magellan discovered the islands in 1521, and since then many attempts were made to colonize them. However, the Spaniards did not actually become established there until 1565 when Don Miguel López de Legazpi, a Viscayan, founded the city of Cebu.[356] Manila was not founded until 1571.

When Magellan disembarked on an island [Mactan] near Cebu, a native who was sent to spy on the Spaniards and who hid behind bamboo thickets and observed them eating their dinner, reported to his chiefs that the newly arrived foreigners were strange men: they were white, they had very long noses, they covered the table on which they served their meals with white cloth, they ate rocks, and they finished their meals by eating fire. Such was his description of the hardtack they ate and the tobacco they smoked.

To convince his countrymen to accept Spanish domination, another native, who was a government representative from the small province of Pampanga on the island of Luzon, wanted his people to imagine the effect and the noise of cannon fire. He told them: "The Spaniards have arms similar to lightning that vomit flames along with very heavy cannon balls. The balls, once fired, fly recklessly from mountain to mountain until they find someone to kill."

* * * * *

There are more than seven thousand Chinese who come from the provinces of Canton and Fukien and who, for the most part, live in the suburb of Manila called Parián [Map 14 – I].[357] There are about four thousand Spaniards, but there are many more mestizos, born of European, Filipinos, and Chinese.

The city of Manila, capital of all the islands, is on a big bay on the island of Luzon [Maps 13 and 14]. It is walled in and protected by ten bastions and a small fort called Santiago. There is a river[358] on its northern side, and the sea is to the west. It is surrounded by a great number of large native communities where, I've been assured, fifty-thousand souls live. Going upriver about four leagues, we saw a lot of hamlets and villages along the banks of the river and the many streams that flow into it after irrigating this beautiful plain. One almost imagines that the cluster of houses spread throughout this vast area forms just one town.

Manila has fourteen immaculate churches, and many of them would be admired in the premier cities of France. The churches in the small towns are well decorated and within they celebrate divine services with great dignity. There is no rural parish that has less than eight or ten musicians. The king of Spain exempts them from paying the tribute that the natives must pay.[359]

One cannot say how far the generosity of the Catholic kings will go when it concerns establishing the reign of Jesus Christ in the places they possess. The zeal that animates them to advance the Christian religion inspires them to seek all possible means so that their new subjects worship the true God.

Every year one hundred thousand écus [silver pesos] are
sent from Mexico,[360] and out of that seventy thousand are
spent to adorn the churches and maintain the missionaries.
Other sums provided for such holy work are even more
considerable. How gratifying for these pious monarchs to
see idolatry eradicated in their vast territories where a little
over two-hundred years ago a great number of humans
were sacrificed to the devil.

Taillandier and Bonnet most likely spent the Christmas of 1708 in Manila. There they would have participated in the traditional festive season celebrating the birth of Jesus Christ. Every evening for the week or two leading up to the 24th of December many of the residents, friends, and their children, would sing Christmas carols all around the city. *Simbang gabi*, or mid-night mass, would be the most attended rite at the Manila Cathedral as well as in the other churches inside and outside the walled city. The priests would have received invitations to go here and there and partake of the local fare such as *rellenong manok*, or roasted chicken, stuffed with Spanish delicacies of chorizo, olives, dried fruits, and nuts. For breakfast they would taste many types of sweet concoctions made from rice, the most popular of which was the *bibinka*, a baked rice flour cake prepared with coconut milk and cane sugar.

After having stayed for seven months on these islands,
which are the most beautiful of lands, the best forested, and
the most pleasant I've ever seen, we boarded a Spanish ship
bound for Malacca with the hope of finding a vessel there
that would sail toward the Coromandel Coast.

On 17 February 1709 Taillandier and Bonnet sailed out of Manila Bay heading west into the South China Sea and then on to Malacca (Map 15).

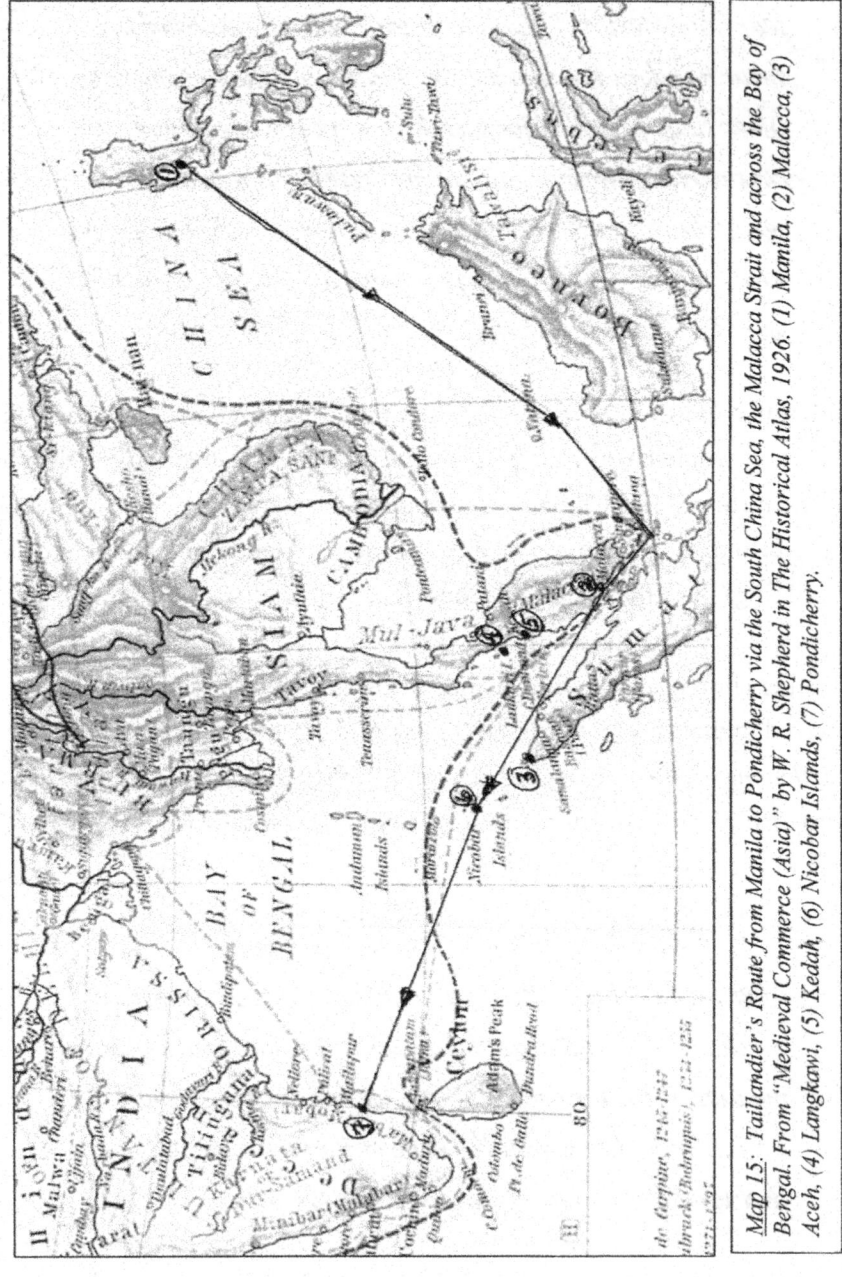

Map 15: *Taillandier's Route from Manila to Pondicherry via the South China Sea, the Malacca Strait and across the Bay of Bengal. From "Medieval Commerce (Asia)" by W. R. Shepherd in The Historical Atlas, 1926. (1) Manila, (2) Malacca, (3) Aceh, (4) Langkawi, (5) Kedah, (6) Nicobar Islands, (7) Pondicherry.*

PART TEN –

Lost and Found

O we can wait no longer,
We too take ship O soul,
Joyous, we too launch out
on trackless seas,
Fearless for unknown shores.

Passage to India
Walt Whitman

MALACCA

The last leg of Pierre Taillandier's epic voyage had just begun, or so he thought. In fact, this part of his journey turned out to be the most difficult chapter of the entire trip.

Malacka. By Johannes Vingboons, c 1665. (Note St. Paul's church on top of the hill. It was originally a Jesuit church under the Archbishop of Goa until the Dutch invaded Malacca in 1641.)

On the 17th of February 1709, we sailed out from the entrance to Manila Bay and on Monday, the 11th of March, we dropped anchor in Malacca's roadstead. During the trip we caught a lot of birds that they call "fous" [stupid], because of the ease by which they are captured. They come to rest on the ship's spars among the crew and *sometimes even on the arms of the mariners themselves. They are captured without making any attempt to fly away.*

I have never seen the sea as calm as it was during the entire trip. A canoe could have made the entire four hundred seventy-five leagues across this sea that is terrifying when the west winds blow.

Had we arrived a few days earlier, we could have boarded a Portuguese or an Armenian ship departing for the Coromandel Coast. Then it would have taken us only a month to sail to Pondicherry.

* * * * *

While Taillandier and Bonnet were sailing to Malacca during the winter of 1709, most of Europe froze. It was the worst winter in 500 years with subzero temperatures lasting for days.[361] France was hit the hardest during what was called "*Le Grand Hiver.*" In Paris "the shortage of bread caused riots…. Louis XIV needed cash to finance the war. He asked for the people to loan him their gold and silver. The king himself melted his gold plate and ate off silver gilt."[362] In fact, the situation was dire. Food was scarce, animals died in their burrows, wheat froze in the ground, rivers and canals became icy boulevards, tens of thousands died from hunger, disease, and the cold, as did Pére de La Chaise, the king's Jesuit confessor. Father Taillandier was too far away, on the other side of the earth, to have known that the situation in his hometown of Lyon and in Paris was grim indeed.

Malacca, the old but teeming entrepot, was a port of call for all sorts of vessels coming from the Spice Islands, the South China Sea, and as far west as the Arabian Sea. Into it flowed muslins and other cotton goods from

India and silk from China. "Malacca was the great centre of that trade, a kind of Alexandria of the Indian Ocean, and consequently the Portuguese [and afterwards the Dutch] valued it highly. Goa was the centre of trade with Persia and Ormuz, from which it received horses, dates, almonds, raisins, silk, pearls, and cotton fabrics. Goa was also the place where expeditions for Lisbon were organized. Yet Goa came in second, after Malacca."[363]

Two-masted Arabian dhow. Oxfordre.com

Having just missed the Portuguese and Armenian ships due to their late arrival in Malacca from Manila, Taillandier and Bonnet were obliged to sail aboard, as Taillandier put it, a "Moorish vessel," likely either an Arabian dhow or an Indonesian jong, for the Coromandel Coast of India. The southeast monsoon had already begun, bringing warm air into the Bay of Bengal, which increased the chances for cyclonic storms to develop. Theirs was the last vessel with two-masts and a chaloupe onboard to depart from Malacca in May of 1709. "A visitor to Achin, Malacca or Batavia, whether in 1650, 1700, or 1750 might have found Chinese junks, Indian and Arab country craft of all types, as well as a Portuguese, English, or Danish East India ship in the roadstead."[364]

Taillandier anticipated sailing for only a few weeks to reach India, but the journey turned out to be a seven-month ordeal! What should have been a pleasant voyage, like the one he just experienced crossing the South China

Sea from Manila, became a nightmare of days and nights without sufficient food or enough water to quench his thirst. As he bravely stated: "We felt happy with just a spoonful of water to temper the sun's heat that burns us."

What unfolded in Pierre Taillandier's letter was a sea story that would have fascinated even an "old salt." His description of the imperilment of the passengers and crew vividly conjures images that gnaw at the bones. One can't help catching his breath when imagining pelting rain rushing in torrents down the flimsy sails into the open mouths of the parched and hungry passengers and crew. His tale is full of the natural ingredients found only at sea with a fantastic cast of characters as diverse as feral cats and city mice.

On his departure from Malacca, Taillandier lamented:

> We had no choice but to sail aboard a Moorish[365] vessel that, for us, turned out to be the cause of fatigue and disasters. Allow me, My Reverend Father, to tell you more about this last leg of our trip. Up to this point, the events I have already mentioned are very common to those who make the journey to the far corners of the world. What remains for me to relate will give Your Reverend an idea of the way in which the Lord sometimes tests the missionaries before employing them to serve Him.

> The ship was small and had only one bridge. It was so full of merchandise that the captain himself often napped in the open air as did the rest of the crew. Imagine, Your Reverend, two missionaries and a Portuguese priest with two black Christian servants in the middle of one hundred Moors or gentiles, all of them black, who watched us with more abhorrence than the most polite European ordinarily would have to live with Negroes.

However, when they launched their chaloupe, they put us in the most comfortable places. A piece of woven mat made from palm leaves sheltered us from the sun in this hot climate. Still, they had to take it from us when there wasn't enough wind to fill the sails.

We were becalmed for many days with the blazing sun over our heads. We also suffered from squalls that seemed like tempests to those who have not seen the sea in all its fury. The rains that accompanied the squalls bothered us greatly on our chaloupe, and we continuously had to fight the wind that tried to tear the protective mats from our hands.

ACEH

ierre Taillandier continued his narrative with not a little sarcasm in his tone as he described the misery they endured aboard their ship:

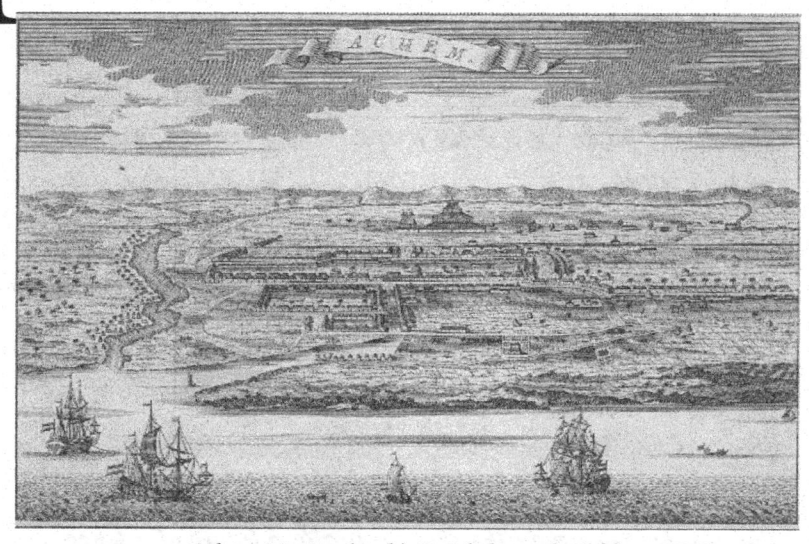

Achem / Atsjien (Aceh). By Jakob van der Schley, c 1753.

After a month of boring and arduous sailing we discovered Aceh, which is only a hundred and fifty leagues from Malacca. Our pilots were so clever that they thought we were at the Nicobar Islands, which actually were two degrees more to the north.[366] They were being so over-confident that, even though we were on the verge of running out of water and food, they wanted to subject us to another three hundred leagues of sailing without having taken aboard more refreshments! The traders and passengers, however, forced the captain to drop anchor in front of a village about three leagues from Aceh. We only had a little water, and we took on some provisions.

On the 15th of April [1709] we set sail, but that same evening the lack of a breeze plus contrary tides forced us to drop anchor off Aceh. The plants and the beautiful forests of Aceh and Malacca would not impress the traveler who has seen the Philippines.

During the night, we put out to sea without losing site of the coast until the 18th. The ordinarily calm weather during this time of the year unnerved our ignorant pilots, who resorted to a thousand superstitions to catch a favorable wind: Sometimes they tossed a little boat filled with rice into the sea as the crew shouted; sometimes they hung a bottle of perfume on the mainsail; at other times, depending on what a sailor or a slave had dreamed, they cast water at the masts, or washed the ship, or made a figure of a horse run across the ship's bridge. In the end, they entrusted themselves to our prayers, and we told them they must renounce their superstitious ways and turn to God alone.

They only gave us a glass of water a day, and the small supply of food we had bought in Aceh was fast disappearing. The lack of water was so great that on the 4th of May we were forced to roast a small amount of rice in the clay pot and eat directly from it. In this dire moment we prayed to almighty God as never before, and our prayers were heard. That very same night we picked up a breeze, and then it rained. We collected the raindrops that rolled down the mats and the sails, and we used this precious resource with much economy to drink only what was necessary to keep us alive. We felt happy with just a spoonful of water to temper the sun's heat that burned us.

On the 6th a violent squall with wind from the stern made us run a course with just one sail. St. Elmo's fire[367] appeared on the ensign pole and at the top of the main mast. On the 9th, the Feast of the Ascension, we lost two of our topmasts during a heavy sea. On the 10th the sea overwhelmed us. We prayed to the Lord with the same faith as before, and in the same merciful manner He heard us. It rained that night, and we saved enough water to last us another week. St. Elmo's fire reappeared and lit up our stays.

The sad predicament we were facing, notwithstanding, we could not contain our laughter when the Portuguese priest told us about the invectives the crew flung at the so-called devil St. Elmo. One of them exclaimed, "What are you doing here? Our merchandise does not belong to you; we did not steal it; it belongs to us, and we paid good money for it!"

"Look," another mariner demanded, "look for the corsairs and pirates who have stolen everything they have aboard their ships, torture them, kill them, but leave the merchants in peace." "Go," yet another mariner shouted, "go and chasten your parents; your father is a thief and your mother and your sisters are denounced for their shameful conduct; your brothers deserve death for their crimes."

Then they armed themselves with sticks and ran around the ship's bridge, climbed the shrouds, shouted at but never actually got near the imaginary devil! In the end, when St. Elmo's fire died out, they congratulated each other as if they had just won a great victory.

On the 19th, the feast of Pentecost, we were entirely out of water. As always, we reached out to Divine Providence for help. Two hours later a lot of rain fell and, based on the amount of water we had allotted each person aboard, we saved enough to last us three weeks. On the 24th the west wind rose again, and we heaved to so as not to lose sight of the coast. The wind grew stronger as night fell, and a heavy swell, hitting the ship broadside, dumped a lot of water into the chaloupe where we slept. It became necessary to run with the wind to prevent a dangerous situation from getting out of hand, since the waves were getting higher and at any moment a high roller could fill our ship and sink it.

We gave ourselves up to Providence, which had saved us on many occasions from the clutches of death.

De Windstoot (The Gust). By Wilhelm van de Velde, the Younger, c 1680.

Despite the rigorous abstinence we kept, our food supply could only last a few more days. Nevertheless, it was necessary to retrace the three hundred leagues that already cost us a lot of suffering and deprivation. But these were not the things distressing the sailors the most. They were preoccupied with the present dangers. The sea was very rough; the high breaking waves chased us. They kept menacing us with the specter of death. One alone would have been enough to entomb us.

It was essential to be alert at all times while manning the tiller to prevent a wave from catching the vessel sideways. That night, the following day, the 25th, and the night after, *the air was filled with ceaseless laments from the fakirs while we were at peace and ready to receive the fate that God had intended for us. We proved then how the faith in God that inspires Christianity is different from the false hope of Mohammedanism.*

Between waiting for the rogue wave that could capsize their ship and witnessing the miracles that kept it afloat, Taillandier must have lost the sense of where they were in relation to the coastline that the helmsman was trying desperately to keep in sight. If the next paragraph of his letter seems confusing, one can only appreciate the fact that despite Taillandier's attention and thoroughness in describing their predicament, the heavy seas and lashing rains on this harrowing voyage probably had rendered the notes in his journal useless, and himself disoriented:

On the 26ᵗʰ the sea settled down and a favorable wind took us back to Aceh. We made this long voyage in seven days. On the 3rd [of June], we passed between the Nicobar Islands, which are at seven degrees of latitude to the north of Aceh. That day there was no rice to eat on the entire ship. We gave the islanders some cloth and tobacco and in exchange they gave us coconuts and iguames, a type of insipid root crop.

At this moment in time, even the best of sailors probably could not have kept track of the vessel's whereabouts. Simply put, it was somewhere between the Andaman Sea and the Strait of Malacca. Likely, they did not pass, as Taillandier stated, "between some of the Nicobar Islands" which were a long distance from Aceh. Having broached to with the force of fierce easterly winds, Taillandier's vessel probably was driven away from Aceh on the northern tip of Sumatra all the way to the islands of Penang and Langkawi off what was then the western coast of Siam.

KEDAH

After a week or so of "ceaseless laments" from the Muslims and silent prayers from the Christians, the battered vessel arrived unexpectedly on the coast of Siam where all aboard had to endure another nine days of hunger and thirst before being rescued!

On the 5ᵗʰ of June we anchored not too far from shore, near the islands of Pulopinam [Penang] and Lancari [Langkawi].³⁶⁸ The sea was becalmed, and we were reduced to sharing two coconuts a day for four people. It was necessary to send the chaloupe out to fetch provisions. So, during the nine days of calm, we were left defenseless against the merciless heat of the sun. The Moors themselves felt sorry for us knowing that, having been born in colder countries, we must suffer more than they. "Why do you spend so much time on prayers?" they asked. "Don't you suffer enough from hunger and the heat? Put down your books, you will say these prayers when you have rested awhile on land."

The chaloupe that was sent to look for provisions returned on the night of the fourteenth. The small amount it brought back restored the spirit and strength of everyone aboard. We commended the benevolence of the Lord who gave us this relief when we had but one coconut and a glass of water left.

On the 16th we entered the Parlis [Perlis] River in the little kingdom of Queda [Kedah].[369] They say it is the same Parlis River where the miraculous battle occurred between the Portuguese and the Acehnese, as prophesied by St. Francis Xavier to all Malaccans. Father Bonnet left in a canoe to find lodging for us in Queda.[370] Since the ship could not navigate upriver until the tide returned, he came back for us aboard a "parau," a sturdy canoe carved from an entire tree trunk with pointed ends. He and I arrived in the town on the 19th where a Muslim trader from Surat had found a house for us.

Their time together at sea, far longer and more perilous than either had anticipated, must have developed in Taillandier and Bonnet a common bond that deepened their friendship. After all, when man first learned to hang a woven mat upon a wooden pole to catch the wind and move his boat across the water, he no doubt felt the same apprehensions and the same thrills the two Jesuits experienced—the excitement of sailing on God's immense oceans.

Malay Village with log canoe.

While they found a bamboo and thatch hut to live in, thanks to the Muslim trader, Taillandier was devastated that they could not celebrate the holy sacrifice of the mass! Nevertheless, from the depths of their reflections they summoned tranquility of mind and spirit amidst the babble of languages and religions and the din of commerce in this bustling port.

So began what turned out to be a seven month stay in a place Taillandier described as barbaric. Sickly and unable to move around much, they bore with equanimity the muezzin's call to "*salat,*" or prayer, repeated five times a day from the mosque's minaret topped with a silver-colored crescent. Merchants and dock workers, not necessarily of the Muslim faith, in the bazaars and stalls by the river's edge were often harshly reminded by religious enforcers to close their shops until prayers were concluded in the mosque.

How then did these two Frenchmen, unable to practice their faith, survive an ordeal *contra natura*? From Taillandier's letter, it was obvious they interacted with the Malaccan crew and the merchants aboard their ship, many of whom were Muslims. Indians from as far away as Surat on the Malabar Coast traded here on the eastern shores of the Bay of Bengal in the same way that Malaccans and Chinese[371] sought business opportunities in the prolific coastal trading centers. But until the return of the seasonal winds, they, too, were stranded in Kedah just like the two Jesuits.

Taillandier and Bonnet could only hope that, while trying to regain their health, they could also plant the cross of Jesus Christ in the hearts of these men. For in showing kindness and love to nameless transients, might not one, perhaps more, be drawn to truly Christian virtues?

As he related it, Taillandier found inspiration in the story of a Frenchman named Martin who, because of the crimes he had committed—armed robbery and murder, was sentenced to death. Martin's life would have been spared if he had converted to Islam. Like the old Christian in Mysore, who, while being cruelly beaten, cried out "My life you can have, my religion never!",[372] Martin demonstrated that it was not the dying for a faith that was difficult, but rather the living up to it. By refusing to convert, Martin won the Jesuit's praise and admiration.

If there was any doubt in Taillandier's rock solid faith in a merciful God, it was dispelled the moment he and Bonnet rescued from slavery a zealous Christian man who had languished in servitude for four years. He believed that God made it possible for them to enter Kedah so that the man, a Chinese merchant from Macao who had come by land from Siam, could obtain his freedom. Not up to the task of fetching water for themselves due to ill health, this former slave descended as a *deus ex machina* and resolved the water supply problem for the priests.

Like Hippocrates, the two Jesuits were bound to keep pure and holy their lives and their art without intentional wrongdoing. Despite all the misgivings that caused Taillandier to decry Kedans as barbaric, wicked, or unholy, he nevertheless took time to describe how the Malays lived and dressed, how they traded with each other, and how they interacted with foreign merchants. He also was fascinated by the flora and fauna that thrived in Kedah, thanks to the ebb and flow of the Perlis River.

Keen to inform, Taillandier plunged himself into scientific questions about the mysterious place where Providence had put him. Aware that his answers would reach many of his colleagues back in France who yearned to know more of the unknown world, he explained:

The kingdom of Queda is a tributary of Siam. The city has seven to eight thousand inhabitants, and in the entire kingdom, there are about twenty thousand. The mouth of the river is at 6 deg. 10 min. North latitude. To the northeast of this mouth, about two or three leagues inland, can be seen Elephant Mountain,[373] so called because from afar it resembles an elephant. Only light vessels can pass over the sand bar, which during high tide would only be two fathoms and a half deep. Along the river up to near Queda, it is four fathoms deep at high water.

The inhabitants are Malays, and all follow the Mohammedan sect of the Turks and the Mogals [Mughals]. Their houses are made of bamboo, and, because of the wetness they are elevated by posts four or five feet from the ground. The houses of the king and of the well-to-do are constructed of wood. Their clothes resemble those worn by the Malays in Malacca, Jor [Johor], and Sumatra. Almost everyone wears his hair long. A piece of cotton cloth or silk is worn around the head without covering it entirely. They always walk around armed with their very sharp swords[374] measuring fifteen to eighteen inches long and two inches wide. Many of these swords are wavy in shape and have gold handles. They also employ small spears, "zagayes," or Moorish arrows, and mousquets [old style harquebuses]. Their shields are round and very light, measuring about two feet and a few inches in diameter. They are made to withstand sword thrusts and gunfire. Many people from the Coromandel Coast live here, and it is easy to spot them because they are darker in complexion and more reserved than the Malays. Also, there are a few Chinese here who came by land from Siam.[375]

The kingdom is sparsely populated. It is covered in dense forests where we see a lot of wild animals, elephants, deer, and tigers. The elephants are captured as in Siam, and they are one of the principal sources of income for the king. The biggest one I saw measured six and a half coudees[376] [more than nine feet] tall. The plains are cut up by many irrigation canals which allow production of different species of rice. Besides the usual fruits that come in from India, the soil here produces many excellent fruits unknown in other parts of the world. Among them the mangoustan [mangosteen] and the durion [durian] are the most prized, even by the Europeans.

The king does not collect taxes from his subjects. He has mines of tin, which is as white as that from England but not as hard. They make coins that weigh a pound but are worth only seven sols.[377] They also fabricate small gold coins of a few carats, round and about one ligne[378] and a half in diameter, on which they inscribe Arabic letters. They take five of these coins for one Spanish écu [escudo]. A small copper coin worth less than one of our deniers[379] circulates among the people. Foodstuffs there are excellent and very cheap. The merchants of Surat come there to buy tin, which in India is called "calin." Those from the Coromandel Coast bring cotton cloth and take, in exchange, tin, gold dust, and elephants.

When we arrived in Queda, we were told that two years earlier a Frenchman, named Martin, had died for the Catholic religion. He was a pilot of a small vessel from Bengal whose captain was an Englishman. After stopping in Aceh and Batavia, he killed the captain and stole all the merchandise aboard. Afraid his crime would be discovered, he considered getting rid of those who had the most reason to challenge him. Accordingly, he abandoned the five Christian sailors he had sent to a deserted island along the coast of Java on the pretext of searching for fresh water. But a little later, forced to put in at Queda, he was denounced by the murdered captain's slave to the king who confiscated the vessel and condemned the pilot to death.

While he was being taken to the place of execution, the king's emissary offered him his life plus a thousand écus in return for converting to Islam. But the pilot, Martin, declared he would rather die than renounce his faith. He died with the crucifix in his hand, pronouncing these Sunday prayer words: "Holy be thy Name." We heard these details from a Portuguese, some Portuguese mestizos, a Malay who served as Martin's interpreter until his last breath, and from the Muslims of Surat themselves, all eyewitnesses of the condemned man's steadfastness and loyalty. I could not help but admire the estimable ways of Providence that does not tire of waiting for us and that in an instant made a martyr for Jesus Christ out of a sinner, guilty of so many crimes.

We were obliged to pass seven months among these barbarians to await the return of the monsoon. I leave it to you, my Reverend Father, to imagine what missionaries suffer when forced to live among depraved men, without any expectation of converting a single soul, and deprived of the only consolation left in this world, which is to celebrate the holy Sacrifice of the Mass.

I do not include among our predicaments that we had to render to ourselves the services one expects from others for the maintenance of life: we could not find a single Moor who would go to the river to fetch water for us. Furthermore, God afflicted Father Bonnet and me with a disease common among Europeans when they live for some length of time in a climate as hot as this one.

Yet, we had the good fortune of rescuing from slavery a Christian from Macao who was not able to win his freedom in four years. But, what do I know, Eh, if it was not to save this zealous Catholic that the Lord permitted all the setbacks we've had since we put in at Queda?

DELIVERANCE

During and after the War of the Spanish Succession, French trading in Pondicherry was reduced while defensive activities took higher priority. Deployment of soldiers, importation of munitions, goods and medicine for the beleaguered town became just as important as trading. This could only be accomplished with the help of the French Navy that escorted the Malouin ships to the French East India Company trading posts along the Coromandel Coast.

French traders continued to sail across the Bay of Bengal to the west coast of Siam into Mergui[380] (now Myeik, Myanmar) and other coastal ports even after the French had been expelled from Siam following King Narai's death. It was through these traders that the Jesuits in Pondicherry learned that Fathers Taillandier and Bonnet were still alive and living in Kedah. Taillandier explained:

> For a long time [since June 1709] we have been asking God to deliver us from this unholy place. He granted our prayer when we least expected it. Three ships from Saint-Malo, unable to make it to Mergui for the winter, were forced to be refitted on the island of Janselou.[381] M. de La Laude, who had embarked at Pondicherry to procure much needed supplies for the ships, sailed the smallest one to Queda

to buy provisions. Hardly had he dropped anchor at the river's mouth when the Muslim merchants from Surat came to congratulate us on the ship's arrival.

We went aboard to visit with the gentlemen. We offered them our house, and to our delight they accepted. The king received them very well, and they were given all they asked for. I went by canoe to pick up the ship's captain who was ill. We had met him aboard the "Saint Esprit" where he was the lieutenant and had treated us with much courtesy.

François-Auguste Magon de La Lande (1679-1761), referred to by Taillandier above, was a Director of the French East India Company and "armateur et corsair du Roi," or shipbuilder and privateer of the King.

The three ships that Taillandier mentioned were the *Saint-Malo*, the *Saint-Jean-Baptiste*, and the *Bien-Aimée*. They belonged to Messrs. Crozat and the Magon de la Landes (François and his father, Jean), who were ship owners in Saint-Malo. On 1 December 1708 the Company authorized Crozat and Magon de la Lande "to send the following in January 1709: one or two ships to Hoogli, Pondicherry and other trading stations on the Coromandel and Malabar Coast, with rights to various privileges of the Company and to the services of its agents in India for the purchase of merchandise, and in France for its sale."[382] Later, the services of a *patache* was deemed necessary, and the ship owners were authorized to add the *"Bien-Aimee"* as a tender ship to navigate the shallow Indian rivers.

In his comprehensive history, *La Compagnie des Indes Orientales*, Paul Kaeppelin catalogued the names, squadron leaders, ports of origin and destinations of the French ships that traded in spices and piece goods from 1665 to 1720.[383] His Table of Arrivals and Departures between 16 February 1709 and January 1710 showed that the following seven ships from Saint-Malo were in the Bay of Bengal: *Saint-Malo, Maurepas, Saint Jean Baptiste, Lys-Brillac, François d'Argouges, Auguste*, and the patache *Bien Aimee*.

Of these ships the *Bien Aimee*, "the smallest in the fleet," according to Taillandier, was the only ship able to navigate the shallows at the mouth of the Perlis River. Her captain, François-August Magon de La Lande, eventually ended the missionaries' miserable seven month stay in Kedah. Providence, it seemed, granted the two Jesuits one more reason to believe that the "courtesies" M. de La Lande had showed them aboard the *Saint Esprit* back in 1707 on their voyage from Saint-Malo to the Canaries, were not a coincidence, but rather a down payment for what the Lord had in store for them.

I noticed the beauty of the river even more. In many places the riverbanks are covered with trees, and in them we saw groups of monkeys jumping from limb to limb from morning until evening. We also saw many crocodiles lying on the sandy shore. One, measuring about twenty feet long, was shot as it approached the canoe, but I believe it got away. M. de La Lande wounded another, about twelve feet long, that was lying on the riverbank. We noticed traces of its blood on the sand, and it had trouble taking three or four steps to get back into the river.

The ship set sail on the 10th of January 1710. On the 24th we passed near the Nicobar Islands[384] that are situated at 8 deg. [N. latitude.] The islanders paddled up in fourteen canoes to offer iguanas, coconuts and chickens in exchange for leaf tobacco. They are almost naked, and their color is a yellowish tan. In the company of Blacks, they could pass for Whites. They make a kind of dough from roots,[385] which takes the place of bread because neither wheat nor rice is cultivated on their islands.

We dropped anchor on the 2nd of February 1710 in the roadstead of Pondicherry.

A masula boat would have ferried Taillandier and Bonnet from their ship through the breakers in front of Fort Louis' battlements that rose above the sand dunes protecting the capital of French India. When the craft beached a few feet from dry land, the boatmen carried the men ashore on their shoulders.

Coming Ashore at Madras. Circle of William John Huggins (1781-1845).

Standing on the beach, Father Guy Tachard, Jesuit Superior of Pondicherry (February 1701-December 1710), would have been jubilant to see the two missionaries whom everyone thought had perished in a shipwreck. He may have considered their rescue nothing short of a miracle. His prayers had been answered. His new initiative to open a mission in Golconda[386] could now be realized. He joyfully embraced the men as they alighted on Indian soil.

PART ELEVEN –

EPILOGUE

The hour of departure has arrived, and we go our ways—I to die, and you to live. Which is the better, only God knows.

Socrates, as quoted by Plato in *Apology*

FRENCH INDIA AND
FRANÇOIS MARTIN

A t the end of the first decade of the 18th century, the French East India Company was no longer the promising entity that had been granted royal patents by Louis XIV back in 1664. By 1714, fifty years after its creation, the merchants of Saint-Malo and their associates had control of the moribund state-run commercial enterprise. The Company's crushing debt could not be eliminated without major concessions to the merchants.

For over thirty years François Martin, more than any other Frenchman, shepherded Pondicherry's rise from a bleak outpost on the Coromandel Coast into the flourishing capital of French India. With his death on 31 December 1706 France lost a brilliant man, a leader, and an entrepreneur who brought not only prosperity to Pondicherry but also the admiration of the Indians in all the trading ports along the Coromandel Coast.

In eulogizing François Martin before a gathering in St. Louis Church,[387] Father Tachard predicted that Pondicherry was destined "to be one day the boulevard of the Christian religion and the foundation of the French Empire in the Indies, words that would bring to mind *la double pensée* (joint thinking) that inspired King Louis XIV and Jean-Baptiste Colbert, the creators of the French East India Company."[388]

That there is a destiny attached to everyman's existence is rooted in the philosophy of ancient scholars. How one passes through life's tribulations to fulfil that destiny might be in God's hands, but certainly its course is guided by stars whose cosmic rays shower him with the particles of life itself. François Martin forged his destiny alongside men who traded, fought, and evangelized for France. Together they shaped a lofty history in south India, particularly in Pondicherry—a city so peculiar that its urbanity evokes wistfulness in its visitors. To those whose ties to French India flow in their veins, the city, with its quaint homes and rues in checkerboard pattern, bonds them in a tender embrace.

A MISSION TO CONVERT THE
NICOBAR ISLANDERS

W hen the weather permitted, the Nicobar Islands were often the place where ships needing provisions stopped on the final leg to India's Coromandel Coast from ports like Malacca farther to the east. The islanders would paddle out to the ships aboard their dugout canoes to barter or sell whatever foodstuffs or produce they had. Yet, no one who had anything to do with evangelization had ever set foot here.

For years since the Jesuits began arriving in India, Jesuit Superior Tachard had wished to evangelize the Nicobarese, but he did not have enough missionaries to assign there until Fathers Faure, Taillandier, and Bonnet landed. Having learned of Father Tachard's new initiative soon after their arrival, Fathers Faure and Bonnet expressed their desire to spread the Word of God to that remote mission on the eastern edge of the Bay of Bengal.

Pierre Faure arrived in the Philippines from Mexico on 30 March 1709. He then proceeded to Pondicherry, arriving several months ahead of Taillandier and Bonnet. Initially assigned to China, Faure encountered some complications with that appointment while in Manila, so instead he proceeded to India. Eventually, having persisted in his quest for a mission post, he, along with Pierre Bonnet, was rewarded with the assignment to evangelize the Nicobarese.

But finding a ship that would sail eastward and leave two missionaries on any of the Nicobar Islands was difficult. It was not until early in 1711 that the opportunity presented itself—four French ships dropped anchor off Pondicherry! Two of the four ships from Saint-Malo, the frigates *Lys-Brillac* and *Maurepas*, were under orders to sail for Malacca. Their captains agreed to accept the missionaries and take them to one of the islands.

*****

Aboard the *Lys-Brillac* on 17 January 1711, Father Faure wrote this emotional letter that presaged his fate and that of Father Bonnet, as if the future had revealed itself to him:[389]

> *Shortly after my arrival in the East Indies, I took a new assignment from the Superiors of that country. They were to initiate a project, formed a long time ago, to announce Jesus Christ to the infidels that inhabit the Nicobar Islands.*

> *When I arrived in Pondicherry, there was already a lot of preparation toward the conversion of the Nicobar islanders; but, since there was no desire to take even a single missionary away from Carnate or from Madurai because they were needed in these places, the Superiors awaited new assistance for this enterprise. Having learned of this, I offered my services to them, even urged them. At last, they gave in to my pleas. I had the good fortune of being selected along with Father Bonnet to put forth the first hand toward a most sacred work as soon as the opportunity to go to the islands presented itself.*

> *We had waited impatiently for some ships to set sail for the Strait of Malacca, when suddenly we saw four of them drop anchor. Two were under orders to pass through the strait. We communicated our intent to go to the Nicobar Islands to M[onsieur] Raoul,*

commander of this small squadron, who, with much grace granted our request to board one of his ships. I went as the ship's chaplain aboard the "Lys-Brillac," commanded by M. du Demaine. M. Raoul, captain of the "Maurepas," chose Father Bonnet to come aboard his ship.

We will soon see the Nicobar Islands where, with the grace of God, I shall dedicate my entire life to the conversion of these poor people who have become my fate. God, who has always been merciful to me, now inspires my total confidence in his ever-powerful protection. In the middle of a barbaric nation, I have become unafraid of the dangers before us.

A thousand times I should be happy … if upon receipt of this letter I would have been privileged to suffer something for Jesus Christ! But you know me well enough that you cannot be persuaded that such grace is reserved only for others more deserving. Whatever the future holds for me you will next year receive news about me: from my own letters, if I am still with life, or from the Fathers at Pondicherry, if I am no longer able to write to you myself.

Seldom is there an account of resolve and audacity as vivid and gut-wrenching as that shown by the two Jesuits who sought to bring, for the first time, the Word of God to the Nicobarese. The amazed crews of the *Lys-Brillac* and the *Maurepas* could not have done anything but watch in silence, stunned and fearful, as the real-life drama of sheer sacrifice unfolded before their eyes.

The commander of the squadron, M. Raoul, most likely composed the following report with the help of eyewitnesses and relayed it to the Jesuit Superior in Pondicherry who summarized it thus:[390]

Here is what has been learned since the two missionaries disembarked on the Nicobar Islands.[391] On the return trip to the Strait of Malacca the two ships passed by the 7th degree of Latitude, in view of one of the islands that M. du Demaine had coasted. He immediately ordered the vessel's launch readied to put the Fathers on the island, but not before many tears were shed by all.

The entire crew became emotional upon seeing how happy the missionaries were to deliver themselves to a wild people on islands so inhospitable and absolutely devoid of things necessary for life.

The vessel hove to, and everyone's eyes followed the launch as it coasted the island for some time without finding a place to disembark. Not finding a landing site, the officer-in-charge considered returning to the ship. The Fathers begged him to continue searching and not to lose hope. And so, they coasted up and down the island for a while until at last they found an opening large enough for them to go in.

The missionaries jumped to shore with a little chest containing the implements to say mass and a sack of rice, a gift from M. du Demaine. Having reached land, they knelt on the shore to pray, and with respect kissed the ground, taking possession of it in the name of Jesus Christ. After hiding the chest and the sack of rice, they plunged into the forest to look for the natives. We will not know their fates until the next ship passes by this place.

Following this report, du Dumaine stated that he...[392]

... saw one of these Barbarians, arrow in hand, proudly watching the missionaries for awhile, then retreat into the woods.

Natives of the Nicobar Islands. Illustrated London News, 1870.

* * * * *

In his capacity as editor of the *LEC*, Jean-Baptiste du Halde wrote the customary introduction to Volume 13 (1718) in which he tried to shed light on the whereabouts of Faure and Bonnet. Relying heavily upon what news Pondicherry could provide, he said that in May of 1715 the Jesuits asked "M. Dardancourt, the Director General of the Royal Company of France in Bengal, to instruct the captain of a brigantine bound for Queda to go to the Nicobar Islands for the purpose of informing himself as to the fate of the missionaries."[393]

Upon the brigantine's return, the journals of the captain and the pilots were examined in the presence of the Director General and the ship's scribe, M. du Douay. They summarized events that took place during the two and a half years the missionaries spent on the island of Chambolan and the ten months they later spent on another island called Nicobary (probably Nancowry today). The journals offered no explanation as to why they left Chambolan. But Faure and Bonnet probably would have wanted to return to Chambolan, perhaps because they felt they could accomplish more for Jesus Christ among the "ferocious and inhumane" people there than with the "gentle, affable, and much more tractable" natives of Nicobary.

"The missionaries were there barely fifteen days when their lives ended," according to du Halde, "doubtless by a violent and cruel death as blamed since then on the inhabitants of Nicobary [who] are still today blaming those of Chambolan: the latter can only defend themselves with evil methods." Two years after the publication of du Halde's report Father Le Caron, in a letter from Pondicherry dated 15 October 1718 but published in 1720, categorically stated: "Fathers Faure and Bonnet were massacred by the Nicobarese."[394]

* * * * *

It must have been in early 1711 when the report of Faure and Bonnet's daring introduction of Christianity to the Nicobarese reached Pondicherry. The establishment of their new mission, though fraught with peril at creation, would also have been expeditiously brought to the attention of King Louis XIV by M. Raoul, the squadron commander, upon his return to Europe.

Informed of the events in the Nicobar Islands, Pierre Taillandier added this comment about Pierre Bonnet, his friend and companion, toward the end of his letter:

> I was saddened by being separated from Father Bonnet, with whom God had united me in a most special way. By now without doubt, Your Reverend must have been informed of his and Father Faure's courage and fortitude on entering the Nicobar Islands, on the 16th of January 1711,[395] to announce Jesus Christ to the barbaric people who inhabit these islands. It does not serve any purpose to repeat the particulars that have already been sent to France.

But Taillandier's grief over the loss of his friend must have been overshadowed by the joyful anticipation of his assignment to Golconda, another new mission territory for the Jesuits of Pondicherry.

THE KINGDOM OF GOLCONDA

As the second decade of the 18th century opened, the ancient fortress-city of Golconda (Appendix A), built on a granite hill 400 feet high, stood in ruins. Some two hundred years later the city was described as "surrounded by a strong crenellated stone wall, over three miles in circumference, with 87 bastions at the angles; some of these still contain large pieces of ordnance bearing Persian inscriptions. Inside the walls are ruins of numerous palaces, mosques, and dwellings, scattered everywhere, while the citadel, or *bala hisar*, is in good preservation." [396]

Golconda Fort. Hyderabadzone.com.

The Golconda citadel was built around gigantic slabs of granite that shaped the hill into a natural cyclopean fortress. It was passed on from the Bahmani Empire[397] to Sultan Kuli, a Shia Muslim, who had migrated to Delhi from Persia at the start of the 16th century. In 1512 he became the Governor of the ancient province of Telangana[398] with the title of Kutb-ul-Mulk.[399] Thus, the dynasty known as the Kutb Shahis, *shah* being the Persian word for king or ruler, was established.

In the years following, the lack of flowing water to the castle forced Sultan Kuli's son and successor, Muhammad Kuli Kutb Shahi, to move his court to the plains below the fortress about five miles to the east. He designated the new town as the capital and seat of government of his kingdom and called it Bhagnagar (present day Hyderabad) in honor of his wife Bhagmati who had converted to Islam and taken the name of Hyder Mahal. The river Musi, a tributary of the Krishna River, "bathes the walls of the town on the southwest side and flows into the Gulf of Bengal close to Masulipatnam [Machilipatnam today]."[400]

The province of Telangana extended to Masulipatnam, which was the principal seaport of the kingdom of Golconda. Into this bustling city, dating back at least to the 1st century BCE, arrived merchandise from countries around the Arabian Sea and the Bay of Bengal as well as from Europe and East Asia. So great was the extent of commerce here and in Bhagnagar that François Martin, during a visit to Bhagnagar in his capacity as Director of the French East India Company, remarked that its streets were filled "with a diversity of nations, and a confusion of carriages, carts, camels, elephants, horses, palanquins, etc."[401]

* * * * *

Pierre Taillandier would have known of Jesuit Superior Bouchet's desire to pursue his predecessor's wish to establish a mission in Golconda. Since 1687, Hyderabad and Golconda were occupied by forces loyal to Aurangzeb after the Sunni Emperor razed these cities, symbols of Shia Muslim power in the Deccan. In 1703 then Jesuit Superior Tachard wrote:

The Muslims, after conquering the kingdom, saw it was almost deserted by the flight of the inhabitants, who feared the avarice and the cruelty of their conquerors, and they have made a small enclosure after tearing down almost all the magnificent pagodas that the gentiles built there... The extent of the territory that the grand Mughal has subjugated and the infinite number of towns that he has taken does not permit him to settle people of his religion there, which is the Mohammedan.... To reward the services of his 'omeraux,' or chosen nobles of the empire, he gives them sovereignty over particular provinces during their lifetime on condition of maintaining for his armies a certain number of horsemen when he needs them.[402]

Before departing for Golconda, Taillandier might have read Abbé Carré's account of his travels in India, in particular to Bijapur and Golconda. We may recall that Louis XIV had sent Carré to India to report on the activities of the French East India Company. When Carré arrived in Hyderabad in 1672, he stopped at the house and church of one of the Portuguese priests in the suburb of the royal city called Millapour, or Malkapur.[403] That priest turned out to be thirty-four-year-old Costudius de Pinho, vicar of the Golconda mission and a Brahmin of the Order of Discalced Carmelites, whom we met along with Abbé Carré in Part FOUR. Since 30 April 1669 de Pinho had served as the Vicar Apostolic in the kingdoms of Idalcan (Bombay), Golconda, and 'Magni Mongolis' (Mughal Empire) in India.[404] Carré spent six days with the Vicar to recover from his journey and to "enjoy the real pleasure of a Christian, in having a priest and a church to fill my soul with the celestial comfort that comes from the ministrations of the Sacraments."[405]

En route to Golconda, Taillandier may have intended to visit Father Pierre Mauduit, who was serving in Carouvepondi, and seek his counsel before proceeding north. He also would have been eager to meet with de Pinho, who would have been close to eighty years old if he were still alive, or with the new Vicar of Golconda.

Mauduit's letter of 1701, written after his journey into the heart of the Carnatic, would have given Taillandier inspiration to undertake his own pilgrimage into the center of the Deccan. Mauduit declared: "We must hurry lest the Muslims, who little by little seize all these kingdoms, force these people to follow their wretched religion. Nothing further edifies these idolaters and commits them more forcefully to embrace the Christian religion than the austere and penitent life that the missionaries lead."[406]

Emperor Aurangzeb's cruel and corrupt policies turned the Rajputs serving his empire into bitter enemies. On his death while pursuing Maratha rebels in 1707, Aurangzeb, the last of the great Mughal Emperors, left behind an empire in chaos and a vast territory with very little loyalty from the governed. From Kabul in the north to the Deccan in the south, a long and fratricidal war of succession among his three surviving sons eventually led to the decline of the Mughal Empire.

It was into this chaotic scene of warring factions that Pierre Taillandier entered.

TAILLANDIER DISAPPEARS ON HIS
WAY TO GOLCONDA

S ometime between late 1711 and 1713, Father Taillandier and two
catechcists bravely sallied forth from Pondicherry to pay "a visit at
the Court of Golconda"[407] and, no doubt, debate Christianity in the
presence of Mughal nobles, Muslim mullahs, Sufis, and Hindu Brahmins.
He would have wanted to spread the Word of God and explain the truths of
his religion in the same manner that his predecessors, Rodolfo Aquaviva and
Antonio de Monserrate, announced Christianity to the Mughal court and
Emperor Akbar in Fatehpur Sikri one hundred and thirty-two years earlier.[408]

Taillandier must have known that lawlessness ran rampant among
countless famished populations in Deccan towns and villages that relied on
the harvest of millet, rice, or barley to survive. In the vast central plateaus of
Golconda, Mysore and the Carnatic, what farmers harvested was all but taken
away by order of the Mughal Princes or their chosen Rajputs who identified
themselves as kings in their little fiefdoms. Like the Romans of ancient times,
the Mughal emperors co-opted Brahmin and Muslim elites and vested them
with tremendous authority in their domains.

From the old city of Golconda, among its granite ruins,[409] the once
elegant minarets of Persian-descended kings quietly pierced the skies. As the
forces of change raged on and Hindu Maratha rebels asserted their independence from the conquering Mughals in the Deccan, living a comfortable life

was exceedingly difficult. For Hindus, their belief in the power of hope and prayer changed quickly into vengeance and banditry.

In Taillandier's day what it meant to be a Hindu was, and still is, greatly influenced by one's social status. His varna dictated his role in Hinduism's complicated social structure. The Brahmins benefitted hugely from this stratification even as the Mughal Empire declined and European East India companies competed for dominance in pursuit of state-sponsored imperialism and mercantilist policies. However, the most marginalized and rejected were the innumerable children of the lower classes who were left alone to fend for themselves. Among them were the pale-faced offspring of itinerant sailors and traders from many lands.

Taillandier would always have remembered the poignant words of the lame mendicant, Ignatius of Loyola, spoken in a chapel within the ancient Eglise Saint-Pierre de Montmartre on the hill above Paris: "We will not be the warriors of the sword, but of the word; we will preach to men, we will teach children; we will make Christians by precepts and by education."

* * * * *

Various Jesuit scholars assert that Father Pierre Taillandier lost his life when he ventured north from Pondicherry sometime in 1711 or as late as 1713. Du Halde wrote in his introduction to the 1715 *LEC* edition in which Taillandier's letter was published: "He departed around the month of June in the year 1712, accompanied by two of his disciples, to go to Golconda, where the needs of the Religion demanded his presence."[410]

What little is known about Taillandier's work and death in India comes from some of his colleagues who served in the turbulent Carnate mission. Writing in 1918 about Taillandier, Jesuit historian Léon Besse reported that he had a pension which Gabriel Petit, the head of the Carnate mission at the time, had requested from the Father General. According to Besse, Petit was told that steps had been taken with the Secretariat of the Provincial of Lyon[411] to secure it.

Meanwhile, Besse wondered what became of Taillandier. Most believe, he stated, that he departed Pondicherry on an expedition toward Golconda (Appendix A). The mission priests never heard more of his fate—not where, nor how, he died. Here Besse interjected that Taillandier died in 1711. But he also pointed out that Carlos Sommervogel, the famed Jesuit bibliographer, claimed he died in 1713 in a shipwreck. Interestingly, Besse continued by citing a letter written by Jean Venance Bouchet (24 September 1714) in which he asserted that Taillandier died along with two of his catechists on the "royal road to Golconda" having been either killed by thieves or drowned while crossing a river.[412]

But Besse acknowledged that Sommervogel's report did not represent "the sentiment of the priests of the mission." Gaston Laurent Coeurdoux echoed this consensus in his letter written in 1732. He stated: "It is not beyond probability that his yearning to witness took Father Taillandier away from this mission. He died too soon. Nothing more was heard about this."[413]

The zeal with which Pierre Taillandier and his fellow missionaries put forth to bring enlightenment even to the poorest of the poor, in a world barely connected but by letters that took months to arrive at their destinations, was untrammeled by any tinge of disillusionment. Such was their faith in the righteousness of their cause—they surrendered their lives in return for the priviledge to bring the gospel of Christ into the hearts of people who spoke different languages and worshipped different gods.

Somewhere on the *route royale* to Golconda, resolved to earth in a muddy riverine shore or to dust in the plains overgrown with yellowing millet, rest Father Taillandier's remains and those of his catechists.

Like most of his predecessors, Pierre Taillandier achieved a life dedicated to his deepest desires. His heroic deeds would have inspired in his neophytes and the children he taught the excitement and love for the sciences worthy of their nascent and grasping imaginations.

FIN

Appendix A: Taillandier's Likely Route from Pondicherry toward Golconda

This map shows the established trade routes of the period. The shortest overland route from Pondicherry to the court of Golconda, and therefore the most probable, began northward along the coast, passed by Madras and turned inland at Nelour (Nellore). A traveler had to cross several rivers along the way, including the Palar, Penna, and Krishna (Coulour).

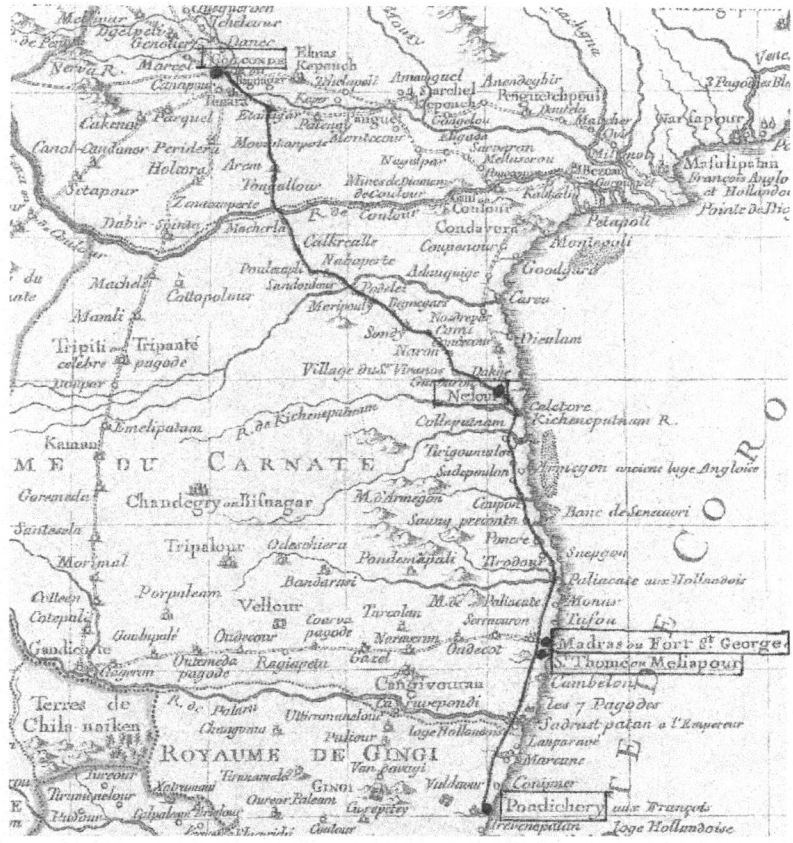

From: *Carte des Côtes de Malabar et de Coromandel* by Guillaume Delisle, 1723.

APPENDIX B: THE TAILLANDIER FAMILY TREE

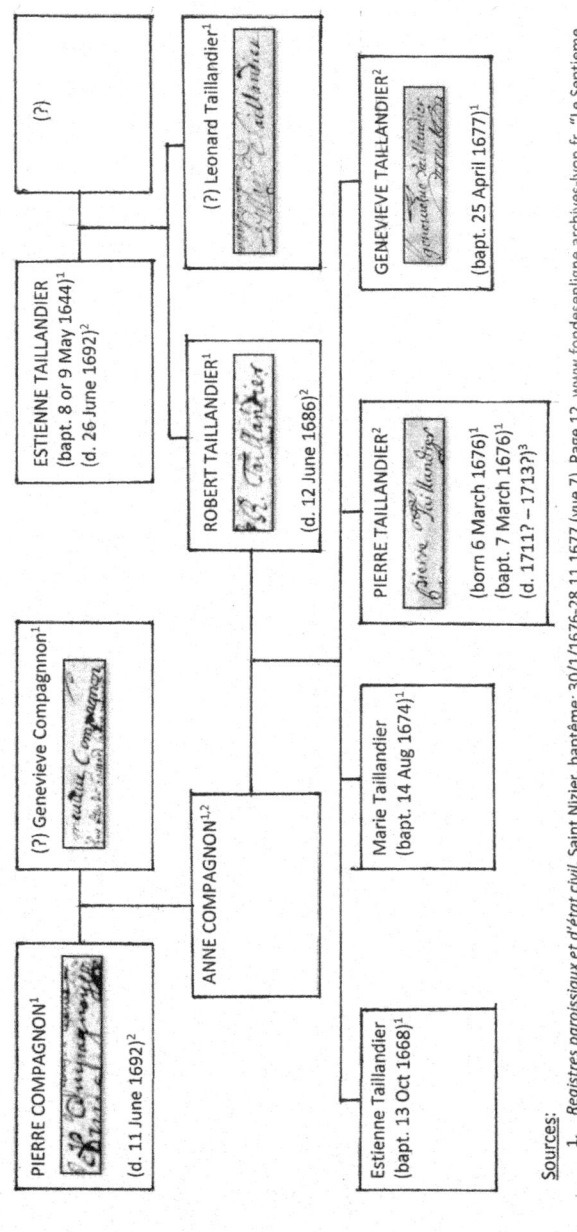

~ TAILLANDIER Family Tree ~
- with original signatures -

PIERRE COMPAGNON[1]
(d. 11 June 1692)[2]

(?) Genevieve Compagnon[1]

ESTIENNE TAILLANDIER
(bapt. 8 or 9 May 1644)[1]
(d. 26 June 1692)[2]

(?)

(?) Leonard Taillandier[1]

ANNE COMPAGNON[1,2]

ROBERT TAILLANDIER[1]
(d. 12 June 1686)[2]

GENEVIEVE TAILLANDIER[2]
(bapt. 25 April 1677)[1]

Estienne Taillandier
(bapt. 13 Oct 1668)[1]

Marie Taillandier
(bapt. 14 Aug 1674)[1]

PIERRE TAILLANDIER[2]
(born 6 March 1676)[1]
(bapt. 7 March 1676)[1]
(d. 1711? – 1713?)[3]

Sources:

1. *Registres paroissiaux et d'état civil*, Saint Nizier, baptême: 30/1/1676-28.11.1677 (vue 7), Page 12. www.fondesenligne.archives-lyon.fr. "Le Septieme mars ... jay baptizé ... Pierre né le 6 ... Robert Taillandier march. libraire ... Anne Compagnon ... Pierre Compagnon aussy marchand." Genevieve (daughter of Robert Taillandier and sister of Pierre) and Catherine Taillandier (daughter of Leonard) are found in the same register.

2. *Inventaires après décès*, 26 June 1692, BP1994, the box in which the original inventories of Robert Taillandier were found at the Archives Départementales du Rhône. http://www.sglb.org/spip/spip.php?page=liste_BP&recherche=%5ET. The address of Robert was recorded as "rue Mercière, that of Pierre Compagnon (Box 2017) was Port du Temple (angle de la rue Ecorche Boeuf et de la rue du ...), and that of Estienne Taillandier (Box 2017) was Lyon - Saint-Genis-Laval.

3. Besse, Léon "Liste Alphabétique des Missionnaires du Carnatic," 237. Carlos Sommervogel and Augustin de Backer, *Bibliotèque de la Compagnie de Jésus*, vol. 7, (Bruxelles: Oscar Schepens, 1896), 1816. Sommervogel also cites the "Necrologe general."

GLOSSARY AND PLACE NAMES

Brahmins: Members of the highest Hindu caste who are priests and teachers. Also: *Brahmans*.

Caste System: the Hindu social hierarchy of four groups from leaders to servers – Brahmin (priests, scholars), Kshatriya (rulers, warriors), Vaishya (merchants, farmers), and Shudra (laborers, artisans, servants).

Chalingue: French term for a masula boat. A long rowboat with high sides and a wide flat bottom made of timber planks which are sewn together with coir (coconut fibers). These boats were used along the Coromandel coast where there were no natural harbors for moving passengers and cargo between ships anchored a mile or two offshore and the beach. The boat was beached in the sand and the passengers and freight were carried to the shore. Also: *chelingue, chalinque, chelinque*.

Comptoir: French trading post. Also: *factory* (English), *feitoria* (Portuguese), *factorerie* (Dutch).

Encomienda: Spanish government grant to a person (encomendero) the right to exact tribute or labor from a specific number of indigenous people (Indios).

Firman: a permit or written order issued by a ruler. Also: *farman*.

Gentiles: Non-Christians in late 17th and early 18th century India. For example, Hindus are often referred to as "gentiles" by religious writers. In the West, though, "gentile" refers to a person who is not a Jew.

League, *Lieue*: an old unit of measure that varied from country to country and over time. It was roughly equivalent to 3 statute miles or 5 kilometers.

LEC: *Lettres Édifiantes et Curieuses, Écrites des Missions Étrangères.*

Livre: A "pound," the basic unit of French currency or account introduced in the 8th century by Charlemagne and in use into the 18th century. Initially, the *livre* was defined as equivalent to a pound of silver. Also: *livre Tournois*.

Malabar: Southwestern coast of India; a native of south India.

Masula Boat: English term for "Chalingue" (see above). Also: *masulah, masoola, massoolah, massulah, mussulah, masuli.*

Modéliar: Broker who served the French East India Company as an intermediary between the company and the native merchants and traders. A Tamil caste of landowners and a title of authority. Also: *mudaliyar.*

Mongols: Persons from Mongolia. Originally, they were subjects of Genghis Khan in the 13th century.

Mughals: Persons originally from Central Asia and descendants of the Mongols who invaded, conquered, and ruled large areas of India from the 16th century. The first Mughal emperor was Babur (r 1526 - 1530). Also: *Moguls, Moghuls.*

Nawab: Native Muslim governor or nobleman serving in the Mughal Empire, could be appointed by a subahdar. Also: *Nabab.*

Nayak: Leader or governor in India. Also: *Naik.*

Pagoda: Hindu temple. An Indian gold coin. Also: *pagode.*

Pariah: A Tamil caste of laborers, "Untouchables." Also: *Paraiyar.*

Raja: Hindu nobleman or chief. Also: *Rajah.*

Rajput: Derived from the Sanskrit "raja-putra," meaning "son of a king." Referred to landowners and warriers in central and northern India, later used to refer to those serving as royal officials.

Ravelin: A small buttress, having a half moon shape.

Subahdar: Governor of a province (*subah*) serving under the Mughal Emperor. Also: *Soubahdar, Soubedar.*

Tali: traditionally a linen cord worn by Brahmins over the left shoulder and across the bare chest.

Ulama: Muslim scholar or theologian. Also: *Ulema.*

Varna: see *Caste System.*

PLACE NAMES AND THEIR SPELLING VARIANTS:

Arcate, Arcot, Alcatile

Batavia, Jakarta

Calcutta, Kolkata

Calicut, Kozhikode

Carnate, Carnata, Karnate, Karnata, Karnatik (Dutch)

Carouvepondi, Carveipondi, Karuveppampoondi

Chandernagore, Chandernagor, Chandannagar

Deccan, Dekan

Gingee, Jingi, Senji, Gingi

Golconda, Golkonda

Hispaniola, Santo Domingo (the island), Saint-Domingue

Kedah, Queda

Krishna River, Coulour

Madras, Chennai

Madurai, Maduré

Malacca, Malaka, Malacka

Masulipatam, Masulipatnam, Machilipatnam

Mousy River, Musi

Mysore, Maisour, Maissour

New Spain, Nueva España, Mexico

Palar River, Palara, Palamalerou

Paliacate, Pulicat

Parlis River, Perlis

Penna River, Pennar, Penner, Penneru, Kichenepatnam

Pondicherry (English), Pondichéry (French), Puducherry (modern Indian English), Puducheri, Ponticheri (W. Dampier, 1691), Pondicheri (1753), Pontichery (1723), Podechery (Dutch)

Ponganour, Punganur

Queda, Kedah

Siam, Thailand

Tarcolan, Tarkolan, Tarcolam, Thakkolam

Velour, Vellore

Visapour, Bijapour

ENDNOTES

PROLOGUE

[1] "LEC": *Lettres Édifiantes et Curieuses, Écrites des Missions Étrangères, par quelques missionaires de la Compagnie de Jésus.*

Charles Le Gobien (1653-1708) compiled, wrote prefaces, and published Vols. 1-8 from 1703 until 1708. Le Gobien's successor, Jean-Baptiste Du Halde (1674-1743), published Vols. 9-26 until his death. In total thirty-four volumes of the French Jesuit missionaries' letters were published between 1703 and 1776.

[2] Also known as Jean-Baptiste Taillandier. Carlos Sommervogel and Augustin de Backer, *Bibliotèque de la Compagnie de Jésus*, vol. 7, (Bruxelles: Oscar Schepens, 1896), 1816. And Petrus Taillandier in Latin records.

[3] War of the Spanish Succession.

PART ONE – Pierre Taillandier

[4] Robert Taillandier died on 12 June 1686. Robert's "Inventaire Après Décès," found in the Archives du département du Rhône in Lyon, described him as a "marchand et maître libraire" (merchant and master bookseller) and gave his address at the time of death as rue Mercière.

[5] Pierre Taillandier might well have been named after his maternal grandfather, Pierre Compagnon.

[6] The "General Inventory" made shortly after Robert died contained a list of the books found in the "shops [*magasins*] and the boutique of Mr. Compagnon and the deceased Robert Taillandier: associated book merchants." Therefore, the two men must have owned more than one bookstore in Lyon.

[7] P. M. Delalain. *Inventaire des Marques d'imprimeurs et de libraires* (Paris: Cercle de la libraire, France), 94. https://play.google.com/books/reader?id=DSJAAAAAMAAJ&hl=en&pg=GBS.PA94.

[8] Jean Baptiste Monfalcon. *Manuel du Bibliophile et de l'Archéologue Lyonnais* (Paris: Adolphe Delahaye, 1857), xxxv. https://books.google.com/books/about/Manuel_du_bibliophile_et_de_l_arch%C3%A9olog.html?id=Vw0CAAAAQAAJ.

[9] Lyon's first printing press was set up in 1471. By the end of the

century there were 45 printers in Lyon established on rue Mercière. By the middle of the 16th century books published there were distributed internationally to Europe and as far away as the West and East Indies. Plaque in the Musée de l'imprimerie de Lyon.

[10] According to the Saint-Nizier parish baptismal records, Pierre had an older brother, Estienne, baptized on 13 October 1668, an older sister, Marie, baptized on 14 August 1674, and a younger sister, Genevieve, baptized on 25 April 1677. Robert Taillandier signed all four entries in these records. See Appendix B: The Taillandier Family Tree.

[11] Pierre Compagnon died on 11 June 1692, six years after Robert Taillandier, his son-in-law. (Interestingly, Robert's father who was Pierre Taillandier's other grandfather, Estienne Taillandier, died a few days later, on 26 June 1692.) According to his "Inventaire Après Décès," Compagnon lived at Port du Temple (angle de la rue Ecorche Boeuf).

[12] Listed in the "Inventaire du Fonds de Librairie Compagnon Taillandier," June 1686, following Robert Taillandier's death.

[13] Giovanni Maffei (1533-1603) was a Jesuit historian for Jesuit missions overseas, especially in the East and Japan.

[14] Sir Thomas Herbert (1606-1682) was an English historian and traveler in Europe, Persia, and India.

[15] The college was founded as a lay institution in 1527 but was taken over by the Jesuits between 1565 and 1595 when it again was administered by secularists until 1604. The Jesuits ressumed leadership from 1604 until 1762. https://data.bnf.fr/en/atelier/12352957/college_de_la_sainte_trinite_de_la_compagnie_de_jesus_lyon/#author.other_forms.

[16] Manonmani Restif-Filliozat. "The Jesuit Contribution to the Geographical Knowledge of India in the Eighteenth Century." *Journal of Jesuit Studies* 6, Issue 1 (11 March 2019): 71. https://brill.com/view/journals/jjs/6/1/article-p71_71.xml?language=en

[17] Thioly's father, Jean Thiolly (also spelled Thioly), was described as "imprimeur de la rue Merciére." Aimé Vingtrinier, *Histoire de l'imprimerie á Lyon, de l'Origine jusqu'a nos Jours* (Lyon: Adrien Storck, 1894), 379. https://gallica.bnf.fr/ark:/12148/bpt6k376391b/f393.image.texteImage.

[18] Sommervogel and de Backer, *Bibliotèque de la Compagnie de Jésus*, vol. 7, 1816.

"Saint-Bonnet's plans were executed under the direction of Fr. Pierre Taillandier, his student and friend...." Pierre de Vregille. *L'Observatoire du Collège de la Trinité, à Lyon* (Paris: Victor Petaux, 1905), 7.

[19] Gilles Adam. "Histoire de l'observatoire de Lyon." https://promenade.imcce.fr/fr/pages5/547.html. Accessed 23 July 2020.

[20] "The galleys, moored in the heart of the city, unloaded the spoils of Europe, Asia and Africa--silks, satins, cotton goods, furs, spices and sandalwood from as far away as Timor..." Henry R. Luce et al, eds., *Life's Picture History of Western Man* (New York: Time, Inc., 1951), 107.

[21] "Sailing in and out was largely dictated by the monsoon winds and storms. The southwest monsoon. occurred from April to September. For the northeast monsoon it was from October to March. October and May had greater chances of cyclonic storms." Sinnappah Arasaratnam, *Merchants, Companies and Commerce on the Coromandel Coast 1650-1740.* (Delhi: Oxford University Press, 1986), 35.

[22] Jordan of Severac, O.P., *Mirabilia Descripta: The Wonders of the East,* c1330, trans Henry Yule (London: The Hakluyt Society, 1863), vi. https://archive.org/details/mirabiliadescrip00jord/page/n19/mode/2up.

[23] "...in 1510 the Island of Goa was occupied by the Portuguese, under Albuquerque leadership, followed by the establishment of Portuguese power on part of the adjoining mainland, and at several points upon the coast, made possible by the almost undisputed Portuguese control of the Indian Seas." George Menachery, "Jesuits in the History of India," December 2002. http://kunjethy.tripod.com/indiajesuits/. Accessed 7 January 2020.

[24] William V. Bangert, SJ, A History of the Society of Jesus (St. Louis, Missouri: The Institute of Jesuit Sources, 1972), 85.

[25] Antonio Monserrate, "Father A. Monserrate's Account of Akbar, 26 November 1582)," trans. Henri Hosten, S.J., *Journal and Proceedings of the Asiatic Society of Bengal,* New Series vol. 8 (May 1912): 185. https://archive.org/details/mobot31753002183835/page/185/mode/2up.

[26] Theatines were priests of the Order of Clerks Regular founded in 1524 in Italy by St. Cajetan and the future Pope Paul IV, Gian Pietro Carafa, who was named Cardinal of Chieti (Latin *Teatinus*), Italy, hence the name Theatines.

[27] Donald F. Lach and E.J. Van Kley, *Asia in the Making of Europe,* vol. 3, Book 1 (University of Chicago, 1998), 228.

[28] Lach and Van Kley, *Asia in the Making of Europe,* vol. 3, Book 1, 228-229.

PART TWO – THE EASTER EFFECT

[29] Richard Tarnas, *The Passion of the Western Mind* (New York: Ballantine Books, 1993), 106.

[30] "For I am not ashamed of the gospel of Christ: it is the power of God to salvation for everyone who believes, to the Jew first and also to the Greek." *Letter from Paul to the Romans*, Romans 1:16 KJV.

[31] "Romans – Introduction – The Letter to the Romans," U. S. Conference of Catholic Bishops. Accessed 5 December 2019. http//www.usccb.org/bible/romans/0.

[32] "In the development of the church from a Jewish Christian origin in Jerusalem, with its roots in Jewish religious tradition, to a series of Christian communities among the gentiles of the Roman Empire, Luke perceives the action of God in history, laying open the heart of all humanity to the divine message of salvation." "Acts – Introduction – The Acts of the Apostles," U. S. Conference of Catholic Bishops. Accessed 6 December 2019. http//www.usccb.org/bible/acts/0.

[33] "To the quickly growing numbers of Christians who now proclaimed their message far and wide in the Roman Empire, what was born of Israel was Christianity." Tarnas, *The Passion of the Western Mind*, 97.

[34] "There were eight major Crusades. They occupied two hundred years and much of the energy of Western Europe. By the end of the thirteenth century nothing was left of the crusaders' kingdoms but the ruins of their feudal fortresses and a surprising number of fair-haired children among the dark natives of the Holy Land." Luce, *Life's Picture History of Western Man*, 42.

[35] "As the morning wore on and the Ottomans realized the truth–that there no longer was any organized resistance–the principles of slaughter became more discriminating. The Ottoman soldiers acted, according to Sad-ud-din, in accordance with the precept, "slaughter their aged, and capture their youth."...The newborn babies were hurled into the squares. ...Women and boys were raped. ...The church treasures–chalices, goblets, and holy artifacts...robes embroidered with much gold and glittering with precious stones and pearls–were carted away and melted down." Roger Crowley, *Constantinople: The Last Great Siege, 1453* (New York: Hachette Books, 2005), 1497-1498. https://archive.org/details/constantinople-the-last-great-siege-1453-roger-crowley/page/n1497.

[36] Pierre Loti, *India*, trans George A. F. Inman (New York: Duffield

& Co, 1906?), 41.

[37] John Shaw Banks, *Our Indian Empire, Its Rise and Growth* (London: Wesleyan Conference Office, 1880), 2. https://books.google.com/books?id=-5ABAAAAQAAJ.

[38] "The Brahmins, crossing the Indus, brought their own language from the west, where it was in constant use–as the ancient inscriptions in Persia testify–and diffused it through the north of India in connection with their religion. It thus became gradually mixed up with the dialects of the different provinces, which at length lost their original distinctions. The word Sanskrit signifies refined, and that language bears every indication of having received the improvements of the literati for many centuries, until it became the most exquisite medium of communication in the world." John Clark Marshman, *The History of India*, Vol 1, (London: Longmans, Green, Reader, and Dyer, 1867), 4. https://books.google.com/books?id=nrwIAAAAQAAJ

[39] The Pariahs are the lowest ranked group in south India. The term derives from the Tamil word "paraiyar," meaning drum. Since the leather used to make drums is considered unclean, only pariahs can touch them. Hence, the Pariahs were also called "Untouchables." They served all the varnas as tanners, cleaners, laundry workers, etc.

[40] Eugène Burnouf and E. V. S. Jacquet, *L'Inde Française*, vol. 1. (Paris: J. J. Chabrelie, 1827), no page. https://gallica.bnf.fr/ark:/12148/bpt6k1041173t/f7.image.

[41] "The European's need to use the pariahs for this job is one of the causes of the extreme contempt that the Hindus bear him among all other foreigners." Burnouf, *L'Inde Française*, vol. 1, no page.

[42] Dharma: "A central word in Hinduism, therefore multi-vocal, untranslatable; usually glossed 'law, righteousness, duty, code, etc.'" U. R. Ananthamurthy, Samskara: *A Rite for a Dead Man*, trans A. K. Ramanujan (New York: New York Review Books, Classics in Literature, 1976), 132.

[43] Paul Féval, *The Jesuits!*, trans. Agnes L. Sadlier, (New York: D & J Sadlier, 1878), 38. https://books.google.com/books/about/The_Jesuits.html?id=Sz0NAAAAYAAJ.

[44] "Book I discusses God, the Trinity, divine guidance, evil, predestination; Book II, angels, demons, the fall of man, grace, sin; Book III, the Incarnation of Jesus Christ, the redemption of sins, virtues, the Ten Commandments; Book IV, the sacraments of the four last things – death, judgment, hell, and heaven." Editors, Encyclopaedia Britannica.

"Peter Lombard," Encyclopaedia Britannica, last modified 25 March 1999. https://www.britannica.com/biography/Peter-Lombard#ref247822. Accessed 3 July 2020.

[45] "Piqued by what he felt was an unfair restriction, especially in view of the acknowledged soundness of his teaching, Ignatius made another of those momentous decisions which opened the door to a unique and fertile phase in his life. He resolved to quit Spain [earlier he was thrown in jail in Alcalá by Inquisitors who had acted on irresponsible gossip about him] and pursue his studies at the University of Paris." Fèval, *The Jesuits!*, 13.

[46] Pierre Favre, Francis Xavier, Simao Rodrigues, Diego Laynez, Alonzo Salmeron, and Nicolas Bobadilla "who committed themselves to his ideal of apostolic action remained faithful to the end." Fèval, *The Jesuits!*, 15.

[47] Fèval, *The Jesuits!*, 15.

[48] Stephen Greenblatt, *The Swerve: How the World became Modern*, (New York: W.W. Norton & Co., 2011), 106.

[49] Greenblatt, *The Swerve: How the World became Modern*, 250.

[50] Bangert, *A History of the Society of Jesus*, 20.

[51] Bangert, A *History of the Society of Jesus*, 21.

[52] Joseph Loconte, "Houses of Worship," *Wall Street Journal*, October 30, 2015, A11.

[53] Lyndal Roper, *Martin Luther, Renegade and Prophet*, (New York: Random House, 2017), 148.

[54] In 1514 in Germany the banking house of Fugger lent Prince Albert of Brandenburg, archbishop of Magdeburg and Halberstadt, a sum of money with which to bribe Pope Leo X in exchange of granting the prince a third Bishopric. "To make sure that the obligation would be met, Pope Leo X had granted to Albert the privilege of selling indulgencies. In Catholic doctrine there is only one way a sinner can be saved from eternal damnation—by confession and contrition. But though he is saved from hell he is still liable to punishment for a period in purgatory." Luce, *Life's Picture History of Western Man*, 146.

[55] The late medieval church was a property church, in which many individuals and institutions had a financial stake. The tithe, paid by the peasants, was a fundamental issue and they sought to have the right to call their own preacher. "But if, as usually the case, the tithe was owned by an individual or an institution, these would take a cut out of whatever was

collected." Roper, *Martin Luther, Renegade and Prophet*, 250.

[56] Roper, *Martin Luther, Renegade and Prophet*, 383.

[57] "In 1522 when the recluse of Manresa was writing his "Exercises" for the purpose of making men better, Luther was...proclaiming the uselessness of the Ten Commandments; and when Loyola was in London begging alms to continue his studies, Luther was coquetting with Henry VIII to induce that riotous king to accept the new Evangel." Thomas J. Campbell, SJ, *The Jesuits, 1534-1921: A History of the Society of Jesus from its Foundation to the Present Time*, vol 1. (New York: The Encyclopedia Press, 1921), 9.

[58] Fèval, *The Jesuits!*, 29.

[59] Fèval, *The Jesuits!*, 30.

[60] "Francis II reiterated three times his injunctions on the subject. Charles IX returned to the charge with no more success. Finally on the 15th of September 1561, the Colloquy of Poissy to which Parliament, taking refuge in subterfuge, had referred the case, solemnly received the Jesuits into France, under some restrictive clauses, afterward removed by Charles IX in 1565, and by Henry III, in 1580." Fèval, *The Jesuits!*, 122-123.

[61] Letters patent (from the Latin *litterae patentes*), always written in the plural, is an open public declaration granting an office, right, title, monopoly or status to a person or corporation. It is in force when the monarch signs it.

[62] Henry IV and the Parliament of Rennes failed in their efforts to steer the Malouins [to Protestantism]. They always answered: "We will die in the Catholic, Apostolic, and Roman faith." "Among the men who directed the affairs of Saint-Malo, for some, it was a matter of good faith; for others a pretext; for all, it was to live free." Charles Cunat, *Saint-Malo Illustré par ses Marins* (Rennes: F. Pèleat, 1857), 16-17. https://archive.org/details/saintmaloillust00cunagoog.

"There is a great deal of evidence to suggest that the transfer of power to the emergent [secular] state was a cause, not the solution, to the wars of the sixteenth and seventeenth centuries." William T. Cavanaugh, *The Myth of Religious Violence*, (Oxford: Oxford University Press, 2009), 162.

PART THREE – THE DECCAN, INDIA

[63] Niccolao Manucci, *Storia do Mogor or Mugal India 1653-1708*, vol. 1, trans. by William Irvine (London: John Murray, 1907), 111. https://

archive.org/details/storiadomogororm01manuuoft/page/n8/mode/2up

[64] The Sunnis believe that the first four caliphs, after Mohammed, were the rightful leaders of all Muslims — and that their heirs are the legitimate religious successors. The Shiites, in contrast, believe that only the heirs of the fourth caliph, Ali, are the legitimate successors of Mohammed.

[65] H.A.R. Gibb, *The Travels of Ibn Battuta*, AD 1325-1354, vol. 2. (London: Syndics of the Cambridge University Press, 1962), 277-278. https://archive.org/details/travelsofibnbatt02harg/.

[66] Chris Lowney, *A Vanished World*, (New York: Free Press, 2005), 169.

[67] That part of Asia south of the Himalayas, which forms a peninsula extending into the Indian Ocean between the Arabian Sea and the Bay of Bengal. This region is now divided between India, Pakistan, and Bangladesh.

[68] "Now the Prangui were abominated because they violated the most respected customs of India, by eating beef, and indulging in wine and spirits; but much as all well-bred Hindus abhorred those things, they felt more disgusted at seeing the Portuguese, irrespective of any distinction of caste, treat freely with the lowest classes, such as the pariahs, who in the eyes of their countrymen of the higher castes, are nothing better than the vilest animals." Joseph Brucker, SJ, "Malabar Rites." T*he Catholic Encyclopedia*. vol. 9. (New York: Robert Appleton Company, 1910). Accessed 13 December 2019. http://newadvent.org/cathen/09558b.htm.

Prangui, an Indian mispronunciation of Frank, i.e. Portuguese, became both in Western and in Southern India the general appellation for the native Christians, as well as the ruling Portuguese. Julius Richter. *A History of Missions in India* (New York: Fleming H. Revell Company, 1908), 56. https://archive.org/details/historyofmission00rich/.

[69] "Perhaps the commonest libel formulated against the Society is the accusation that it is the teacher, if not the author, of the immoral maxim: 'the end justifies the means,' which signifies that an action, bad in itself, becomes good if performed for a good purpose. If the Society ever taught this doctrine, at least it cannot be charged with having the monopoly of it." Campbell, *The Jesuits, 1534-1921*, 287.

[70] Bangert, *A History of the Society of Jesus*, 153.

[71] "The missions concerned are not those of the coast of southwestern India, to which the name Malabar properly belongs, but those of inner

South India, especially those of the former kingdoms of Madura, Mysore and Carnatic. The question of Malabar Rites originated in the method followed by the Jesuits since the beginning of the 17th century, in evangelizing those countries." Brucker, "Malabar Rites." *The Catholic Encyclopedia*. vol. 9.

[72] "In the last letter he sent to the Madurai mission, Aquaviva (Jesuit Father General) encouraged de Nobili, lifted the restrictions on his work except the matter of the tuft of hair (*codhumbi*) and the white cord (*tali*) since at the moment they were under consideration at the Vatican." Bangert, *A History of the Society of Jesus*, 154.

[73] "This stood in marked contrast to the long tradition of free trade that had been the source of Kozhikode's prosperity, and the ruler responded (in the words of the Portuguese chronicler) that he could not comply, 'for it was unthinkable that he expel 4000 households of them, who lived in Calicut as natives, not foreigners, and who had contributed great profits to his Kingdom.'" Sebastian R. Prange. "Where the Pepper Grows," *Saudi Aramco World Magazine*, January/February 2008. https//archive.aramcoworld.com/issue/200801/where.the.pepper.grows.htm.

[74] "At the time of his death, Fr. Criminali, who was but twenty-nine years old, had been a Jesuit for seven years." Joseph N. Tylenda, SJ, *Jesuit Saints and Martyrs*, (Chicago: Loyola University Press, 1984), 156.

[75] Tylenda. *Jesuit Saints and Martyrs*, 36.

John de Britto was born in Lisbon, Portugal on March 1, 1647. In 1669 he wrote to the Jesuit General Giovani Paolo Oliva requesting that he be sent to India. He arrived in Madurai in 1673 after a brief stint in Goa. In Tamil Nadu de Britto is known as Arul Anandar.

[76] "The king of the Maravas is the only one among many rulers within the great expanse of the Madurai Mission who has shed the blood of missionaries." Pierre Martin to P. Villette, 8 November 1709, Marava in Madurai Mission. *LEC*, vol. 10 (1713), 79.

[77] François Martin. *India in the 17th Century, 1670-1694 (Social, Economic, and Political): Memoirs of François Martin*, Vol. 2, Part 2, trans. Lotika Varadarajan (New Delhi: Manohar Press, 1985), 1496.

[78] Pierre de la Lane to P. Mourgues, January 30, 1709, Pondicherry. LEC, vol. 10 (Paris: Jean Barbou, 1713).

"In southern India, the boundaries of Mughal authority were continually shifting; Hindu and Muslim princes were engaged in a constant struggle to maintain their independence vis-à-vis their neighbors as well as the Mughal." Holden Furber. *Rival Empires of Trade in the Orient,* 1600-1800, vol. 2 (Minneapolis: University of Minnesota Press, 1976), 10.

[79] Although the *Carte des Missions* (Map 2) is clearly attributed to Bouchet, who was the Superior of the Carnate mission at the time he sent the original to France, there is some evidence that the original data and perhaps the original version of the map was based on work produced by two other Jesuits: Father Louis-Nöel de Bourzes and Friar Claude Moriset. Manonmani Restif-Filliozat. "The Jesuit Contribution to the Geographical Knowledge of India in the Eighteenth Century." *Journal of Jesuit Studies* 6, Issue 1 (11 March 2019): 71-84.

[80] "The Muslim kings, the Grand Mughal of India, the Turkish sultans, tried to demonstrate political authority despite separatist tendencies by their provincial governors to enrich themselves by all means, including tyranny and extortion. But they themselves struggled with endless indiscipline of their local chiefs and against the lawlessness unleashed. The abused people, robbed of their harvests in the field, lost all initiative for work. Agriculture and trading were reduced to just what was necessary." Angelo Ghirelli. *El Renacimiento Musulman.* Barcelona: Montaner y Simón, S.A., 1948), 29.

[81] D. Ferroli, SJ. *The Jesuits in Mysore.* Kozhikode, India: Xavier Press, 21 June 1955. Archive.org. Accessed 21 September 2020.

[82] Ferroli. *The Jesuits in Mysore,* 12.

[83] Ferroli. *The Jesuits in Mysore,* 20.

[84] Ferroli. *The Jesuits in Mysore,* "Foreword" by Thomas Pothacamury.

[85] As a military leader Timur allied himself with the Khan of the Chagatai Khanate in Transoxiana. After marrying a princess of the Chagatai clan, he assumed the tile of Amir, meaning general. Timur could not claim the title of *khan* because he was not a descendant of Genghis Khan.

[86] A Persian derivation or mispronunciation of the word "Mongol".

[87] The Mughal rulers were: Babur (1526-1530), Humayan (1530-1556), Akbar (1556-1605), Jahangir (1605-1627), Shah Jahan (1627-1658), and Aurangzeb Alamgir (1658-1707).

[88] "The application of laws derived from Sanskrit classical texts leveled the community of Hindus to include all those who were not Muslims or Christians, and it absorbed under the category of 'Hindu' both outcastes and members of religions as diverse as Buddhists, Jainism,

Sikhism, Judaism, and Zoroastrianism. Gauri Viswanathan. *Outside the Fold: Conversion, Modernity, and Belief* (Princeton, New Jersey: Princeton University Press, 1998), 78.

[89] From the Sanskrit *raja-putra*, or son of a king.

[90] Dacca (Dhaka), then the Mughal capital of Bengal, is now the capital of Bangladesh.

[91] "In many countries, kings and their dependent aristocracy loved to adorn their bodies with this unique piece of cloth." V. B. Kulkarni. *History of the Indian Cotton Textile Industry* (Bombay: Millowners' Association, 1979), 1.

[92] Akbar and his son Jahangir received a gift of the history of the apostles in Persian from Jerònimo Xavier (grandnephew of Francis Xavier), a Spanish Jesuit missionary (1549-1617), who arrived in Goa in 1581. He was sent to Lahore when Akbar "called for a mission of Jesuit priests to court, where he arrived on May 5, 1595." Lach and Van Kley, *Asia in the Making of Europe*, vol. 3, Book 1, 394.

"The emperor read, with great pleasure, a 'Life of Christ' composed in Persian, and a picture of the Virgin, copied from the Madonna del Popolo in Rome, was by his orders taken to the palace that he might show it to the women of his household." Campbell, *The Jesuits, 1534-1921*, 230

[93] Lach and Van Kley, Asia in the Making of Europe, vol. 3, Book 1, 394.

[94] Ines G. Zupanov, "The Historiography of the Jesuit Missions in India (1500-1800)" in Jesuit Historiography Online, 2016. Accessed on 28 September 2019. https://referenceworks.brillonline.com/entries/jesuit-historiography-online/the-historiography-of-the-jesuit-missions-in-india-15001800-COM_192579.

[95] Manucci, Storia do Mogor or Mugal India 1653-1708, vol 1, 159.

[96] "The Mughal emperor was Shah-an-Shah, 'king of kings', rather than king of India. He was the highest manifestation of sovereignty, the court of final appeal, for Muslims an earthly successor to aspects of the authority of the Prophet Muhammad. Yet many of the attributes of what we would call the state pertained not to the emperor or his lieutenants, but to the Hindu kings of the localities, the rajas or the notables who controlled resources and authority in the villages." C. A. Bayly. "Indian Society and the Making of the British Empire" in The New Cambridge History of India, vol. 2, part 1 (Cambridge: Cambridge University Press,

1998), 13. Cambridge Histories Online.

[97] Estienne Le Gac to Fr. Charles Porée, January 10, 1709, Chinnabalabaram. *LEC*, vol. 10 (1713), 253.

[98] "The whole interior of the Deccan is a lofty table land, the home of large kingdoms, and enjoying of course a cooler climate than the narrow plains which stretch thence to the sea. The mountains of this plateau are called *ghauts* (steps)." Banks, *Our Indian Empire, Its Rise and Growth*, 1.

[99] Also known as Tarkolan or Tarcolam, but today as Thakkolam.

[100] Pierre de la Lane to P. Mourgues, 30 January 1709, Pondicherry. *LEC*, vol. 10 (1713).

[101] Also called Karnatic, Karnataka, and Karnatika. "Scholars have tried to interpret Karnataka in various ways…. A popular view is that the land is of black soil (*kari* + *nadu*) and from this is derived 'Karnadu.' But the most accepted view is that the word 'Karnata' is derived from *karu + nadu,* the big land or an elevated land. Major parts of Karnataka are situated in the Deccan Plateau and are therefore an elevated country". Lalit Chugh. *Karnataka's Rich Heritage – Art and Architecture: From Historic Times to the Hoysala Period* (Chennai: Notion Press, 2016), 16-17.

[102] Arasaratnam, *Merchants, Companies and Commerce on the Coromandel Coast 1650-1740*, 65-67.

[103] Since the 1650s The Dutch East India Company (VOC) brutally controlled the production and transport to Europe of cloves, mace, and nutmeg in the Spice Islands. A rebellion by local farmers and the planting of the trees on other islands gradually weakened the Dutch monopoly. A century or so later the French succeeded in planting nutmeg trees in Mauritius.

[104] Sommervogel and de Backer, *Bibliotèque de la Compagnie de Jésus*, vol. 7, 1802-1805.

[105] Tachard recalled that the King Louis XIV, through François de la Chaise, the king's confessor, chose fourteen Jesuits from the five provinces, including two from Lyon (Rochette and de la Bruille), to serve as ambassadors to the court of the king of Siam. They were summoned to Paris to met with de la Chaise and then were sent to the Academie des Sciences. There they met with the scientists so that they would be better prepared to make "bonnes Sciences" (good studies) in Siam. The subjects studied were: mathematics, anatomy, navigation, herbs, how to paint the plants and animals they found, and other observations to be made there. Guy Tachard, SJ. *Second Voyage du Père Tachard et des Jésuites au Royaume*

de Siam (Paris: Daniel Horthemels, 1689), 1-4.

[106] "The priests of the Paris Foreign Mission Society [Mission Étranger de Paris, or MEP] expelled from Siam, likewise began to work at Pondicherry in 1689. Tachard, the Jesuit, slowly gave up his hope of reviving the Siam mission. Urged on by de Britto, he finally decided in 1692 to concentrate on a French mission to the interior of India, which would take off where the Madurai mission ended and expand northward into the Telugu country." Lach and Van Kley, *Asia in the Making of Europe*, vol. 3, Book 1, 258.

[107] A French *lieue*, league, was an old unit of measure equivalent to about 3 statute miles or 5 kilometers.

[108] About 200 km southwest of Pondicherry.

[109] "When I arrived in Pondicherry, on my fifth trip, I found Fr. Mauduit, who had already begun a settlement [in Carouvepondi] about 30 or 40 leagues from here to the NW after having left the Madurai mission... Before leaving for France, this last time, I learned from the Father General that Father Bouchet returned to our new French mission." Guy Tachard to A. M. Le Comte de Crecy [Louis de Verjus, signer of the Treaty of Ryswick and Jesuit benefactor], 4 February 1703, Pondicherry. *Lettres Édifiantes et Curieuses Concernant l'Asie, l'Afrique et l'Amérique* (hereafter *LECC*), vol. 2, 325. This two-volume collection was edited by M.L. Aimé Martin and published in Paris in 1840 by Auguste Desrez.

[110] Pierre de la Lane to P. Mourgues, 30 January 1709, Pondicherry, *LEC*, vol 10 (1713).

[111] "It has been nearly five weeks since I arrived in Pondicherry with Fr. Tachard. You will see by the relation he sent to France, how our voyage was happy and which route we took. To come from the site of our landing at Pondicherry, we had to pass through the small kingdom of the Maravas, which is a dependency of the Madurai mission. You have often heard of this mission as one the most blessed and the most glorious in Jesus Christ that we have in India." Gabriel Petit to P. de Trevou, 12 February 1702, Pondicherry, *LECC*, 316.

[112] Pierre de la Lane to P. Mourgues, 30 January 1709, Pondicherry, *LEC*, vol. 10 (1713).

[113] Walter Scott Seton-Karr. *Selections from Calcutta Gazettes of the Years 1784-1823*, vol. 2. (London: Longmans, Green, Reader and Dyer, 1865), 288.

[114] Estienne Le Gac to P. Charles Porée, 10 January 1709,

Chinnabalabaram. *LEC*, vol. 10 (1713).

[115] "One of the converts baptized at Krishnapuram by Fr. Le Gac was one Rangappa, the first Christian parent of the Bhimashetty family of Krishnapuram whose descendants are now settled at Kondramutia. ... He lived many more years...He died on Good Friday, 4th April, 1738. The people say that the grave of Fr. Le Gac, in Krishnapuram, is the holiest. He is called Sarijinathaswamilavaru." Henry Heras, SJ. *Jesuits of Old Days in Andhradesa.* docplayer.net/84463407-Jesuits-of-old-days-in-andhra-desa/html. Accessed November 2019.

[116] "The French Father Jean Venantius Bouchet worked for twelve years in Madurai, chiefly in Trichinopoly, during which time he baptized about 20,000 infidels. And it is to be noted that the catechumens, in these parts of India, were admitted to baptism only after a long and careful preparation." Brucker, "Malabar Rites." *The Catholic Encyclopedia.* vol. 9.

[117] Hing, a favorite staple of the Mughal Sultans, originally came from Persia. Its garlicky flavor when cooked in oil is a good substitute for onions and garlic, which is avoided by devout Hindus.

[118] Prévost, Antoine-François, Abbé. *Histoire Générale des Voyages, Collection de Toutes les Relations*, vol. 13, Book 3. (La Haye: Pierre de Hondt, 1755), 459. Google Books.

[119] Father Heras, a Catalan, was born Enric Heras de Sicars but later preferred to use the Anglicized version of his name. He died in Bombay in 1955 at age sixty-seven.

[120] Gabriel Petit to P. du Trevou. 12 February 1702, Pondicherry, *LECC*, 316.

[121] Brucker. "Malabar Rites." *The Catholic Encyclopedia.* vol. 9.

[122] "By this method, and no less by the prestige of his pure and austere life, the missionary [Fr. de Nobili] had soon dispelled the distrust and before the end of 1608, he conferred baptism on several persons conspicuous for nobility and learning. While he obliged his neophytes to reject all practices involving superstition or savoring in any wise of idolatrous worship, he allowed them to keep their national customs, in as far as these contained nothing wrong and referred to merely political or civil usages. Accordingly, Nobili's disciples continued for example, wearing the dress proper to each one's caste; the Brahmins retaining their codhumbi [tuft of hair] and [*tali*] cord [cotton string slung over the left shoulder]; all adorning as before, their foreheads with sandalwood paste, etc. yet, one condition was laid on them, namely, that the cord and

sandal[sandalwood paste], if once taken with any superstitious ceremony, be removed and replaced by others with a special benediction, the formula of which had been sent to de Nobili by the Archbishop of Cranganore." Brucker, "Malabar Rites." *The Catholic Encyclopedia.* vol. 9.

[123] "Since Indian ascetics, *pandara suami*, were able to approach individuals of all castes, Fr. [de] Britto established himself as one of them. He lived as they lived: he ate only a few handfuls of rice a day; he used a mat on the floor for his bed. He also dressed as they dressed in a red cloak and turban. He set up small retreats in the wilderness, similar to hermitages, where interested Indians could visit him. In time he was accepted pandara suami; his reputation grew and he converted many." Tylenda. *Jesuit Saints and Martyrs*, 36.

[124] In 1630, after he became Mughal Emperor, Shah Jahan having "not forgotten the repulse he received from Portuguese Governor Rodrigues at Hooghly [four years earlier to assist him with some guns and artillerymen to fight a rebellion in Bengal], ordered the expulsion of the Portuguese idolaters from his dominions." Marshman *The History of India,* 138.

[125] Information about these "Jesuit martyrs" is etched on wall headstones at the memorial and cemetery in Karuveppampoondi Olugari Post Kanchipurem, Madam, Tamil Nadu 631603.

[126] Besse, Léon, SJ. "Liste Alphabétique des Missionnaires du Carnatic de la Compagnie de Jésus au XVIIIe Siécle," *Revue Historique de l'Inde Française,* vol 2 (Pondicherry: Société de l'Histoire de l'Inde Française, 1918), 222. https://babel.hathitrust.org/cgi/pt?id=mdp.39015030172251&view=1up&seq=252&q1=222.

[127] P. Bouchet to M. Cochet de Saint-Vallier, (no date or place). *LEC,* vol. 11 (1715), 3-4.

[128] Estienne Le Gac to Fr. Charles Porée, 10 January 1709, Chinnabalabaram. *LEC,* vol. 10 (1713).

[129] Dhruv Raina, "French Jesuits in India: Historical Astronomy in the Discourse on India, 1670-1770," *Economic and Political Weekly.* 34, no. 5 (Jan. 30 – Feb.5, 1999): PE36. https://www.jstor.org/stable/4407606. Accessed 16 June 2019.

[130] "They [Brahmins] count four ages since the beginning of the world." Pierre de la Lane to P. Mourgues, 30 January 1709, LEC, vol. 10 (1713).

[131] "Three different interests [citing Catherine Jami in this essay] converged in the formation of French Jesuit missions and subsequently

deciding their research agenda. In the first instance the director of the Paris observatory in the 1670s Gian-Domenico Cassini (1624-1712) submitted a proposal to send Jesuits to China to make some astronomical observations, and to advance their knowledge of latitudes, longitudes and magnetic declinations. Secondly, the French king was compelled by French Jesuit interests to augment support for Catholic missions abroad." Raina, *French Jesuits in India*, PE30-31.

[132] Rao, N. Kameswara and Christina Louis. "Father Richaud and Early Telescope Observations in India." Bulletin of the Astronomical Society of India 12, no.1, (1984): 82. http://adsabs.harvard.edu/full/1984BASI...12...81K. Accessed 25 September 2019.

[133] R. K. Kochlar. "French Astronomers in India during the 17th-19th Centuries." *Journal of the British Astronomical Association* 101, no. 2 (1990): 95. http://adsabs.harvard.edu/full/1991JBAA..101...95K. Accessed 5/14/20.

[134] Adrien Launay, *Histoire des Missions de l'Inde: Pondichéry, Maissour, Coimbatur*, vol. 1. (Paris: Ancienne Maison Charles Douniol, 1898), 456.

[135] At this time China represented the Western concept of East Asia. For example, the term *nao de China* was used to describe the Spanish galleons serving between Manila (ie. Asia) and Acapulco.

[136] Jacques Cassinni, Letter 10 January 1705. "Reflections on the observations of the variation of the needle, made in the pope's legate's voyage to China in the year 1703," trans. Ephraim Chambers. *The Philosophical History and Memoirs of the Royal Academy of Sciences at Paris*, vol. 2. (London: John and Paul Knapton, 1742): 239-240.

[137] J. V. Bouchet. *Old, Antique map of Southern India*, published in Germany in 1726. Found among the Sanderus Antique Maps. sanderus@sanderusmaps.com. Accessed 1 January 2020.

Although the German edition of the map is attributed to Bouchet, the original version may have been created by Louis-Noël de Bourzes with Frère Claude Moriset. Manonmani Restif-Filliozat. "The Jesuit Contribution to the Geographical Knowledge of India in the Eighteenth Century:" *Journal of Jesuit Studies* 6, Issue 1 (11 March 2019): 71.

[138] Jean V. Bouchet to (Unknown), 19 April 1719, Pondicherry, *LECC*, 548.

[139] In 1906 Bernard Brunhes, Director of the Geophysical Observatory of Puy de Dome, discovered the inversions of the earth's magnetic field by

measuring reverse magnetization in samples from basaltic lava flow and other sediments in Pont Farin near Auvergne, France. Jacques Kornprobst and J.-F. Lénat. "Centenary of the Discovery of Earth's Magnetic Field Reversals" EOS, 4 November 2014. https://eos.org/articles/centenary-discovery-earths-magnetic-field-reversals. Accessed 19 December 2019.

PART FOUR – THE FRENCH EAST INDIA COMPANY

[140] Arasaratam. *Merchants, Companies, and Commerce on the Coromandel Coast* 1650-1740, 22-23.

[141] G. B. Malleson. *History of the French in India* (London: W. H. Allen & Co. Ltd., 1893), 6.

[142] Colbert "is one of those men who stamp their name on the age in which they live." Malleson, *History of the French in India*, 10.

[143] *Mémoire sur l'implantation de la Compagnie des Indes à partir de 1664 (1664/1725).* http://anom.archivesnationales.culture.gouv.fr/ark:/61561/ou533f0y31a.num=500.start=801. Accessed 7 March 2020.

[144] For perspective on the magnitude of the original capital account: 600,000 French livres tournois in 1715 was the equivalent of about 12,000,000 US dollars in 2015. Historicalstatistics.org. Accessed 6 November 2020.

[145] "The urban areas contained a large class of feudal gentry whose refined tastes and love of luxury ensured the prosperity of the textile industry. The karkhanas mostly catered to their tastes and throve on royal patronage. In a country where social divisions are largely based on this profession, the textile workers were divided into numerous mutually exclusive sub-castes. The carders, the spinners, the weavers, the dyers, the bleachers, and the printers formed themselves into distinct groups and functioned accordingly." Kulkarni, *History of the Indian Cotton Textile Industry*, 2.

[146] Dirk van der Cruysse. *Siam and the West, 1500-1700.* Trans by Michael Smithies. Chiang Mai, Thailand: Silkworm Books, 2002. (No page). At this time Martin was engaged as an "under-merchant" with a salary of six hundred *livres* per year.

[147] "Though the French were forced, after several trials, to abandon their hold on Madagascar, it was only … to seize and secure the smaller islands [Mauritius and Reunion] contiguous to it, the possession of which from 1672 to 1810 proved to them a tower of strength in their wars with England; a festering thorn in the sides of their maritime rivals." Malleson, *History of the French in India*, 9.

[148] During the Dutch War (July 1672-September 1674) France and England were allied against Holland.

[149] Barthélemy Carré, *The Travels of the Abbé Carré in India and the Near East, 1672-1674,* trans. Charles Fawcett and Richard Burn (New Delhi Asian Educational Services, 1990), 328.

[150] "The interdictions imposed by the Ming emperors when they decided to change their policy of overseas expansion (literally turning their backs on the sea towards the middle of the 15th century) did not prevent a great number of Chinese from emigrating to Indo-China, Malaya, and Indonesia." Auguste Toussaint, *History of the Indian Ocean,* trans. June Guicharnaud (Chicago: Chicago University Press, 1966) 84.

[151] Quoted in: M. K. Agarwal, *Bharata to India*: vol. 1: *Chrysee the Golden* (Bloomington, Indiana: IUniverse, Inc., 2012), 518.

[152] Martin. *India in the 17th Century, 1670-1694 (Social, Economic, and Political): Memoirs of François Martin,* Vol. 2, Part 2, 1431.

[153] There is evidence that from around 1 AD the Romans established a trading post at a site called Poduca (Puduke) which is believed to be the recently excavated town of Arikamedu on the Ariankuppam River about 4 km south of today's city of Pondicherry. Toussaint, *History of the Indian Ocean,* 36.

[154] Martin. *India in the 17th Century, 1670-1694 (Social, Economic, and Political): Memoirs of François Martin,* Vol. 2, Part 2, 1233.

[155] Governor of Coromandel under the Dutch.

[156] Martin. *India in the 17th Century, 1670-1694 (Social, Economic, and Political): Memoirs of François Martin,* Vol. 2, Part 2, 1523.

[157] Martin. *India in the 17th Century, 1670-1694 (Social, Economic, and Political): Memoirs of François Martin,* Vol. 2, Part 2, 1565.

[158] That same month Pierre Taillandier entered the novitiate at the Collège de la Trinité in Lyon. There must have been talk there of the French defeat and repatriation of the Jesuits once this news reached Paris.

[159] "The first French hospital was built by the Jesuits in the White Town in 1690. François Martin constructed a second in 1699. A third came into existence in 1738 for sick military. Past soldiers or sailors with scurvy, but also asylum for the old soldiers and families of the Company des Indes remain here." Pierre Aubry and Bernard Gaüzére, "Histoire de la Santé dans l'océan Indien: soins, prévention, enseignement et recherche du XVIIe siécle au milieu du XXe siécle." *Medecine et Santé Tropicale,* 26,

no. 2 (April – June 2016): 122-129.

[160] "Fort Louis finally finished and "inaugurated" with ceremony: cannon fire from bastions in August of 1705." Paul Kaeppelin, *La Compagnie des Indes Orientales et François Martin: Étude sur l'Histoire du Commerce et des Établissements Français dans l'Inde sous Louis XIV (1664-1719)* (Paris: Augustin Challamel, 1908), 521.

PART FIVE – Tilting at Windmills

[161] "The Dutch are also at the origin of the separation between Ville noire and Ville blanche (Black Town and White Town). In the French plan dated 1700, the western settlement is called Ville neuve; in the other one, dated 1714, a distinction is made between 'la ville haute habitee la plus grande partie par des noirs' and 'les deux basses villes occupiee en partie par des François.'" Deloche, *Origins of the Urban Development of Pondicherry*, 41. White Town still exists on today's maps of Pondicherry, and Black Town is now called Heritage Town.

[162] The Dutch map of Pondicherry dated 1694 describes the Jesuit residence as the "former place of the Jesuits" and their gardens as the "King's gardens." Deloche, *Origins of the Urban Development of Pondicherry*, 34.

[163] They built a third church on the site beginning in 1728. It, too, was destroyed by invaders, this time the British in 1761. By the end of the century the fathers completed the fourth church which survives today as the Immaculate Conception Cathedral of the Roman Catholic Archdiocese of Pondicherry and Cuddalore.

[164] This pagoda is clearly labelled on the Dutch plan of Pondicherry, dated 1694, as "Malabar pagoda." Deloche, *Origins of the Urban Development of Pondicherry*, 34.

It also appears on De Nyon's 1716 plan, but not on later ones; therefore, it must have been torn down.

[165] "There are three churches in Pondicherry; the first [a chapel] is at the fort serving the garrison and Company employees, the second is in the town, a Capuchin church for Europeans – the reverend Capuchin Fathers conduct service in both these churches – and the third is run by the reverend Jesuit Fathers for those dressed in Indian clothes." (This statement is attributed to a Chevalier d'Albert who visited Pondicherry in 1726.) Raphaël Malangin, *Pondicherry that was Once French India* (New Delhi: Lustre Press/Roli Books, 2015), 37.

[166] "Since the French had settled at that place (Pondicherry), the spiritual care of the colonists was in the hands of the Capuchin Fathers,

who were also working for the conversion of the natives. The Bishop of Mylapore, or San Thomé, to whose jurisdiction Pondicherry belonged, resolved in 1699, to transfer it entirely to the Jesuits of the Carnatic mission, assigning to them a parochial church in town and restricting the ministry of the Capuchins to the European immigrants, French or Portuguese. The Capuchins were displeased by this arrangement and appealed to Rome. The petition they laid before the pope in 1703, embodied not only a complaint against the division of parishes made by the bishop, but also an accusation against the methods of the Jesuit mission in South India." Brucker, "Malabar Rites." *The Catholic Encyclopedia*. vol. 9.

[167] "Malabar" in this context was a term used to identify the natives of south India.

[168] "The marriage and death records, kept by Capuchins who acted as the Catholic population parish priests, revealed that the town's residents hailed from all over the globe: various locales in South Asia, the Indian Ocean island colonies, Bagdad, Isfahan, Ireland, England, Germany, Venice, and as far afield as Canada." Danna Agmon, *A Colonial Affair: Commerce, Conversion, and Scandal in French India*, (Ithaca, New York: Cornell University Press, 2017), 13.

[169] In an earlier but similar affair, the Jesuits in China under Matteo Ricci (1552-1610), founder of the missions in China, had amalgamated Confucian practices and customs into Catholicism to effect conversion. This thoroughly complicated de Tournon's relations with the Emperor after the latter learned that the decision against the [Malabar] rites had been given since 20 November 1704, but not yet published in Europe, as the pope wished that it should be published first in China... "When the Emperor learned of this decree, he ordered Mgr. de Tournon to be brought to Macao and forbade him to leave there before the return of the envoys who he himself sent to the pope to explain his objections to the interdiction of the rites. While still subject to this restraint, the legate died in 1710." Brucker, Joseph, SJ, "*Matteo Ricci.*" *The Catholic Encyclopedia*, vol. 13. (New York: Robert Appleton Company, 1912). Accessed 2 January 2020. http://www.newadvent.org/cathen/13034a.htm.

[170] Bangert, *A History of the Society of Jesus*, 329.

[171] "While cultural differences indeed played a major role, the three missions [Madurai, Mysore, and Carnatic] were ravaged by such fierce conflict because the adoption of native social hierarchies had been the main condition that the missionaries had negotiated with the local elites in order to 'open the door' to Christianity.... Paolo Aranha, "The Social

and Physical Spaces of the Malabar Rites Controversy," in *Space and Conversion in Global Perspective*, eds. Giuseppe Marcocci, et al (Leiden, The Netherlands: Koninklijke Brill, NV, 2015), 218.

[172] Bangert, *A History of the Society of Jesus*, 330.

[173] "The very first Jesuit mission started in India…, a geographical term, today corresponding to South Asia, but which in the early modern period often encompassed the entire Asia or at least what the Portuguese, who were the patrons of the Jesuit missions, called *Estado da Índia*." Zupanov, "The Historiography of the Jesuit Missions in India (1500-1800)," In *Jesuit Historiography Online*.

[174] The first six volumes of *Lettres Edifiantes et Curieuses*, organized by Charles Le Gobien, S.J., were already in print by the time Taillandier departed for India. It is very likely that these books were made available to the missions from the Collége Louis le Grand (founded by the Jesuits in 1563 as Collége de Clermont within the campus of the University of Paris) where Le Gobien might have resided. It is also likely that an outbound missionary was introduced to his correspondent here. Taillandier's correspondent was Father Willard.

[175] Launay, *Histoire des Missions de l'Indes*, 107.

[176] Launay, *Histoire des Missions de l'Indes*, 107-108.

[177] Stephen Neil, *A History of Christianity in India, 1707-1858*, vol. 2 (Cambridge: Cambridge University, 1985), 76.

[178] AMDG ("For the Greater Glory of God") served as the epigraph for the Society of Jesus since its formation.

[179] Ferroli. *The Jesuits in Mysore*, 131.

[180] Louis Phélypeaux, Comte de Pontchartrain, Chancellor of France from 1699 to 1714.

[181] Mudaliyar [modéliar] is a Tamil term for a person of honor and authority.

[182] *Réglements fait par la Compagnie des Indes pour Pondichéry, et confirmé par sa Majesté, 14 February 1711*, 51. http://anom. archivesnationales.culture.gouv.fr/ark:/61561/ou533f0y5yw.num=100. start=841.form=simple.

[183] "The Company traders-administrators sought to sustain the profitable status quo and insert themselves into long standing trading networks based on kinship and confessional affiliation – a preservationist strategy. French Jesuits, on the other hand, even as they practiced the

strategy of accommodation among their own converts, espoused an ideology of disruption and radical change in the city at large, in an effort to fundamentally reconfigure the local spiritual and social hierarchies." Danna Agmon, *An Uneasy Alliance: Traders, Missionaries and Tamil Intermediaries in the 18th Century French India.* (PhD dissertation, University of Michigan, 2011), 4. https://deepblue.lib.umich.edu/bitstream/handle/2027.42/89720/danna_1.pdf?sequence=1&isAllowed=y

[184] Over the years and tenure of François Martin, he obtained the "aldées of Calapet (1703), to the north and Oulgaré (1706), to the west of Pondicherry." Kaeppelin, *La Compagnie des Indes Orientales et François Martin*, 662.

[185] "The Jesuits, one cannot deny their high intellectual culture but also their great spirit of domination, believed themselves bound at that time to propose, and if need be, to impose their domination, either directly or indirectly, on established powers." Alfred Martineau's introduction in Paul Olagnier's *Les Jésuites à Pondichéry et L'Affaire Naniapa* (Paris: Societe de L'Histoire des Colonies Françaises, 1932), 8. https://gallica.bnf.fr/ark:/12148/bpt6k58400179/f12.image.texteImage.

[186] From the beginning Lazaro de Mota Tanapa Modeliar (also spelled Lazzaro de Motta Thanappa Mudaliar) was influential in French efforts to establish themselves in Pondicherry. For example, as early as 1686 he provided the funds to build the first church there for the Capuchins. It was dedicated to his patron saint, St. Lazarus. He accompanied François Martin when he left Madras for Pondicherry in 1674 and acted as Martin's interpretor and negotiator with the Tamils.

[187] Olagnier, *Les Jésuites à Pondichéry et L'Affaire Naniapa*, 15.

[188] Olagnier, *Les Jésuites à Pondichéry et L'Affaire Naniapa*, 21.

During early 1700s, 10,000 pagodas had the equivalent value of 50,000 livres. https://.historicalstatistics.org/Currencyconverter.html Accessed 1 March 2020.

[189] *Réglements fait par la Compagnie des Indes pour Pondichéry, et confirmé par sa Majesté, 14 February 1711.*

[190] Olagnier, *Les Jésuites à Pondichéry et L'Affaire Naniapa*, 24.

[191] "This man, Chavoury, (Tamil: Savari), was, according to council documents, expected to act conjointly and in concert with Nayiniyappa." Agmon, *A Colonial Affair*, 29.

[192] "Such conduct would have surprised us had we not been aware of the nature of the Brahmins who are devoid of gratitude and show

themselves full of insolence when they feel that they are in a stronger position or when success is theirs." Martin. *India in the 17th Century, 1670-1694 (Social, Economic, and Political): Memoirs of François Martin,* Vol. 2, Part 2, 1482.

[193] The "Chalingue [French term for *masula*] is a small boat which is used in India, that doesn't have ribs except in the bottom, and that is hardly longer than wide. It has no iron in its construction, not even nails. The upper planks are sewn only with coconut rope. They are strong, light and have high sides, they respond to the oar. The boat is used in the Malabar and Coromandel coasts." Denis Diderot and Jean le Rond d'Lambert, *L'Encyclopédie ou Dictionnaire des sciences, des arts et des métiers,* vol. 3 (Paris: Chez Briasson, *et al,* 1753), 39. https://gallica.bnf.fr/ark:/12148/bpt6k505351/f40.item.r=chalingue.texteImage.

[194] Malangin, *Pondicherry that was Once French India,* 29.

[195] "Father Tachard's Jesuits came to Pondicherry in 1689 and they embarked upon educational and evangelical work with Indians of all castes and with people of mixed race who were rejected by both [native and European] communities." Malangin, *Pondicherry that was Once French India,* 38.

[196] Guy Tachard to Reverend P. de la Chaise, King's Confessor. September 30, 1703, Pondicherry *LECC,* 328.

[197] "It was largely from the Mogul Empire of India, - from Bengal and the coasts of Coromandel and Malabar, - that came the fine cottons which, especially in the last century of the traffic, filled so important a place in the cargoes." William Lytle Schurz, *The Manila Galleon* (Manila: Manila Conservation Society, 1985), 34.

[198] "With little of value to offer Asian markets, European traders paid for their purchases with precious metals…. It was essential that the Coromandel be kept well provided with cash specie and goods, said Batavia's Dutch governor-general, Jan Pieterzoon Coen in 1617. In the first half of the 17th century, the Spanish silver real became the most widely accepted currency in SE Asia." Sunil S. Amrith, *Crossing the Bay of Bengal: The Furies of Nature and the Fortunes of Migrants* (Cambridge, Massachusetts: Harvard University Press, 2013), 53.

"In 1701, François Martin asked the Directors of the Company in Paris to send well cut dies made in France" to counter the illegal copies of French *fanams* struck by local artists." Later he "got authority to mint pagoda (gold) … stamped with the figure of the Hindu goddess Lakshmi for big commercial transactions. However, as the Jesuits objected to the image of Lakshmi, Martin was forced to mint the new gold pagodas with the French symbol of a fleur-de-lis." Sandeep Kumar Verma, "Currency System in Pondicherry under the Rule of the Compagnie des Indes Orientales, 1674-1761," *International Journal of Applied Research* 1, no 8, Part C (2015), 112. http://www.allresearchjournal.com/archives/2015/vol1issue8/PartC/1-8-86-154.pdf.

[199] Derived from the Arabic word *mausim* or season of winds, referring to reversing prevailing winds.

[200] Coromandel textiles "became a link in a trade cycle which embraced the Mediterranean, the Red Sea and the Persian Gulf, western India, Malabar and Coromandel, Malacca, Java and the Spice islands. In this trade Coromandel textiles were used to barter for the spices of the Moluccas or to acquire purchasing power for the acquisition of spices for the Mediterranean and West Asian markets. Arasaratnam, *Merchants, Companies and Commerce on the Coromandel Coast 1650-1740*, 97.

[201] Amrith, *Crossing the Bay of Bengal*, 53.

[202] By1704 the city side of the fort was protected substantially by "three bastions whose escarpments and counter-escarpments were covered with brick and whose moat was filled with about 5-6 feet of water. On the seaside, … Martin constructed two temporary earthen bastions and another in the form of a priest's cap or double pincer to protect the roadstead and prevent any landing. These were well fortified with artillery." Kaeppelin, *La Compagnie des Indes Orientales et François Martin*, 506.

[203] Pondicherry was founded near the mouth of tidal lagoons surrounding marshy lands and sand dunes. "It is near the mouth of the main brook called Uppar, which flows into the Ariankuppam lagoon that the town originated. This water course, which appears to have been relatively large in the second half of the 17th century, at the beginning of the European occupation, followed roughly the course of the present *petit canal* towards the east and then the *grand canal* towards the south." Deloche, *Origins of the Urban Development of Pondicherry*, 13.

[204] "A catamaran (in Tamil *kattamaram*, from *kattal*, 'to tie or bind,' and *maram*, 'wood,' literally tied wood, or timber lashed together) is a raft, from twelve to fifteen feet long, composed of three spars or logs of light wood, lashed together; and managed by two or three *kareiars*, or beachmen, persons of the same caste as those employed in the *Masoola* boats." Elijah Hoole, *Madras, Mysore, and the South of India* (London: Longman, Brown, Green and Longmans, 1844), 29-30.

[205] Richter. *A History of Missions in India*, 66.

206 Barbara Bartoli. "Pondicherry: Modern Technologies Approach in the Message of the Past." In *Proceedings of the 5th International Conference: Analysis of Historical Constructions*. New Delhi, 2006. http://www.hms.civil.uminho.pt/sahc/2006/1973.pdf. Accessed 13 May 2021.

207 According to Paolo Aranha, a noted authority on the Malabar Rites in southern India, this letter to Father Willard of 20 February 1711 was not the only one Taillandier composed and dispatched from Pondicherry that month. Aranha reported in an email to the authors that he read the original letter in which Taillandier weighed in on the "internal politics" of the French Jesuits "in relation to the French colonial authorities and the various religious actors implied in the Malabar Rites controversy." Paolo Aranha, Personal communication, 19 September 2015.

208 Dava Sobel, *Longitude* (New York: Walker and Company, 1995), 25.

209 At least one source reports that Taillandier made astronomical observations while in Pondicherry. Vregille, *L'Observatoire du Collège de la Trinité*, 7.

210 "Born in Lyon, April 18, 1652, Jean de Saint-Bonnet entered the novitiate on 12 January 1672. He had expertise in grammar and the humanities, two years rhetoric, six years philosophy, and ten years mathematics and physics. He was associated with the celebrated astronomer Dominique Cassini, who urged him to have an observatory built on the church of the College of the Trinity in Lyon. The 'consulat' or government granted funds for this purpose, and for a long time Father Saint-Bonnet devoted the pension he received from his family to it. As he gave orders to the workmen who were doing the construction, he was carried away by the rope of a crane and fell down on the forecourt of the church. He died from the fall on 6 March 1702." Sommervogel and de Backer, *Bibliotèque de la Compagnie de Jésus*, vol. 7, 411.

211 "At the Collège de la Trinité at Lyon, one of the colleges in France with the strongest tradition in teaching mathematics from 1605, an observatory was founded in 1701. Jean de Saint-Bonnet (1652-1702) oversaw the construction, built upon one tower of the church of the college, but he died in an accident during the works. The first director was Pierre Taillandier (1676-1713), who made observations until 1707, when he was sent to India." Agustin Udías, *Jesuit Contribution to Science, A History,* (chapter 2, item 2.2, provided by the author). Springer, 2015.

212 Joseph Picot. Les *Jésuites à Lyon de 1604 à 1762*. (Lyon: Editions aux Arts, 1995) 104.

[213] https://patrimoine.auvergnerhonealpes.fr/dossier/observatoire-du-college-de-la-trinite/bdef0ce3-c1b9-4491-aa5a-4a1be27765d9. Accessed 10 March 2021.

[214] Pierre Taillandier to Fr. Willard, 20 February 1711, Pondicherry. *LEC*, vol. 11 (1715), 92.

[215] "Father Martin, having heard the news of my imprisonment, ... entered the house of the governor, and in a modest but firm and vigorous voice told him that having heard his senior Brother was in jail he had come to die with him, if he was guilty, but if he was innocent, asked the governor to set him free." P. Bouchet to M. de Saint-Vallier, *LEC*, vol. 11 (1715), 69.

[216] "Father Dacunha is the first missionary Your Reverend has sent to the Mission of Mysore since you started as provincial. Despite being in the middle of many persecutions, he cultivated for three years this new vineyard with indefatigable zeal, but recently lost his life as a result of the wounds he received defending the truths of the faith." Père Sant-Yago to Manoël Saray, Provincial of the Province of Goa, 8 August 1711, Capinagati, *LEC*, vol. 10 (1713), 98.

"In two months and a half I baptized more than 1,100 pagans; I heard the confessions of more than 6,000 neophytes. This country was afflicted by hunger and by epidemics, doubling my hardship and anguish; the many sick and dying did not allow me an opportunity for even a short rest." Pierre Martin to P. Villette, 8 November 1709, Marava in Maduré Mission. *LEC*, vol. 10 (1713), 80.

[217] "After the wreckage of our mission in Siam, the majority of our fathers withdrew to Pondicherry on the Coromandel coast, where I joined them after my third voyage to France. On seeing the great number of idolaters which surround us to the west and north, we were touched by a true desire to work on their conversion. The great progress that the Portuguese Jesuits had made toward the south, where they had formed a Christendom of nearly 200,000 souls, we find that by employing the same methods for the conversion of the Indians living to the north of Pondicherry, we could perhaps with time obtain from our Lord the same blessings." Tachard to A. M. Le Comte de Crecy, 4 February 1703, Pondicherry, *LECC, 325.*

[218] Guy Tachard to A. M. Le Comte de Crecy, 4 February 1703, Pondicherry, *LECC*, 325.

[219] Ferroli. *The Jesuits in Mysore*, 12.

[220] The *kombu* is a south Indian semi-circular trumpet-like horn.

"This instrument that irritates the delicate ear of a European is one that wins the favor of the Indians...." Burnouf, *L'Inde Française*, vol. 2, no page.

[221] "Sri Manakula Vinayagar Temple was in existence before the French came and settled in Pondicherry, i.e., before 1666. According to Sasthra, Lord Ganesha is named in 16 types based on his various forms of which the god facing the east coast of Bengal has been named as Bhuvaneshar Ganapathey, now called as Manakula Vinayagar.... The Jesuits and missionaries wanted to demolish Manakula Vinayagar, but they could not. During 1700 the French prohibited performing poojas and festivals, particularly on Fridays in the temple. All the Hindus who were worshipping Lord Vinayagar objected and migrated to Moratandi English territory [about 8 km NW of this temple]. Arulmigu Manakula Vinayagar Devasthanam. "Manakula Vinayagar Temple, Puducherry." http://www.manakulavinayagartemple.com/. Accessed 31 May 2020.

[222] Pierre Loti, who visited a temple at the invitation of the Maharajah of Travancore toward the end of the 19th century, described a typical temple feast that might have occurred in Pondicherry, or elsewhere in South India: "The enclosure is square and large enough to contain a town. In the middle of each of the four blank walls a huge pylon rises, under which a door has been hallowed out, but, except for this, these walls are as gloomy as those of a citadel. The place we are in is sacred and must not be trod by common men. We pass dark masses, which look like pedestals... These are the chariots in which the gods are placed on feast days, when thousands of frenzied arms push them along the ground...As we retrace our way under the avenues of palms whose dark heads are bent in all directions, a clamor of religious frenzy breaks over us, and the hallow sound of tom-toms fills the serene night air; horns bray like monsters, and barbarous noises fill us with a sense of terror." Loti, *India*, 26.

PART SIX – THE LONG VOYAGE

[223] By 1706 Pierre Genthon, Jean Gardel, and Jean Chiquet were the new operators of the "ferme des coches, carrosses, diligences et messagerie de Lyon," succeeding the previous owner, François de la Bruyére, who had messagerie (courier service) rights to Normandy and other areas. Two citations: 1) Eugéne d'Auriac, *Histoire Anecdotique de l'industrie française*, (Paris: Libraire de la Société des Gens de Lettres, 1861), 205 and 2) Maurice Prou, *Recherches sur les hôtels de l'archevêché de Sens à Paris*, (Sens, France: Charles Duchemin, 1882), 16-17.

[224] "In April 1594 Henry IV created the position of Superintendent of 'coches et carrosses publics' to protect the safety of the carriages and the travelers because the roads were so poorly maintained." d'Auriac, *Histoire Anecdotique de l'industrie française*, 193.

[225] Anne Conchon, "Road Construction in Eighteenth Century France." https://www.arct.cam.ac.uk/Downloads/ichs/vol-1-791-798-conchon.pdf, 791. Accessed 6 January 2019.

[226] The Lyon-Paris grand route overland was also known as the "route du Bourbonnais." Taillandier would have left Lyon via La Tour de Salvagny, then passed through Tarare, Roanne, Never, Pouilly, Briare, Montargis, Nemours, Fontainebleu, and entered Paris via Villejuif. Or, if not, then he might have entered Paris having traveled west through Orleans, or east via Dijon. Two citations: 1) Charles Estienne, *La Guide de Chemins de France* (Paris, Charles Estienne, 1553). https://books.google.com/books?id=N-87AAAAcAAJ&printsec=frontcover&source=gbs_ViewAPI#v=onepage&q&f=false 2) *Liste Generale des Postes de France* (Paris: Chez le Sr. Jaillot, 1741). https://books.google.fr/books?id=iOV_0Juv_XQC&printsec=frontcover&hl=fr#v=onepage&q&f=false.

[227] "By the early 1700s these roads typically were 20 meters wide with ditches on either side and they were lined with trees. The middle was paved with stones to a width of 6.5 meters. The remainder of the road was dirt, which was the favored surface in good weather because it was smoother." Patrick Marchand, "Voyager en France au Temps de la Poste aux Chevaux," in *Le Maître de poste et le messager, les transports publics en France au temps des chevaux.* (Paris: Belin, 2006), 2. https://www.laposte.fr/chp/mediasPdf/PMarchand.pdf. Accessed 14 January 2020.

[228] Two citations: 1) https://data.cerl.org/thesaurus/cnp00065654 and 2) Sommervogel and de Backer, *Biblioteque de la Compagnie de Jesus*, vol. 2. (Bruxelles: Oscar Schepens, 1891), 1035.

[229] "Saint Bonnet was commissioned by Cassini to build an astronomical observatory on top of the Lyon College; he died in an accident during the construction." *Giovanni Domenico Cassini (1625-1712).* In *Jesuit Science Network*, Version 03/11/2018. http://jesuitscience.net/p/711/. Accessed 14 January 2020.

And, Saint-Bonnet's father provided him a pension of 3,000 livres annually which he dedicated to the construction of the observatory. Picot. *Les Jésuites à Lyon de 1604 à 1762*, 102.

[230] The chapel was destroyed by Charlemagne in the 9th century. "A new chapel dedicated to St. Aaron was built in the area by Cardinal de

Montfort in 1431. By 1618 it was crumbling…. In 1621 a new chapel was consecrated and the devotion to St. Aaron redoubled.", Èduoard Prampain, *Saint Malo Historique* (Amiens, France: Piteux Frères, 1902), 190.

[231] "Mismatched wall rubble, unequal in height and strength, topped the battlements, crowned with 'machicoulis' [floor opening between supporting corbels through which stones could be dropped on attackers at the base of the wall], 'echauguettes' [overhanging turrets] and…latrines, cantilevered, reinforced, different periods, with numerous towers…such was the strange appearance of this enclosure." Prampain, *Saint Malo Historique*, 50.

[232] Cunat. *Saint-Malo Illustré par ses Marins*, 20.

[233] William Lytle Schurz, "Mexico, Peru, and the Manila Galleon," *The Hispanic American Historical Review* 1, no. 4 (November 1918): 394. https://www.jstor.org/stable/2505890?seq=1#metadata_info_tab_contents. Accessed 6 June 2020.

[234] Ilocos, a region or province of northern Luzon in the Philippines.

[235] "The Saint Malo Shipwrecks: Les Épaves Corsaires de la Natiére." https://archeologie.culture.fr/epaves-corsaires/fr/mediatheque. Accessed 7 January 2020.

[236] A 16thc statue of the Virgin Mary, "Notre-Dame de la Croix du Fief," stood in a niche outside the house across the square from the Duguay-Trouin house, built in the 17th c. "All Malouins greatly venerate her" reads the plaque hanging next to the statue in the Cathedral.

[237] The Malouins always considered the English their enemy. Around the year 1433 after the battle for Mont Saint Michel in which Malouins helped defeat the English fleet, a post on a wall in the intra-muros read: "This enemy (the English), they are our most hated mortal enemy." Cunat. *Saint-Malo Illustré par ses Marins*, 7.

[238] In the middle of the 17th century, "the fishing for cod employed six thousand fishermen from Saint-Malo, Saint Brieuc, and Granville. Our establishments in Canada commenced to catch more and prosper." Cunat, *Saint Malo Illustré par ses Marins*, 25.

[239] *L'activité maritime à Saint Malo dans la seconde moitié du XVIII siècle,* Collection Documents pour l'Histoire de Saint-Malo, Dossier No. 4, (Archives Municipales de Saint-Malo, 1992), 8.

[240] At present called the Lycée Emile Zola.

[241] "With the agreement of Canon de Kournoual, they petitioned the

Chapter and obtained the chapel by donation, as well as the little house next door, by means of keeping a chaplain there, pay an annuity of thirty pounds to the holder of the property, and make the reposoir (temporary altar) for the Feast of Corpus Christi (18-21 August 1631.)" Prampain, *Saint Malo Historique*, 192.

[242] *L'activité maritime à Saint Malo dans la seconde moitié du XVIII siècle*, 9.

"On 6 January 1708, two warships of 600 tonnes, carrying 50 and 40 cannons, *Le Curieux* and *Le Diligent*, commanded by two Malouin captains, went to Moka and made their return on 12 May 1710. They brought back coffee, myrrh, incense, aloe, balm from Mecca and various other drugs." Cunat, *Saint Malo Illustré par ses Marins*, 32.

"East India companies chartered by European governments were the chief means whereby commerce between Europe and Asia were carried on." Furber, *Rival Empires of Trade in the Orient 1600-1800*, 3.

[243] "Jean de Chatillon street [near the Croix du Fief], with its beautiful large houses all chiseled with fine sculptures, was the aristocratic street. This street bordered the sea and when its rich residents opened their picturesque windows of colored stained glass, they saw at their feet the lovely Mer Bonne cove where, by a long channel dug in the granite, the elegant galleys and the fishing boats were protected, against the winds blowing offshore." Eugéne Herpin, *La Cote d'Emeraude, Saint Malo, Ses Souvenirs* (Rennes: Hyacinthe Cailliére, 1894), 309-310. Note: after 1708 the Mer Bonne shoreline here was filled in (See Map 7.) to enlarge the city.

[244] Henri-Georges Gaignard, *Connaitre Saint- Malo* (Paris: Èditions Fernand Lanore, 1973), 103.

[245] Prampain, *Saint Malo Historique*, 65.

[246] Prampain, *Saint Malo Historique*, 104.

[247] *L'activité maritime à Saint Malo dans la seconde moitié du XVIII siècle*, 10.

[248] Today a copy stands in its place and the original is displayed in the St. Vincent's Cathedral.

[249] Prampain, *Saint Malo Historique*, 66.

[250] E. W. Dahlgren. "Voyages Français à Destinations de la Mer du Sud avant Bougainville, 1695-1749." *Nouvelles Archives des Missions Scientifique et Litteraire*, vol 14, (Paris: Imprimerie Nationale, 1907), 476. https://babel.hathitrust.org/cgi/pt?id=inu.30000093666208&view=1up&

seq=548.

[251] "The souls of Sir Clowdisley's lost sailors precipitated the famed Longitude Act of 1714, in which Parliament promised a prize of £ 20,000 for a solution to the longitude problem. Sobel, *Longitude*, 16.

[252] Elizabeth Heaphy Murray, *Sixteen Years of an Artist's Life in Morocco, Spain and the Canaries*, vol. 1 (London: Hurst and Blackett, 1859), 209-210.

[253] "Few who have visited Santa Cruz will ever forget the desolate and savage appearance of the rocks of Paso Alto, which extend to the outskirts of the town." Murray, *Sixteen Years of an Artist's Life in Morocco, Spain and the Canaries*, vol. 1, 211-212.

[254] "Beginning in the 18th century and continuing until colonial independence in the 1820s, Spain loosened its grip, forced by the growing discontent among colonists and merchants at home. Canarian ships regularly travelled to Havana, Santiago de Cuba, Santo Domingo, La Guaira, Cumaná, Chagres, Portobelo, Riohacha, Santa Marta, Cartagena, Vera Cruz, Campeche, Omoa, and several smaller ports." John M. Lipski, "The Spanish of the Canary Islands." http://www.personal.psu.edu/jml34/Canary.htm. Accessed 28 February 2018.

[255] "Unique to the Valley of La Orotava is its system of vine training, *el cordon trenzado*, the braided cord. Vines' branches are braided together in large bunches of multiple strands. Vine lengths vary from 3 meters up to 15 in the case of old established vines. This method of vine training evolved due to space constraints on the island. Traditionally, el cordon trenzado allowed branches to be moved easily, leaving the earth below to be utilized for potatoes, which were essential for feeding the island's inhabitants." "Valle de la Orotava Wine." https://www.wine-searcher.com/regions-Valle+de+la+Orotava. Accessed 28 February 2018.

[256] Located at 1, Calle de Colegio. "Erected in the second half of the XIX century the house was previously called casa Díaz Flores but now we know it as the casa Brier, a neoclassic style building erected over the site once occupied by the Jesuit College." Jesús Rodríguez Bravo, *Los Jesuitas y las Artes en la Orotava*. Santa Cruz de Tenerife: Le Canarien Ediciones, 2015), 65-66.

[257] Murray, *Sixteen Years of an Artist's Life in Morocco, Spain and the Canaries*, vol. 1, 339.

[258] "The Port of La Orotava [Puerto de la Cruz] ...to it arrives around 80% of the commercial shipping of the second half of the XVII century,

thanks above all to the export of wines to England and Portugal." Bravo, *Los Jesuitas y las Artes en la Orotava*, 30.

"It is thought that 30,000 pipes (12.5 million liters) of Malmsey, a sweet wine made from white malvasía grape, were exported through the Puerto de La Orotava in one year, with the English, Dutch, and Germans being the biggest consumers." "Valle de la Orotava Wine." www.wine-searcher.com/regions-Valle+de+la+Orotava.

"Shakespeare writes about Malmsey wine in Love's Labor Lost (5.2.240) and Henry IV (2.1.36). But the most famous reference to Malmsey in all of literature can be found in Richard III, when Richard orders the execution of his brother, the Duke of Clarence. Richard's hired assassins decide to drown Clarence in a large cask (butt) of the brew... Similar to malmsey, canary wine was a sweet white variety with a yellow tint... Shakespeare refers to canary wine in Twelfth Night (1.3.74) and The Merry Wives of Windsor (3.2.83). Amanda Mabillard. "Shakespeare's Drinking," *Shakespeare Online*. http://www.shakespeare-online.com/faq/shakespearedrinking.html. Accessed 16 January 2020.

[259] "Practically nothing visible remains about the Jesuits in La Orotava. As if time wanted to erase any or all traces of their accomplishment here; as if it wanted to prolong a historical tragedy to a point as to forget the Jesuits had come. It is therefore important to pursue artistic archaeology and other methods of exhaustive analysis to assure future investigators of the reconstructed history." Bravo, *Los Jesuitas y las Artes en la Orotava*, 17.

[260] El Teide is one of only sixteen volcanoes in the world classified as a "Decade Volcano" by the International Association of Volcanology and Chemistry of the Earth's Interior. These volcanoes have been designated as such because of their history of destruction and their proximity to population centers. Pico del Teide is the highest point in Spain at 12,188 feet (3715 m).

[261] "The king gave them [Jesuit mathematicians sent to Siam] some instruments: 2 quadrants, 2 observation pendulums, an "anneau astronimique," a "machine paralytique," several "demicircles," and many other instruments." Tachard, *Second Voyage du Pere Tachard et des Jesuites au Royaume de Siam*, 4.

[262] A toesa, an ancient French measure of length, was equivalent to about 2 meters. 1300 toesas would be roughly equivalent to 2600 meters. The discrepancy between Teide's actual height of 3,718 meters compared to Taillander's estimate could be attributed to a misestimate of the horizontal distance between his sighting location and the volcano and

the atmospheric conditions at the top of the volcano.

[263] Antonio de Pigafetta, Magellan's faithful scribe said this in his memoires: "Then we departed [from San Lucar in Spain] and came to a port called Monterose [Punta Rosa, Tenerife], where we remained two days to furnish ourselves pitch... Know that among the other islands which belong to the said Grand Canary, there is one where no drop of water coming from the spring or river is found, save that once a day... there descends from heaven a cloud which encompasses a great tree... and from the leaves is distilled great abundance of water, so that at the foot of the tree there is so great a quantity of water that seems a living fountain." Antonio Pigafetta. *Magellan's Voyage, A Narrative of the First Circumnavigation*, trans. R. A. Skelton (New York: Dover Publications, 1969), 41.

[264] "Due to *"les hostilitiés"* she captured, near sight of the coast of Brazil, a Portuguese ship, the Bon Jesus-de Boisses, captained by Miguel Sousa de Pinto, whom Captain Avice escorted to the St. Anne Islands. The Saint Esprit, weakened by worms that damaged it, was sold in Callao in 1710." Dahlgren. "Voyages Français à Destinations de la Mer du Sud avant Bougainville, 1695-1749," 476.

[265] "The bay is the southern edge of the area to which humpback whales come from the north Atlantic to calf and mate every year during winter." Lubos Kordac, *Historic Shipwrecks of the Dominican Republic and Haiti* (Merritt Island, Florida: Signum Ops, 2009), 95.

[266] The cosmographer's art "was based on the application of the study of the stars to the practical concerns of navigation, above all through the calculation of latitude from the observation of the height (*altura*) or angle of the sun with the horizon at noon. To navigate by alturas, that is, through calculating latitude by the sun, was the latest word in scientific navigation of the epoch. The determination of longitude remained, for the moment, subject to estimates based on the course and the distance traveled, and it would not be solved in a scientific manner until the second half of the eighteenth century." Pablo Perez Mallaina, *Spain's Men of the Sea* (Baltimore: Johns Hopkins University), 232-233.

[267] "The camellia, *Camellia sinensis* [from China], is also known as tea. The Empire of China had a near complete monopoly on tea, as it was the only country to grow, pick, process, cook, and in all other ways manufacture, wholesale, and export 'the liquid jade.'" Sarah Rose, *For All the Tea in China* (New York: Penguin Books, 2010), 1.

The Portuguese physician and Jesuit Luis d'Almeida, writing from

Oita Prefecture, Japan, on 14 October 1564 was the first European to describe the habit of drinking tea, or *cha*, in Japan.

[268] Malick W. Ghachem, *Our Crown and Glory: The Jesuits in Haiti, 1704-1763*. Radcliffe Institute for Advanced Studies, 2018-2019. https://www.radcliffe.harvard.edu/fellowship-program/research-partnership-opportunity/our-crown-and-glory-jesuits-in-haiti-1704-1763. Accessed 30 January 2020.

[269] The word tobacco is believed to be derived from the Taíno language (tabako), as are a few other words, such as hurricane (hurakan), canoe (canoa) and barbecue (barbacoa).

[270] "The first commercial production of sugar in the New World was undertaken in 1550, when the Portuguese *Donatarios* built mills near Pernambuco and São Vicente along the Atlantic coast of Brazil." Mark Johnston, *The Sugar Trade in the West Indies and Brazil Between 1492 and 1700*. https://www.lib.umn.edu/bell/tradeproducts/sugar.

[271] A supersaturated sugary liquid is heated "until crystals begin to appear in the liquid and then must be separated out. The hot crystal-containing solution was then poured into conical containers with a hole at the pointy part on the bottom. As it cooled, the solid sugar would stick to the sides and the liquid molasses would drip out the bottom. What was left was a solid cone of sugar." "Primitive Sugar Production," Bacardi Sugar Spirit Project, 1 September 2011. https://www.alcademics.com/2011/09/primitive-sugar-production.html. Accessed 3 February 2020.

[272] "... manufacturing the dye required considerable equipment and skill. Indigo makers soaked and drained their harvest in a series of large masonry tanks.... Although the putrid basins were said to spawn deadly diseases, merchants paid well for the dark powder left when the water drained away." John D. Garrigus, *Before Haiti: Race and Citizenship in French Saint Domingue* (New York: Palgrave Macmillan, 2006), 29.

[273] Philip P. Boucher, *France and the American Tropics to 1700: Tropics of Discontent* (Baltimore, Johns Hopkins University Press, 2010), 240.

[274] M. L. E. Moreau de Saint Mercy, *Description topographique, physique, civile, politique et historique de la partie française de l'isle Saint Domingue* (Paris: Chez Dupont, 1797), 372.

[275] Benoît Roux. "De insulis Karaybicis relations manuscriptae: Adrien Le Breton, The Last Missionary in the 'Carib Island' of St. Vincent." *In Communities in Contact. Essays in archaeology, ethnohistory and*

ethnography of the Amerindian circumCaribbean (Leiden: Sidestone Press, 2011), 344, 349. https://halshs.archives-ouvertes.fr/halshs-01598281. Accessed 8 June 2020.

[276] Its many articles regulated the life, marriages, death, and treatment of slaves by their masters in all French colonies until they gained their freedoms. It prohibited slaves from owning property for they had no legal capacity, prompting Voltaire, the French intellectual and philosopher during the age of Enlightenment, to write that "the Black Code only serves to show that the legal scholars consulted by Louis XIV had no ideas regarding human rights." Slavery in all French colonies was finally abolished in April 27, 1848. Kelly Buchanan, "Slavery in the French Colonies: Le Code Noir of 1685," *Custodia Legis,Law Librarians of Congress,* 13 January 2011. https://blogs.loc.gov/law/2011/01/slavery-in-the-french-colonies/ .Accessed 8 June 2020.

[277] A grant conferred by the Spanish crown to conquistadors or settlers, which gave them the right to exact labor and tributes from native populations in the Americas and the Philippines. The encomenderos were responsible for the protection and the religious (Roman Catholic) instruction of the natives they oversaw.

[278] Lewis Hanke, *The Spanish Struggle for Justice in the Conquest of America* (Dallas: Southern Methodist University Press, 2002), 17.

"'Turk' was largely a pejorative term applied by the nation-states of the West, the name Turkey unknown to them until borrowed from Europe to create a new Republic in 1923. The Ottomans, literally tribe of Osman, called themselves just that, or simply Muslims." Crowley, *Constantinople: The Last Great Siege, 1453,* 52.

[279] Hanke, *The Spanish Struggle for Justice in the Conquest of America,* 22.

[280] The Pracel (paracel or placel) are the islets or sand bars along the northern coasts of Yucatán, Cuba, and Jamaica. M. Bonne and M. Desmarest, *Atlas Encyclopedique, contenant a geographie ancienne* (Paris: Hôtel de Thou, 1788), 92.

Also defined as "banks of sand or rocks in the sea," in the Velazquez Spanish Dictionary.

[281] Taillandier misspells the fort's name. It is "El Castillo de los Tres Reyes Magos del Morro." "Morro" here refers to the "rock" or "promontory" on which the fort was built.

[282] In fact, the entrance to Havana's harbor is so narrow (about 250

m wide and 1.5 km long) that the Spanish installed a heavy copper cable from El Morro across the channel to La Punta to protect the town. This cable could be raised when enemy ships approached the harbor.

²⁸³ While Taillandier does not mention the Jesuit presence in Havana, we know that the diocese dates from the early 1500s. Beginning in 1569, the Jesuits initiated plans to establish a school on the banks of the Canal de la Entrada not far from the port docks. By 1689, under the direction of Bishop Diego Evelino de Compostela, they established the Colegio San Ambrosio.

²⁸⁴ Pedro González García, *Discovering the Americas: The Archive of the Indies* (New York: Vendome Press, 1997), 116.

²⁸⁵ Francisco Hernández de Córdoba, Spanish conquistador and discoverer of the Yucatán Peninsula, died in 1517 after his ill-fated expedition. Coincidentally, another conquistador of the same name founded Nicaragua in 1524, after the conquest of Mexico by Hernán Cortés.

²⁸⁶ Whisking melted chocolate between two hands by means of a small wooden paddle while heating the liquid in a tall clay pot (*chocolatero*).

"Etymologists trace the origin of the word 'chocolate' to the Aztec (Nahuatl) word 'xocoatl,' which referred to a bitter drink brewed from cacao beans." Amanda Fiegl. "A Brief History of Chocolate," *Smithsonian Magazine*, 1 March 2008. https://www.smithsonianmag.com/arts-culture/a-brief-history-of-chocolate-21860917/.

²⁸⁷ Havre de Grace is now called Le Havre, the port city at the mouth of the Seine. Port Louis, on the northwestern coast of France (Brittany), was where the French East India Company was established in 1664. The shipyards, across the bay, were known as L'Orient.

M. du Casse (Admiral Jean Baptiste du Casse) started out as a privateer and later became governor of Saint Domingue from 1691 to 1703.

²⁸⁸ This French ship is not listed on the French maritime history website "La flotte française en 1707." http://www.netmarine.net/bat/listes/flot1707.htm. Therefore, it is possible the *Saint-Jean Baptiste* was constructed in a French occupied port in the Americas, such as New Orleans, Louisiana.

PART SEVEN – THE TREK TO MEXICO CITY

²⁸⁹ San Juan de Ulúa. Derived from two names combined: Joan

(or Juan), the captain of an earlier expedition to Mexico commissioned by Gov. Velázquez of Cuba, and Ulúa, the name of the place where the expedition landed.

[290] Velázquez was the first governor of Cuba who sailed to the New World on the second voyage of Columbus in 1511. As *adelantado*, Velázquez was portrayed by Bartolomé de las Casas as perpetrating acts of horrific brutality on the native Cubans until the island was completely colonized in 1514.

[291] Two other writers, Francisco López de Gomara and Gonzalo de Illescas, wrote about the conquest, but their versions were dubious or third hand. They were never in the field of battle according to Díaz del Castillo. He finished his memoires in Santiago de Guatemala after serving as *regidor*, or governor of Chiapas, a post awarded to him by Cortés for his services as a conquistador.

[292] On the mainland and known as Chalchihuecan.

[293] Cochineal, also known as Carmine Red dye, is a pigment derived from the crushed bodies of female cochineal insects. The dye was first used by the Aztecs as far back as a thousand years, but it was the Spanish who exploited the dye for commercial purposes after they conquered Mexico. It is still in use today in such far-ranging applications as textiles, cosmetics, food and medical research. Bill Norrington. *Cochineal – A Little Insect Goes a Long Way* (UCSB Geography Department, no date.). https://geog.ucsb.edu/cochineal-a-little-insect-goes-a-long-way/. Accessed 28 July 2020.

[294] "The reservoirs and cisterns went dry. The crops, which grew in terraces cut into jungle hills, died. Starvation set in; millions perished for lack of water with which to irrigate farms and feed enormous populations in Guatemala, Belize, and the Yucatán. Eventually the survivors gave up hope and left, migrating to the coast or to lakes in the north." Will Hunt, "Cave of the Crystal Maiden," *Discover Magazine*, December 2014, 36.

[295] "In all the battles fought in New Spain, Tlaxcala, and Mexico, Doña Marina was a very helpful woman and being a linguist, she was always at Cortés' side." Bernal Díaz del Castillo, *Historia Verdadera de la Conquista de la Nueva España* (Mexico City: Editores Mexicanos Unidos, SA, 2014), 39.

[296] B. C. Álvarez. "La Ciudad de Veracruz." https://www.otromundoesposible.net/la-ciudad-de-veracruz/ Accessed 4 February 2021.

[297] Today the road distance from Vera Cruz to Mexico City is 402.7 km. or 252 miles. Taillandier said the distance he traveled was 80 leagues, or about 240 miles.

[298] Montezuma II who reigned from 1502 to 1520.

[299] Internal strife between the indigenous inhabitants and collaboration with them were decisive factors in the speed of the conquest of the New World. García, *Discovering the Americas: The Archive of the Indies*, 53.

[300] "In 1609 occurred a serious revolt among the negroes in the Vera Cruz district. Tired of their masters' yoke, a number of slaves escaped from different towns and plantations to unite with their free brethren near the present town of Córdoba." Hubert Howe Bancroft, *History of Mexico*, vol. 3 (New York, The Bancroft Company, 1900?), 11.

[301] The dormant volcano, Pico de Orizaba, also known as Citlaltépetl (star mountain), is the highest mountain in Mexico at 18,491 ft.

[302] Puebla de los Angeles is at 7,000 ft. above the sea level. Construction of Puebla's cathedral began in 1575. The locals believe that the heavy bells in the campanile of the cathedral could only have been carried up by angels, hence the name of the city.

[303] Psalm 118, verse 20: "Ésta es la puerta del Señor; los justos entrarán por ella."

[304] Taillandier may not have recalled the geography between Puebla and Tlaxcala correctly. Cholula is WNW of Puebla (i.e., to the left) and Tlaxcala is north of there.

[305] Taillandier saw the volcanoes Popocatepetl (elev. 17,802 ft.) and Iztaccihuatl (elev. 17,159 ft.). The Popo, or "smoking mountain" in Nahuatl, was known to have erupted on 20 October 1697, but the stop date is unknown. Therefore, it is probable volcano was still smoking in 1708.

[306] The focal point and center of the Aztec Empire, the Templo Mayor dedicated to the Aztec gods Huitzilopochtli and Tlaloc, dominated the skyline of Tenochtitlan since 1427 during the reign of Itzcoatl, Montezuma's grandfather.

[307] Díaz del Castillo, *Historia Verdadera de la Conquista de la Nueva España*, 83.

Montezuma allowed Cortés and his entourage to stay in the Palace of Atzayácatl in November 1519.

308 *El quinto real*, the tribute equivalent to 20% of any treasure discovered on the high seas. "This royal tribute was to be levied on metals, precious stones and pearls, regardless of whether they came from mines, fisheries, burial grounds or temples." García, *Discovering the Americas: The Archive of the Indies*, 176.

309 "Having opened the road to Tenochtitlan, the siege of the city was able to commence. It began on 21 May 1521 and lasted until 13 August." García, *Discovering the Americas: The Archive of the Indies*, 55.

310 The Parián market, *El Mercado del Parián*, in existence since 1694, was named after a similar marketplace created by Spanish authorities in Manila to control and manage the activities of Chinese merchants. The author believes the word Parián is derived from a combination of the Spanish word *para*, meaning "for or to," and the Tagalog word diyan, meaning "there or that place."

311 "Men like Thomas Gage and Gemelli Careri, and, in later times, Alexander von Humboldt, actually saw the luxury and display of Mexico. 'Both men and women,' says [Gage], 'are excessive in their apparel, using more silks than stuffs and cloths.' And, writing of the 2,000 or more coaches that rolled back and forth each afternoon in the *Alameda*, 'full of gallants, ladies and citizens, to see and be seen, to court and to be courted,' he observes that, 'they spare no silver, nor precious stones, nor cloth of gold, nor the best silks from China to enrich them.'" Schurz, *Mexico, Peru, and the Manila Galleon*, 390.

312 Maria Waldinger, "The Long-Run Effects of Missionary Orders in Mexico," *Journal of Development Economics* 127 (Online version, July 2017), 7. http://eprints.lse.ac.uk/68841/1/Waldinger_The%20Long%20Run%20Effects.pdf. Accessed 12 June 2020.

313 Today the colleges have been converted to museums: Antiguo Colegio San Ildefonso/ Museo de la Luz and Colegio Máximo is now the Museum of the Constitutions of Mexico.

314 "With this concept, the Franciscan, Augustinian, Dominican, and the merciful could evangelize the most distant communities from the viceroyalty capital or that they might be secluded in the convents." http://radiopuap.com/2016/01/los-jesuitas-en-la-nueva-españa/.

Before the Jesuits were expelled from Mexico in 1767 they numbered 678, including 468 natives, and they had more than forty colleges or seminaries, six missionary districts with ninety-nine missions. J. H. Pollen, "The Jesuits after the Restoration (1814-1912)," In *The Catholic Encyclopedia,* vol. 14 (New York: Robert Appleton Co., 1912).

https://www.newadvent.org/cathen/14100a.htm. Accessed 13 June 2020.

PART EIGHT – THE TREK DOWN TO ACAPULCO

[315] Taillandier's "New Town" is now called Tuxpan (place of rabbits) in Guerrero state. Tuxpan is a name derived from the Nahuatl language. The lake is Laguna de Tuxpan.

[316] Today Palula is part of the city of Tepecoacuilico de Trujano. But in the past, it was the midpoint of the route which brought valuable merchandise from the naos de China that had been sold in Acapulco to the merchants in Mexico City. There might be up to 100 carts carrying these goods at any one time. For the benefit of the owners, a watch tower was erected on top of Calvary Hill. Guards with spyglasses awaited the approach of the carts during the day, and at night the cart conductors were obligated to light "*luces de bengala*," or torches, for the benefit of the guards on the hill. https://www.guiaturisticamexico.com/municipio.php?id_e=12&id_Municipio=01073. Accessed 13 June 2020.

[317] Louis XIV was given a 4 inch high specimen for his garden in early 1700s and by 1716 it had grown to 23 feet. M. de Jussieu, "Description du cierge épineux du Jardin du Roy," in *Histoire de l'Academie Royale des Sciences*, 1716 (Paris: Imprimerie Royale, 1718), 146-147.

[318] "…every Indian wears a long towel over his shoulders, and with the end of it they are continually driving away the gnats, and yet I saw their legs were raw with their stings." This description is attributed to Fr. Domingo Navarrete (1610 -1689), a Dominican priest who left Spain in 1646 for the Philippines via Mexico. Awnsham and John Churchill, A *Collection of Voyages and Travels*, Vol.1, Book 6 (London: Awnsham, and John Churchill, 1704), 232. https://babel.hathitrust.org/cgi/pt?id=aeu.ark:/13960/t59c7fq9j&view=1up&seq=349.

[319] Robert C. West. "Early Silver Mining in New Spain, 1531-1555." In *Mines of Silver and Gold in the Americas*, ed. Peter Bakewell (New York: Routledge, 2020), np.

[320] The Sierra Madre del Sur range extends parallel to the Pacific Coast for about 1,000 km from the province of Michoacán southeast to Oaxaca.

[321] Probably the *Amazona oratrix*, 14 to 15 inches in length, about 18 ounces in weight, and living up to 60 years. The yellow feathers are confined to the forehead and crown when fully grown at six years. Also called Yellow Headed Amazon parrot – now an endangered species. Endemic to Mexico and N. Central America on both coasts. https://www.

naturalista.mx/taxa/18998-Amazona-oratrix.

[322] "This port is worth to the Castellan 20,000 pieces of eight a year, and a little less to the comptroller. The Curate makes 14,000 pieces of eight a year. The trade of this place being for millions of pieces of eight, every man in his way gets much, and a black will scarce be satisfied with a piece of eight a day [a Spanish silver dollar marked with a figure eight, of value equal to eight reals]. Edward Cooke, *A Voyage to the South Sea, and Round the World, Performed in the Years 1708, 1709, 1710, 1711* (London: B. Lintot and R. Gosling), 397-398. https://archive.org/details/voyagetosouthsea01cook/page/n9/mode/2up?q=20%2C000.

Upon his arrival in Acapulco in 1646 (the same route Taillandier took more than 60 years later), Domingo Navarrete ends his voyage with these words: "It pleased God we came safe to Acapulco, which in the country language signifies 'mouth of hell.'" Dominick Fernandez Navarette, "An Account of the Empire of China," in *A Collection of Voyages and Travels*, vol.1, Book 6, trans. A. and J. Churchill (London: Awnsham and John Churchill, 1704), 233. https://babel.hathitrust.org/cgi/pt?id=aeu.ark:/13960/t59c7fq9j&view=1up&seq=350.

[323] Giovanni Francesco Gemelli Careri, "Giro del Mondo (Around the World)," Part 6, Book 1, in *A Collection of Voyages and Travels*, vol. 4, trans. A. and J. Churchill (London: A. and J. Churchill, 1704), 502. https://archive.org/details/dli.bengal.10689.1427/page/n519/mode/2up?q=acapulco.

[324] "After the registered cargo had been accounted for in accordance with the certified invoices, the goods found to be consistent with their bills of lading were removed to the warehouses, where they were stored, in bond as it were, until the opening of the fair." Schurz, *The Manila Galleon*, 307.

PART NINE – ACROSS THE PACIFIC

[325] García, *Discovering the Americas: The Archive of the Indies*, 42.

[326] "*Cette navigation est tres douce*, wrote Pere Taillandier, a French Jesuit who crossed by this way to China in 1709 with twenty-two others of the Society." Schurz, *The Manila Galleon*, 226.

[327] "Galeones de Manila (III Parte)," *La América española*, last modified 26 February 2016. https://laamericaespanyola.wordpress.com/2016/02/26/galeones-de-manila-iii-parte/.

[328] Francisco Fernández de la Cueva, 10th Duke of Albuquerque (1666-1724).

329 "The *situados* were funds transferred yearly to the Philippines to help that colony's fiscal situation." Josep M. Fradera, Filipinas, La Colonia Más Peculiar (Madrid: Consejo Superior de Investigaciones Científicas, 1999), 62.

"Governor Anda [1762-1764] said that from 1,500,000 to 2,000,000 pesos were taken each year from Mexico to Manila." Schurz, *The Manila Galleon*, 156.

330 Schurz, *The Manila Galleon*, 263.

331 Schurz, *The Manila Galleon*, 34.

332 Philip II specifically meant "the Philippines and others, which are outside of the Line of Demarcation within our side," for "we do not wish to run counter to our agreement with the most serene King of Portugal." James R. Moriarty and Mary S. Keitsman, "Philip II Orders the Journey of the first Manila Galleon," *The Journal of San Diego History* 12, no. 2 (April 1966). https://sandiegohistory.org/journal/1966/april/galleon/ Accessed 13 May 2021.

333 García Jofre de Loaysa was the captain of the 16th century expedition in search of the Spice Islands after Magellan was killed in Cebu. The fleet, composed of seven ships and 450 men, met its fate between the Strait of Magellan and the Celebes Sea when bad weather and storms prevented the ships from sailing together. Loaysa died of scurvy on 30 July 1526. Juan Sebastian Elcano, a survivor of the Magellan expedition, died a few days later. Andres de Urdaneta and a few others were captured by the Portuguese in the Moluccas but eventually returned to Spain in 1536.

334 Schurz, *The Manila Galleon*, 206.

335 Diego Luis de Sanvítores, with five other Jesuits "island hopping" from Manila, landed on Guam on 16 June 1668. "The natives responded readily to the teaching of the missionaries, and in one year, on Guam alone, some 6,500 received baptism, while practically all the others were catechumens. Within three years troublemakers aroused sharp opposition to the Jesuits and turned the Marianas [named after the Queen Regent of Spain, Mariana of Austria] into the most dangerous mission of the Society. By 1685...twelve Jesuits were killed including Sanvítores himself who was only forty-five years old." Bangert, *A History of the Society of Jesus*, 261.

336 Succeeded Antonio de Saravia in 1683 as Governor of the islands. "By 1695 the resistance of the [Chamorro] natives [to a Christian life and religious instructions] was everywhere broken and the entire population was settled in Saipan and Guam." Lach and Van Kley, *Asia: In the Making*

of Europe, vol. 3, Book 1, 1558.

[337] "Canoe-like dugouts called *paraos*, made from whole timber up to thirty feet long and provided with an outrigger on one side." Lach and Van Kley, *Asia: In the Making of Europe*, Vol. 3, Book 1, 1553.

"I verily believe they may run 20 mph...for they passed by us like a bird flying. They have but one mast, which stands in the middle, and a man sits at each end with a paddle to steer her, so that when they go about, they don't turn the boat as we do to bring the wind on the other side, but only change the sail...." Woodes Rogers, *A Cruising Voyage Round the World* (London: A. Bell, 1712), 367.

[338] Embocadero, or embocadura, meaning the mouth, or narrow part. "Continued favorable winds would carry a galleon on rapidly to the Embocadero at the entrance of the Philippines, unless she should reach this area after the southwest monsoon had set in, in which case she might have considerable difficulty in getting into the islands." Schurz, *The Manila Galleon*, 200.

[339] "At twelve degrees [latitude] ... the northern end of the island [Samar] facing Manila is the usual channel through which ships coming from Acapulco enter. This channel is called San Bernardino after an islet by that name located almost in its center. The natives call the island *Tagbaloran*, from the word for wave, *balod*, meaning a place where treacherous waves occur." "Alzina's Historia de las islas é Indios de Bisayas...1668," *Leyte-Samar Studies*, Vol. 4, no. 1 (1970).

[340] In 1709, the year following Taillandier's voyage to the Philippines, the *NS del Rosario y SVF* was wrecked in the Straits of San Bernardino on her next trip from Acapulco. Charles H. Cunningham, *The Audiencia in the Spanish Colonies as Illustrated by the Audiencia of Manila* (1583-1800) (Berkeley: University of California Press, 1919), 158.

[341] Pedro Murillo-Velarde, *Historia de la Provincia de Philipinas de la Compañía de Jesús, Segunda Parte* (1616-1716) (Manila: Nicolas de la Cruz Bagay, 1749), 29.

[342] Murillo-Velarde, *Historia de la Provincia de Philipinas*, 5.

[343] By 1696, the Jesuit personnel in Carigara and Dagami (Leyte); Catbalogan and Palapag (Samar) numbered twenty-six men. Horatio De la Costa, SJ, *Jesuits in the Philippines (1581-1768)* (Cambridge, Massachusetts: Harvard University Press, 1961). 438.

[344] José S. Arcilla. "Jesuit Historians of the Philippines." *Philippine Studies 44*, no. 3 (Third Quarter 1996): 379.

Francisco Colín incorporated much of Chirino's unedited literary material to produce his manuscript, *Historia de la Provincia de Philipinas de la Compañía de Jesús*, in 1663.

[345]Murillo-Velarde's *La Segunda Parte de la Compañía de Jesús en Filipinas*, published in 1749, "evoques the unedited work of Chirino," according to Eduardo Descalzo Yuste in his PhD thesis: "La Compañía de Jesús en Filipinas (1581-1768)" Universidad Autónoma de Barcelona, 2015), 31.

[346] De la Costa, SJ, *Jesuits in the Philippines* (1581-1768), 5-9.

PART TEN – LOST AND FOUND

[347] The Spanish colonists who arrived first with Magellan in 1521, and then with Legazpi in 1565, called the indigenous people of the Visayas (Cebu, Leyte, Negros, Panay, Samar, and Bohol) "Pintados" because they tattooed their bodies.

[348] Letter addressed to Juan Martin, S.J., Jesuit General's assistant for the Spanish provinces. De la Costa, SJ, *Jesuits in the Philippines (1581-1768)*, 458.

[349] In addition, the Jesuits founded the Escuela de Niños in 1595 to educate Spanish boys. By 1610 there were three Jesuit educational institutions in the Intramuros.

"In the year 1623, a Bull from Pope Gregory XV and a Réal Cedula from Philip IV arrived so that in our College of Manila the courses in Philosophy and Theology can be given." Murillo-Velarde, *Historia de la Provincia de Philipinas*, 26.

"Sometime after the canonization of St. Ignatius of Loyola in 1622 it began to be called the College of San Ignacio." De la Costa, SJ, *Jesuits in the Philippines (1581-1768)*, 568.

[350] De la Costa, SJ, *Jesuits in the Philippines (1581-1768)*, 502.

[351] The Czech Jesuit and pharmacist George Kamel (1661-1706) established this garden to supply the pharmacy he founded at the College of Manila.

[352] Often teak wood was used for the galleon's framework, molave for the "ribs and knees, the keel and rudder," and *lanang* for the sheathing. Schurz, *The Manila Galleon*, 196. These woods are remarkable for their strength and resistance to insects and fungi. Pine trees were used for the masts as they were both straight and flexible. Estimates are that at least 2,000 trees were used to construct one galleon, and all had to be harvested

and carried from deep in the forest to the shipyards, such as in Cavite.

[353] Taillandier is probably referring to the Aeta, an indigenous people living in scattered communities in the mountains of Luzon. The Spaniards called them Negritos, for their small stature and dark skin. They had little interaction with the Spanish authorities or the Catholic missions throughout the Spanish rule.

[354] "The earliest human remains known in the Philippines are the fossilized fragments of a skull and jawbone of three individuals who are collectively called Tabon Man. Physical anthropologists are agreed that the Tabon skullcap belonged to modern man – that is homo sapiens. What this basically means is that Tabon Man was 'pre-Mongoloid.' Mongoloid being the term anthropologists apply to racial stock which entered SE Asia during the Holocene and absorbed earlier peoples to produce the modern Malay, Indonesian, Filipino and Pacific peoples." William Henry Scott, *Pre-Hispanic Source Materials for the Study of Philippine History*, Quezon City, Philippines: New Day Publishers, 1984), 14-15.

[355] It is obvious that Father Taillandier did not visit the southern islands of the Philippines (South Mindanao and Sulu archipelago), or he would have concluded that the natives living there were just as "cruel and ferocious" as the Malays.

[356] Cebu is in the Visayan region of the Philippines. In 1564 Legazpi was sent by the Viceroy of New Spain to claim the islands for Spain. At the time Cebu was already an important port for trade with East Asia, particularly China and Siam, and the Celebes Islands (now Indonesia).

[357] A little over a hundred years after Taillandier's visit to Manila, the American naval officer John White wrote the following: "Manila, within the walls, is rather a gloomy, cheerless place, inhabited principally by haughty and austere patricians, who maintain every appearance of state and ceremony, amidst the solemn grandeur of papal power and monastic observances. Parian, on the contrary, is a lively, pleasant, airy place, and possesses no small degree of community activity, with good society." John White, *A Voyage to the China Sea* (Boston: Wells & Lilly, 1823), 113.

[358] Pasig River.

[359] Taillandier here made the same observation attributed by de la Costa to a visiting Austrian Jesuit, Andreas Mancker, regarding the Philippine musicians and their exemption from tribute for providing music at church services. De la Costa, SJ, *Jesuits in the Philippines* (1581-1768), 467-468.

³⁶⁰ Taillandier is referring to the yearly subsidy sent from Mexico, known as the *situado*.

³⁶¹ One theory links the coldest winter in Europe to the earlier eruption of Teide, the volcano Taillandier saw when he passed through the Canary Islands in 1707, and two other volcanoes (Santorini and Vesuvius) in the Mediterranean. Juan José Sánchez Arreseigor, "Winter is Coming: Europe's Deep Freeze of 1709," *National Geographic History*, January-February, 2017. https://www.nationalgeographic.com/history/magazine/2017/01-02/1709-deep-freeze-europe-winter/.

In mid-January 1709 temperatures in the Paris area fell to below 15 degrees Celsius.

³⁶² Nancy Mitford, *The Sun King* (London: Sphere Books Limited, 1966), 24.

³⁶³ Toussaint, *History of the Indian Ocean*, 114.

"The turning point in the rooting of Islam in SE Asia came at the beginning of the 15ᵗʰ century with the conversion of Malacca, the region's foremost trading center in 1419." Amrith, *Crossing the Bay of Bengal*, 37.

³⁶⁴ "Malacca was the great emporium where Chinese and Malay worlds met." Furber, *Rival Empires of Trade in the Orient*, 19.

³⁶⁵ *Moor* was the term used by Europeans to refer to African, Indian, and Asiatic Muslims.

³⁶⁶ About 1500 km north of Aceh.

³⁶⁷ St. Elmo is the patron saint of sailors. The "fire" named after him is a bluish continuous electrical spark called a "glow discharge."

³⁶⁸ *Pulopínam* means "Island of Pinam," or Penang. *Lancarí*, or Lankari, is now known as Langkawi Island. Both islands belong to Malaysia today.

³⁶⁹ Queda (Kedah) refers to the kingdom (now a state and a city), through which the Perlis flows. Perlis also refers to the northernmost Malaysian state which is bordered by Kedah to the south.

³⁷⁰ Bonnet probably went upstream to Kota Sena, then the seat of the sultanate and now known as Kangar, the capital of the state of Perlis. Taillandier referred to the town as Queda.

³⁷¹ Cultural and economic relations between China and India date back to ancient times. The Silk Road not only served as a major route for trade but is also credited for facilitating the spread of Buddhism from India to East Asia.

[372] Ferroli, *The Jesuits in Mysore*, 221.

[373] "...a hill, north of town and island, called Elephant, favours the navigator's approach." Thomas Forest, *A Voyage from Calcutta to the Mergui Archipelago* (London: J. Robson, 1792), 25.

[374] Taillandier wrote: "cry," meaning the Malay kris. If he had visited Mindanao while in the Philippines, he would have reported that the inhabitants of Davao, Cotabato, Zamboanga and other Muslim communities along the coasts had the same type of armaments, headdresses, and houses.

[375] "Kedah was an entrepot for both maritime trade... and trans-peninsular trade to the Gulf of Siam. The most important of several routes was that to Pattani. Travelers moved across by foot, river boats and elephants. Some of these traders continued on to the major ports of Siam and eastward to ports in China." Maziar M. Falarti, *Malay Kingship in Kedah: Religion, Trade, and Society* (Plymouth, U. K.: Lexington Books, 2013), 148.

[376] A *coudée*, an ancient unit of measurement, equals approximately 1.5 ft. or 46 cm.

[377] The sol was a copper coin in France. Generally, 20 sols equal 1 livre (silver coin). The sol was later referred to as a sou.

[378] 1 ligne is equivalent to 2.3 mm or 0.09 inch.

[379] 12 deniers were equivalent to 1 sol.

[380] "M. de Bruant had been instructed to build a fort at Mergui for which a plan had been entrusted to him in Siam." Martin, *India in the 17th Century, 1670-1694 (Social, Economic, and Political): Memoirs of François Martin*, Vol. 2, Part 2, 1180.

Mergui was not only important as a port for ship building and repair, but also it was the starting point of an overland trail used by traders and travellers wishing to reach the Siamese court in Ayutthaya.

[381] Janselon is most likely Phuket Island, south of Mergui, yet north of Kedah. In earlier times the island was called "Junk Ceylon" or "Jung Ceylon," corruptions of the Malay name *Tanjung Salang* or Cape Salang.

[382] "The three ships departed on February 16, 1709, and [having dropped off the rescued Jesuits in Pondicherry] returned, well laden, to Port Louis [France] on August 23, 1710." Kaeppelin, *La Compagnie des Indes Orientales et François Martin*, 578.

[383] Kaeppelin, *La Compagnie des Indes Orientales et François Martin*,

653.

[384] Today the Nicobar Islands are a union territory of India as are the Andaman Islands to the north.

[385] Possibly yams, the most popular root staple today among indigenous tribes in the Nicobar Islands.

[386] "The kingdom of Carnate should not be solely taken to mean where the mission is located, although it carries the name. The kingdom includes many provinces and dominions, within a vast extension of lands... The kingdom's principal states of which I know are Carnate, Visapour [Bijapur], BIjanogaran, Ikeyeri, and Golconda. Pierre de la Lane to P. Mourgues, Pondicherry, 30 January 1709, *LEC*, vol. 10 (1713).

PART ELEVEN – EPILOGUE

[387] St. Louis Church inside the fort was the original Capuchin church in Pondicherry. Later in 1707, they built the Church of Our Lady of the Angels outside the fortress as an annex to this church. http://catholicchurches.in/directory/pondicherry-churches/our-lady-of-angels-church-notre-dame-des-anges.htm. Accessed 13 October 2021.

[388] Kaeppelin, *La Compagnie des Indes Orientales et François Martin*, 523.

[389] Pierre Faure to Fr. de la Boesse, aboard the *Lys-Brillac*, at the mouth of the Strait of Malacca, 17 January 1711, *LEC*, vol. 10 (1713), 47.

[390] This report was included in an unsigned postscript to Faure's letter. Given the details, it seems likely that M. Raoul relayed the message to the Jesuit Superior in Pondicherry who in turn passed it on to du Halde, the editor of *LEC*, vol. 10. Addendum to the letter from Faure to de la Boesse, 1711, *LEC*, vol. 10, (1713), 73.

[391] "It was on the big island of Nicobar called Chambolan [now called Great Nicobar], the nearest to Aceh, that the two missionaries first landed." J. B. Du Halde, "Epistre," *LEC*, vol.13 (1718), xvi-xxii.

[392] Du Halde, Addendum to the letter from Faure to de la Boesse, 1711, *LEC*, vol. 10 (1713), 76.

[393] Du Halde, *LEC*, vol. 13 (1718), xvi-xix.

[394] Pere Le Caron, 15 October 1718, Pondicherry, *LEC*, vol. 14 (1720), 484.

Le Caron arrived in Pondicherry on 20 August 1718. Unlike Taillandier who took the western route via Manila ("la nouvelle route qu'il fut oblige," according to du Halde), Le Caron sailed around the African cape. As he explained, the voyage took only five months and was the "most beautiful and the happiest voyage ever, without storms, without disease." Once in Pondicherry, Le Caron, like Taillandier, studied the Telugu language before his assignment to the Carnatic mission.

395 Taillandier must be in error here as Faure's letter from the Strait of Malacca is dated 17 January 1711. Therefore, Faure and Bonnet must have landed sometime after the 17th.

396 "Golconda," *Imperial Gazetteer of India*, vol. 12 (Oxford: Clarendon Press, 1908) 309-310. Accessed 8 November 2019. https://dsal. uchicago.edu/reference/gazetteer/pager.html?objectid=DS405.1.I34_V12_315.gif.

397 The Bahmani Sultanate was a medieval Muslim state in the Deccan founded by Persians in the 14th century, but it collapsed during the 15th.

398 From Telugo Angana, or a place where Telugo is spoken.

399 W. H. Moreland, Editor, "The Kingdom of Golconda," *Relations of Golconda in the Early Seventeenth Century* (London: The Hakluyt Society, 1931), xvi. https://archive.org/details/in.ernet.dli.2015.63333/page/n15/mode/2up.

400 Jean-Baptiste Tavernier, *Tavernier's Travels in India*, vol 1, trans. Valentine Ball (New Delhi: Asian Educational Services, 2004), 122.

At the height of the Roman Empire, Masulipatnam, then known as Maisolos, was the export center for highly prized Indian textiles destined for Rome. Much later, diamonds mined in the interior near Golconda became a significant export, as well as iron and steel. https://www.livehistoryindia.com/cover-story/2019/03/16/machilipatnam-port-with-the-midas-touch. Accessed 22 August 2020.

401 Carré, *The Travels of Abbé Carré in India and the Near East, 1672-1674*, 329 (footnote #2).

402 Tachard to A.M. Le Comte de Crecy, 4 February 1703, Pondicherry, *LECC*.

403 This may have been the suburb now known as Malkapur in western Hyderabad between it and Golconda. Carré, *The Travels of Abbé Carré in India and the Near East*, 1672-1674, 326 (footnote #5).

404 "Costudius de Pinho (1638-1697) was born in Salsette, a kingdom belonging to Portugal, the island on which Mumbai is located."

Conrad Eubel, *Hierarchia Catholica Medii et Recentioris Aevi*, vol 5 (Patavii, Italy: Typis Libraiae, 1952), 219-220. https://archive.org/details/hierarchiacathol05eubeuoft/page/n5/mode/2up. Accessed 5/13/2021.

[405] Carré, *The Travels of Abbé Carré in India and the Near East, 1672-1674*, np.

[406] Pierre Mauduit, "Relation: D'un voyage [from Carouvepondi beginning 3 September 1701]… à l'Ouest du Royaume de Carnate en 1701," LEC, vol. 6 (1723), 17.

[407] "…un cinquième [Taillandier] se rendait á la cour de Golconde." LEC, Jean Venance Bouchet to the Father General, 24 September 1714, Pondicherry, as cited in: Léon Besse, SJ. "Liste Alphabétique des Missionnaires du Carnatic de la Compagnie de Jésus au XVIIIe Siécle," *Revue Historique de l'Inde Française*, vol 2, 186. https://babel.hathitrust.org/cgi/pt?id=mdp.39015030172251&view=1up&seq=216.

[408] "Father Anthony Monserrate was Blessed Rudolf Aquaviva's companion during the first Jesuit Mission to Akbar's court. They had left Daman for Surat on 13th December 1579 and arrived at Fatipur Sikri on 27th February 1580." Monserrate, "Father A. Monserrate's Account of Akbar, 26th November 1582," 185.

[409] "At the corner of one of the outlying streets of Hyderabad, this inscription can be read upon an old wall – "Road to Golconda." Loti, *India*, 151. It would also have been true to have written: "Road to Silence and Ruin."

[410] Du Halde, "Epistre," *LEC*, vol. 11 (1715), v.

[411] Besse, "Liste Alphabétique des Missionnaires du Carnatic," 237. https://babel.hathitrust.org/cgi/pt?id=mdp.39015030172251&view=1up&seq=267.

[412] Besse, "Liste Alphabétique des Missionnaires du Carnatic," 237.

Sommervogel cites the "Necrologe general." Sommervogel and de Backer, *Bibliotèque de la Compagnie de Jésus,* vol. 7, 1816.

Further, the Society's "Defuncti Secundi Saeculi Societatis Jesu, 1641-1740" states: Petrus Taillandier - "Naufragio periit, anno 1713" ("Died on a sinking ship in 1713"). Josephus, Fejér, *Defuncti Secundi Saeculi Societatis Jesu, 1641-1740*, vol. 5 (Rome: Curia Generalitia SJ Institutum Historicum SJ, 1990), 167.

Taillandier's exact route to Golconda is unknown. But, if he traveled overland, he would have crossed rivers (Palar, Penna, and Krishna) in the typical Indian *coracle*, a small, unstable, bowl-shaped rowboat made of reeds covered with animal skin. The monsoon season in this part of India can last from mid-June through mid-October. If a storm arose during the river crossing, he could easily have fallen overboard. If he traveled by sea, say from Pondicherry to Madras or even farther north to Bezoar, then he might have perished aboard a masula. This boat is also somewhat unstable in high waves. See Appendix A for a map of his possible route based on the known trade routes of the day.

[413] *Il n'est pas hors de probabilité que l'envie d'observer a enlevé le P. Taillandier à cette mission, il s'avança trop avant. On n'en a plus entendu parler.* Besse, "Liste Alphabétique des Missionnaires du Carnatic," 237.

BIBLIOGRAPHY

ARCHIVED MATERIALS, PRIMARY SOURCES

Inventaire Aprés Décès, Robert Taillandier. (1686) Lyon: Archives Départementales du Rhône (BP 1994).

Inventaire du Fonds de Librairie Compagnon Taillandier. June, 1686. Lyon: Archives Départementales du Rhône (BP 1994).

Inventaire Aprés Décès, Pierre Compagnon. (1692). Lyon: Archives Départementales du Rhône (BP 2017).

Registres paroissiaux et d'état civil: Saint Nizier: Baptême, 1676 – 1677. Lyon: Archives Municipals de Lyon. www.fondsenligne.archives-lyon.fr.

LETTRES ÉDIFIANTES ET CURIEUSES

Bouchet, Pere to M. Cochet de Saint-Vallier, Président des Requêtes du Palais à Paris. (No Date or Place) *Lettres édifiantes et curieuses, écrites par quelques missionnaires de la Compagnie de Jésus* (Hereafter referred to as: "*LEC.*"). Vol. 11. Paris: Nicolas Le Clerc, 1715. Google Books.

Bouchet, Venance to (unknown), 19 April 1719, Pondicherry. *Lettres Édifiantes et Curieuses Concernant l'Asie, l'Afrique et l'Amérique* (Hereafter referred to as "*LECC.*"). Vol. 2. Edited by M. L. Martin. Paris: Société du Panthéon Littéraire, 1843. Google Books.

Bouchet, Venance. Letter to the Father General, 24 September 1714. Cited in Besse, Léon, SJ, "Liste Alphabétique des Missionnaires du Carnatic de la Compagnie de Jésus au XVIIIe Siécle." In *Revue Historique de l'Inde Française.* Vol. 2. Paris: Societé de l'Histoire de l'Inde Française. 1918. HathiTrust.

De la Lane, Pere to Pere Mourgues, 30 January 1709, Pondicherry. *LEC*. Vol. 10. Paris: Jean Barbou (le College de Louis le Grand), 1713. Google Books.

—1705, Tarkolan. *LEC*. Vol. 10. Paris: Jean Barbou, 1713. Google Books.

Du Halde, Jean-Baptiste. "Epistre," *LEC*. Vol 11. Paris: Nicolas Le Clerc, 1715. Google Books.

—"Epistre," *LEC*. Vol 13. Paris: P. G. Le Mercier, 1718. Google Books.

Faure, Pierre to P. de la Boesse, 17 January 1711. Aboard the *Lys-Brillac* at the mouth of the Strait of Malacca. *LEC*, Vol. 10, Paris: Jean Barbou, 1713. Google Books.

Le Caron, 15 October 1718, Pondicherry. *LEC*, Vol. 14. Paris: Nicolas le Clerc, 1720. Google Books.

Le Gac, Estienne to his brother, 30 November 1713, Devandapalli. As referenced in Besse, Léon, SJ. "Liste Alphabétique des Missionnaires du Carnatic de la Compagnie de Jésus au XVIIIe Siècle." In *Revue Historique de l'Inde Française*, Vol. 2. Pondicherry, India: Société de l'Histoire de l'Inde Française, 1918. HathiTrust.

—to P. Charles Poree, 10 January 1709, Chinnabalabaram. *LEC*. Vol. 10. Paris: Jean Barbou, 1713. Google Books.

Martin, Pierre, to P. Villette, 8 November 1709, Madurai. *LEC*. Vol. 10. Paris: Jean Barbou, 1713. Google Books.

Mauduit, Pierre, SJ. "Relation: D'un voyage que le P. Mauduit, Missionnaire de la Compagnie de Jésus a fait à l'Ouest du Royaume de Carnate en 1701." *LEC*, Vol. 6. Paris: Nicolas Le Clerc, 1723. HathiTrust.

Petit, Gabriel to P. de Trevou, 12 February 1702, Pondicherry. *LECC*.

Sant-Yago, SJ, to Manuel Saray, Provincial of the Province of Goa, 8 August 1711. Capinagar. *LECC*.

Tachard, Guy to A. M. Le Comte de Crecy, 4 February 1703, Pondicherry. *LECC*.

—to Reverend P de la Chaise, Confessor to the King, 30 September 1703, Pondicherry. *LECC.*

Taillandier, Pierre to P. Willard, 20 February 1711, Pondicherry. *LEC.* Vol. 11. Paris: Nicolas Le Clerc, 1715.

ONLINE SOURCES

Álvarez, B. C. "La Ciudad de Veracruz." https://www.otromundoesposible.net/la-ciudad-de-veracruz/. Accessed 2 February 2021.

Buchanan, Kelly. "Slavery in the French Colonies: Le Code Noir of 1685." in Custodia Legis, Law Librarians of Congress (Blog), 13 January 2011. https://blogs.loc.gov/law/2011/01/slavery-in-the-french-colonies/

Chavan, Akshay. "Machilipatnam: Port with the Midas Touch," 16 March 2019. https://www.livehistoryindia.com/cover-story/2019/03/16/machilipatnam-port-with-the-midas-touch. Accessed 22 August 2020

Conchon, Anne. "Road Construction in Eighteenth Century France." https://www.arct.cam.ac.uk/Downloads/ichs/vol-1-791-798-conchon.pdf, p 791. Accessed 6 January 2019.

Edel, Matthew. "The Brazilian Sugar Cycle of the Seventeenth Century and the Rise of West Indian Competition. *Caribbean Studies* 9, no. 1 (1969): 24-44. https://www.jstor.org/stable/25612106?seq=1.

"Galeones de Manila (III parte)," *La América Española* (Blog). https://laamericaespanyola.wordpress.com/2016/02/26/galeones-de-manila-iii-parte/. Accessed 2 July 2020.

Ghachem, Malick W. "Our Crown and Glory: The Jesuits in Haiti, 1704-1763." Research Partnership Opportunity, Radcliffe Institute for Advanced Study Harvard University, 2018-2019 https://www.radcliffe.harvard.edu/fellowship-program/research-partnership-opportunity/our-crown-and-glory-jesuits-in-haiti-1704-1763. Accessed 30 January 2020.

Heras, Henry, SJ. (No Date). *Jesuits of Old Days in Andhra Desa.* https://docplayer.net/84463407-Jesuits-of-old-days-in-andhra-desa.html. Accessed 14 July 2020.

Johnston, Mark. "The Sugar Trade in the West Indies and Brazil Between 1492 and 1700." https://www.lib.umn.edu/bell/tradeproducts/sugar. Accessed 10 June 2020.

Kornprobst, Jacques and J. F. Lénat. "Centenary of the Discovery of Earth's Magnetic Field Reversals," 4 November 2014. https://eos.org/articles/centenary-discovery-earths-magnetic-field-reversals. Accessed 23 January 2020.

Lipski, John M. "The Spanish of the Canary Islands." Penn State University. http://personal.psu.edu/jml34/Canary.htm. Accessed 28 February 2018.

Lombard, Peter. "Sententiarum Libri IV, Four Books of Sentences." *The Encyclopaedia Britannica.* Last modified: 25 March 1999. https://www.britannica.com/biography/Peter-Lombard#ref247822.

Mabillard, Amanda. "Shakespeare's Drinking," *Shakespeare Online.* http://www.shakespeare-online.com/faq/shakespearedrinking.html. Accessed 16 January 2020.

Mémoire sur l'implantation de la Compagnie des Indes à partir de 1664 (1664/1725). http://anom.archivesnationales.culture.gouv.fr/ark:/61561/ou533f0y31a.num=500.start=801. Accessed 7 March 2020.

Menachery, George. "Jesuits in the History of India." Paper presented in December 2002 in the Seminar: *In the Footsteps of Francis Xavier: Jesuits in India.* Alto Porvorim, Goa, India: Goa University, Xavier Centre of Historical Research. http://kunjethy.tripod.com/indiajesuits/. Accessed 7 January 2020.

Norrington, Bill. *Cochineal – A Little Insect Goes a Long Way* (UCSB Geography Department, no date.) https://geog.ucsb.edu/cochineal-a-little-insect-goes-a-long-way/. Accessed 28 July 2020.

Pollen, John H. "The Jesuits after the Restoration (1814-1912)." In *The Catholic Encyclopedia*. Vol. 14. New York: Robert Appleton Co., 1912. http://www.newadvent.org/cathen/14100a.htm. Accessed 6 July 2020.

"Primitive Sugar Production." *Bacardi Sugar Spirit Project*. 1 September 2011. https://www.alcademics.com/2011/09/primitive-sugar-production. html. Accessed 3 February 2020.

"Réglements fait par la Compagnie des Indes pour Pondichéry, et confirmé par sa Majesté, 14 Février 1711." http://anom.archivesnationales. culture.gouv.fr/ark:/61561/ou533f0y5yw.num=100.start=841. form=simple.

"Sri Manakula Vinayagar Temple." (No date). http://www. manakulavinayagartemple.com. Accessed 6 July 2020.

"Tepecoacuilco de Trujano." (No date). https://www.guiaturisticamexico. com/municipio.php?id_e=12&id_Municipio=01073. Accessed 6 July 2020.

"The Saint Malo Shipwrecks: Les Épaves Corsaires de la Natiére – Calculating Latitude." https://archeologie.culture.fr/epaves-corsaires/en/ calculating-latitude. Accessed 6 July 2020.

"The Saint Malo Shipwrecks: Les Épaves Corsaires de la Natiére – An Underwater Graveyard." https://archeologie.culture.fr/epaves-corsaires/fr/mediatheque. Accessed 6 July 2020.

U. S. Conference of Catholic Bishops. "*Acts – Introduction – The Acts of the Apostles.*" http://www.usccb.org/bible/acts/0. Accessed 6 December 2019.

U. S. Conference of Catholic Bishops. "*Romans – Introduction – The Letter to the Romans.*" http://www.usccb.org/bible/romans/0. Accessed 5 December 2019.

"Valle de la Oratava Wine." www.wine-searcher.com/regions-Valle+de+la+Orotava. Last modified 8 May 2004.

BOOKS AND JOURNALS

Agarwal, M. K. *Bharata to India*: Vol. 1. *Chrysee the Golden*. Bloomington, Indiana: iUniverse, 2012.

Agmon, Danna. *A Colonial Affair: Commerce, Conversion, and Scandal in French India.*" Ithaca, New York: Cornell University Press, 2017

—*An Uneasy Alliance: Traders, Missionaries and Tamil Intermediaries in the 18th Century French India.*" PhD diss, University of Michigan, Ann Arbor, 2011.

"Alzina's Historia de las islas é Indios de Bisayas…1668." (Chapter 5: "Location, Characteristics, and Climate of these Islands of the Bisaias). Translated by Cantius J. Kobak. *Leyte-Samar Studies* 4, no. 1 (1970): 21-28. (Courtesy of Victoria Sievert Salazar, Divine Word University, Tacloban City).

Amrith, Sunil S. *Crossing the Bay of Bengal: The Furies of Nature and the Fortunes of Migrants*. Cambridge, Massachusetts: Harvard University Press, 2013.

Ananthamurthy, U. R. *Samskara: A Rite for a Dead Man*. Translated by A. K. Ramanujan. New York: New York Review Books, Classics in Literature, 1976.

Aranha, Paolo. "The Social and Physical Spaces of the Malabar Rites Controversy." in *Space and Conversion in Global Perspective*, edited by Giuseppe Marcocci, *et al*, 214-232. Leiden, The Netherlands: Koninklijke Brill, NV, 2015. Academia.edu.

Arasaratnam, Sinnappah. *Merchants, Companies and Commerce on the Coromandel Coast 1650 – 1740*. Delhi: Oxford University Press, 1986.

Arcilla, José S. "Jesuit Historians of the Philippines." *Philippine Studies* 44, No. 3 (Third quarter 1996): 374-391. Jstor.org.

Aubry, Pierre and Bernard Gaüzére. "Histoire de la Santé dans l'océan Indien: soins, prévention, enseignement et recherche du XVIIe siécle au milieu du XXe siécle." *Médecine et Santé Tropicales* 26, no. 2 (April - June 2016): 122-129.

Bancroft, Hubert Howe. *History of Mexico*. Vol. 3. New York: The Bancroft Company, 1900 (?). HathiTrust.

Bangert, William V., SJ. *A History of the Society of Jesus*. St. Louis, Missouri: The Institute of Jesuit Sources, 1972.

Banks, John Shaw. *Our Indian Empire, its Rise and Growth*. London: Wesleyan Conference Office, 1880.

Bartoli, Barbara. "Pondicherry: Modern Technologies Approach in the Message of the Past." In *Proceedings of the 5th International Conference: Analysis of Historical Constructions*. New Delhi, 2006.

Bayly, C. A. "Indian Society and the Making of the British Empire." In *The New Cambridge History of India*. Vol. 2, Part 1. Cambridge: Cambridge University Press, 1988. Cambridge Histories Online, 2008.

Besse, Léon, SJ. "Liste Alphabétique des Missionnaires du Carnatic de la Compagnie de Jésus au XVIIIe Siècle." In *Revue Historique de l'Inde Française*, Vol. 2. Pondicherry, India: Société de l'Histoire de l'Inde Française, 1918. HathiTrust.

Bonne, M. and Desmarest, M. *Atlas encyclopédique, contenant la géographie ancienne*. Paris: Hôtel de Thou, 1788. Google Books.

Boucher, Philip P. *France and the American Tropics to 1700: Tropics of Discontent*. Baltimore: Johns Hopkins University Press, 2010.

Bravo, Jesús Rodríguez. *Los Jesuitas y las Artes en la Orotava*. Santa Cruz de Tenerife: Le Canarien Ediciones, 2015.

Brucker, Joseph, SJ. "Malabar Rites." In *The Catholic Encyclopedia*. Vol. 9. New York: Robert Appleton Company, 1910. New Advent.

—"Matteo Ricci." In *The Catholic Encyclopedia*. Vol. 13. New York: Robert Appleton Company, 1912. New Advent.

Burnouf, Eugène and E. V. S. Jacquet. *L'Inde française, ou Collection de dessins lithographiés représentant les divinités, temples, costumes, physionomies, muebles, armes, et ustensiles, des peoples Hindous....* Vols. 1 and 2. Paris: J. J. Chabrelie, 1827 (Vol. 1) and 1835 (Vol. 2). Gallica.bnf.fr.

Vol. 1 Table: https://gallica.bnf.fr/ark:/12148/bpt6k1041173t/f375. image.r=Eugene%20burnouf%20l'Inde%20francaise

Vol. 2 Table: https://gallica.bnf.fr/ark:/12148/bpt6k1041175n/f345. image.r=Eugene%20burnouf%20l'Inde%20francaise

Campbell, Thomas J., SJ. *The Jesuits, 1534-1921: A History of the Society of Jesus from its Foundation to the Present Time.* Vol. 1. New York: The Encyclopedia Press, 1921.

Careri, John Francis (Giovanni Francesco) Gemelli. "A Voyage Round the World (Giro del Mondo)." In *A Collection of Voyages and Travels,* Vol. 4. Compiled and translated by A. and J. Churchill. London: Awnsham and John Churchill, 1704.

Carré, Barthélemy, Abbé. *The Travels of the Abbé Carré in India and the Near East, 1672-1674.* Vol. 2. Translated by Sir Charles Fawcett and Sir Richard Burn. New Delhi: Asian Educational Services, 1990.

Cassini, Jacques. Letter dated 10 January 1705. Translated by Ephraim Chambers. In *The Philosophical History and Memoirs of the Royal Academy of Sciences at Paris.* Vol. 2. London: John and Paul Knapton, 1742. Google Books.

Cavanaugh, William T. *The Myth of Religious Violence.* Oxford: Oxford University Press, 2009.

Charton, Èdouard. "Duguay-Trouin: Sa Maison a Saint-Malo." *Le Magasin Pittoresque*, Année 51. Paris, Bureaux d'Abonnement et de Vente, 1881. HathiTrust.

Chugh, Lalit. *Karnataka's Rich Heritage – Art and Architecture: From Historic Times to the Hoysala Period.* Chennai: Notion Press, 2016.

Cooke, Edward. *A Voyage to the South Sea, and Round the World Performed in the Years 1708, 1709, 1710, and 1711.* London: B. Lintot and R. Gosling, 1712. Internet Archive.

Crowley, Roger. *1453 – The Holy War for Constantinople and the Clash of Islam and the West*. New York: Hachette Books, 2005. Internet Archive.

Cruysse, Dirk van der. *Siam and the West, 1500-1700*. Translated by Michael Smithies. Chiang Mai, Thailand: Silkworm Books, 2002.

Cunat, Charles. *Saint-Malo Illustré par ses Marins*. Rennes: F. Péalat, 1857. Internet Archive.

Cunningham, Charles H. *The Audiencia in the Spanish Colonies as Illustrated by the Audiencia of Manila (1583-1800)*. Berkeley: University of California Press, 1919. HathiTrust.

Dahlgren, E. W. "Voyages Français à destination de la Mer du Sud avant Bougainville (1695-1749)." *Nouvelles Archives des missions Scientifique et Littéraire*. Vol. 14. Paris: Imprimerie Nationale, 1907. HathiTrust.

D'Auriac, Eugène. *Histoire Anecdotique de l'industrie française*. Paris: Libraire de la Société des Gens de Lettres, 1861.

De la Costa, Horatio, SJ. "Jesuit Education in the Philippines." In *Philippine Studies* 4, No. 2 (1956): 127 – 155. Jstor.org.

—*Jesuits in the Philippines (1581-1768)*. Cambridge, Massachusetts: Harvard University Press, 1961.

Deloche, Jean. *Origins of the Urban Development of Pondicherry according to Seventeenth Century. Dutch Plans*. Pondicherry, India: French Institute of Pondicherry, 2004.

Descalzo Yuste, Eduardo. "La Compañía de Jesús en Filipinas (1581-1768)." PhD Thesis, Universidad Autónoma de Barcelona, 2015.

Díaz del Castillo, Bernal. *Historia Verdadera de la Conquista de la Nueva España*. Mexico City: Editores Mexicanos Unidos, SA, 2014.

Diderot, Denis and Jean Le Rond d'Lambert. *L'Encyclopédie ou Dictionnaire des sciences, des arts et des métiers*. Vol. 3 (Ch-Cons). Paris: Chez Briasson, et al, 1753. Gallica.bnf.fr.

Estienne, Charles. *Liste Generale des Postes de France,* 3rd Edition. Paris: Charles Estienne, 1553. Google Books.

Eubel, Conrad. *Hierarchia Catholica Medii et Recentioris Aevi.* Vol 5. Patavii, Italy: Typis Libraiae, 1913. Internet Archive.

Falarti, Maziar M. *Malay Kingship in Kedah: Religion, Trade, and Society.* Plymouth, U. K.: Lexington Books, 2013.

Fejér, Josephus, SJ. *Defuncti Secundi Saeculi Societatis Jesu, 1641-1740.* Rome: Curia Generalitia SJ, Institutum Historicum SJ, 1990.

Ferroli, Domenico, SJ. *The Jesuits in Mysore.* Kozhikode, India: Xavier Press, 1955. Archive.org.

Féval, Paul. *The Jesuits!* Translated by Agnes L. Sadlier. New York: D & J Sadlier, 1878. HathiTrust.

Fiegl, Amanda. "A Brief History of Chocolate." *Smithsonian Magazine,* 1 March 2008.

Forest, Thomas. *A Voyage from Calcutta to the Mergui Archipelago.* London: J. Robson, 1792. Internet Archive.

Fradera, Josep M. *Filipinas, La Colonia Más Peculiar.* Madrid: Consejo Superior de Investigaciones Científicas, 1999.

Furber, Holden. *Rival Empires of Trade in the Orient, 1600-1800.* Europe and the World in the Age of Expansion Series, Vol. 2. Minneapolis: University of Minnesota Press, 1976.

Gaignard, Henri-George. *Connaître Saint- Malo.* Paris: Éditions Fernand Lanore, 1992.

García, Pedro González. *Discovering the Americas: The Archive of the Indies.* New York: Vendome Press, 1997.

Garrigus, John D. *Before Haiti: Race and Citizenship in French Saint Domingue.* New York: Palgrave Macmillan, 2006.

Ghirelli, Angelo. *El Renacimiento Musulman.* Barcelona: Montaner y Simón, SA, 1948.

Gibb, H. A. R. *The Travels of Ibn Battuta, AD 1325-1354,* Vol. 2. London: Syndics of the Cambridge University Press, 1962. Internet Archive.

"Golconda." *Imperial Gazetteer of India*. Vol. 12. Oxford: Clarendon Press, 1908.

Greenblatt, Stephen. *The Swerve: How the World Became Modern*. New York: W. W. Norton & Co, 2011.

Gribble, J. D. B. *A History of the Deccan*. Vol. 1. London: Luzac & Co., 1896. Google Books.

Hanke, Lewis. *The Spanish Struggle for Justice in the Conquest of America*. Dallas: Southern Methodist University Press, 2002.

Heijmans, Elisabeth. *The Agency of Empire: Connections and Strategies in French Overseas Expansion (1686-1746)*. Boston: Brill, 2019.

Herpin, Eugéne. *La Cote d'Emeraude, Saint Malo, Ses Souvenirs*. Rennes: Hyacinthe Cailliére, 1894. Google Books.

Hoole, Elijah. *Madras, Mysore, and the South of India, 2nd Edition*. London: Longman, Brown, Green and Longmans, 1844. Google Books.

Hunt, Will. "Cave of the Crystal Maiden." *Discover Magazine*, December 2014.

Jordan of Sévérac, O.P. (Friar Jordanus). *Mirabilia Descripta: The Wonders of the East*. Translated by Henry Yule. London: The Hakluyt Society, 1863. Internet Archive.

Jussieu, M. de. "Description du cierge epineux du Jardin du Roy." In *Histoire de l'Academie Royale des Sciences, 1716*. Paris: Imprimerie Royale, 1718. Google Books.

Kaeppelin, Paul. *La Compagnie des Indes Orientales et François Martin: Étude sur l'Histoire Du Commerce et des Établissements Français dans l'Inde sous Louis XIV (1664-1719)*. Paris: Augustin Challamel, 1908. Google Books.

Kochhar, R. K. "French Astronomers in India during the 17th - 19th Centuries." *Journal of the British Astronomical Association* 101, no. 2 (1990): 95-100.

Kordac, Lubos. *Historic Shipwrecks of the Dominican Republic and Haiti."* Merritt Island, Florida: Signum Ops, 2009.

Kulkarni, V. B. *History of the Indian Cotton Textile Industry*. Bombay: Millowners' Association, 1979.

Lach, Donald F. and E. J. Van Kley. *Asia in the Making of Europe*. Vol. 3, Book 1. University of Chicago Press, 1993.

"L'activité maritime à Saint-Malo dans la seconde moitié du XVIII siècle." *Collection Documents pour l'Histoire de Saint-Malo*, Dossier No. 4. Archives Municipales de Saint-Malo, 1992.

Launay, Adrien. *Histoire des Missions de l'Inde: Pondichéry, Maissour, Coimbatur*. Vol. 1. Paris: Ancienne Maison Charles Douniol, 1898. Google Books.

Lavallé, Bernard. *Bartolome De Las Casas: Entre la Espada y la Cruz*. Translated by Marta Pino Moreno. Barcelona: Ariel, 2009.

Liste Generale des Postes de France. Paris: Chez le Sr. Jaillot, 1741. Google Books.

Lockman, John. *Travels of the Jesuits into Various Parts of the World: particularly China and the East-Indies*. Vol. 2, 2nd Edition. London: T. Piety, Rose and Crown, 1762. Google Books.

Loconte, Joseph. "Houses of Worship." *Wall Street Journal*, 30 October 2015.

Loti, Pierre. India. Translated by George A. F. Inman. New York: Duffield & Co., 1906 (?)

Lowney, Chris. *A Vanished World*. New York: Free Press, 2005.

Luce, Henry R, ed. *Life's Picture History of Western Man*. New York: Time, Inc., 1951.

Malangin, Raphaël. *Pondicherry that was Once French India*. New Delhi: Lustre Press/Roli Books, 2015.

Mallaina, Pablo Perez. *Spain's Men of the Sea*. Baltimore: Johns Hopkins University, 1998.

Malleson, George Bruce. *History of the French in India: from the founding of Pondichery in 1674 to the capture of that place in 1761.* London: W. H. Allen & Co., Ltd., 1893. Google Books.

Manucci, Niccolaò. *Storia do Mogor or Mogul India 1653-1708.* Vol. 1. Translated by William Irvine. London: John Murray, 1907. Internet Archive.

Marchand, Patrick. "Voyager en France au Temps de la Poste aux Chevaux." In *Le Maître de poste et le messager, les transports publics en France au temps des chevaux.* Paris: Belin, 2006.

Marshman, John Clark. *The History of India: From the Earliest Period to the Close of Lord Dalhousie's Administration.* Vol. 1. London: Longmanns, Green, Reader & Dyer, 1867. Google Books.

Martin, François. *India in the 17th Century (Social, Economic and Political): Memoirs of François Martin, 1670-1694.* Vol 2, Part 2. Translated by Lotika Varadarajan. New Delhi: Manohar Press, 1985.

Martineau, Alfred. Introduction to: *Les Jésuites A Pondichéry et L'Affaire Naniapa (1705 à 1720).* Paris: Societe de L'Histoire des Colonies Francaises, 1932.

Mitford, Nancy. *The Sun King.* London: Sphere Books Limited, 1966.

Monfalcon, Jean Baptiste. *Manuel du Bibliophile et de l'archéologue Lyonnais.* Paris: Adolphe Delahaye, 1857. Google Books.

Monserrate, Antonio. "Father A. Monserrate's Account of Akbar, 26 November 1582." Translated by Henri Hosten, SJ. *Journal and Proceedings of the Asiatic Society of Bengal*, New Series Vol. 8 (May 1912): 185-189. Internet Archive.

Moreau de Saint-Mercy, M. L. E. *Description topographique, physique, civile, politique et historique de la partie française de l'isle Saint Domingue.* Vol. 1. Paris: Chez Dupont, 1797. Internet Archive.

Moreland, W. H. (ed). "The Kingdom of Golconda." In *Relations of Golconda in the Early Seventeenth Century.* London: The Hakluyt Society, 1931. Internet Archive.

Moriarty, James R. and Mary S. Keistman. "Philip II Orders the Journey of the first Manila Galleon." *The Journal of San Diego History* 12, no. 2 (April 1966).

Murillo-Velarde, Pedro, SJ. *Historia de la Provincia de Philipinas de la Compañía de Jesús, Segunda Parte.* Manila: Nicolas de la Cruz Bagay, 1749. Internet Archive.

Murray, Elizabeth Heaphy. *Sixteen Years of an Artist's Life in Morocco, Spain and the Canaries.* Vol. 1. London: Hurst and Blackett, 1859. Google Books.

Navarette, Dominick Fernandez. "An Account of the Empire of China." In *A Collection of Voyages and Travels.* Vol. 1. Translated by A. and J. Churchill. London: Printed for Awnsham and John Churchill, 1704. HathiTrust.

Neill, Stephen, *A History of Christianity in India, 1707-1858.* Vol. 2. Cambridge: Cambridge University Press, 1985.

Olagnier, Paul. *Les Jésuites à Pondichéry et L'Affaire Naniapa (1705 à 1720).* Paris: Societe de L'Histoire des Colonies Françaises, 1932. Gallica. bnf.fr.

Picot, Joseph. *Les Jésuites à Lyon de 1604 à 1762.* Lyon: Editions aux Arts.

Pigafetta, Antonio. *Magellan's Voyage, A Narrative of the First Circumnavigation.* Translated by R. A. Skelton. New York: Dover Publications, 1969.

Prampain, Èduoard. *Saint Malo Historique.* Amiens, France: Piteux Frères, 1902. Google Books.

Prange, Sebastian R. "Where the Pepper Grows," *Aramco World Magazine* (January/February 2008).

Prévost, Abbé Antoine-François. *Histoire* Générale des Voyages, Nouvelle Collection de *Toutes les Relations de Voyages*, Vol. 13, Book 3. La Haye: Pierre de Hondt, 1755. Google Books.

Prou, Maurice. *Recherches sur les hôtels de l'archêveché de Sens* à *Paris*, Sens, France: Charles Duchemin, 1882. Google Books.

Raina, Dhruv. "French Jesuits in India: Historical Astronomy in the Discourse on India, 1670-1770." *Economic and Political Weekly* 34, no. 5 (Jan. 30 - Feb. 5, 1999). Jstor.org.

Rao, N. Kameswara, A. Vagiswari and Christina Louis. "Father Richaud and Early Telescope Observations in India." *Bulletin of the Astronomical Society of India* 12, no. 1 (1984): 81-85.

Renouard, Michel, et al. *L'activité maritime à Saint-Malo dans la seconde moitié du XVIIIe siècle.* Saint-Malo: Mairie de Sant-Malo, Service Educatif des Archives départementales l'Ille-et Vilaine, 1992.

Restif-Filliozat, Manonmani. "The Jesuit contribution to the Geographical Knowledge of India in the Eighteenth Century." *Journal of Jesuit Studies* 6, Issue 1 (11 March 2019): 71-84. Brill.com.

Richter, Julius. *A History of Missions in India.* Translated by Sydney H. Moore. New York: Fleming H. Revell Company, 1908. Internet Archive.

Rogers, Woodes. *A Cruising Voyage Round the World.* London: A. Bell, 1712. Google Books.

Roper, Lyndal. *Martin Luther, Renegade and Prophet.* New York: Random House, 2017.

Rose, Sarah. *For All the Tea in China.* New York: Penguin Books, 2010.

Roux, Benoît. "De insulis Karaybicis relations manuscriptae: Adrien Le Breton, The Last Jesuit Missionary in the 'Carib Island' of St. Vincent." In *Communities in Contact. Essays in archaeology, ethnohistory and ethnography of the Amerindian circum-Caribbean*, 343-359. Leiden: Sidestone Press, 2011. Halsh.archives-ouvertes.fr.

Sánchez Arreseigor, Juan José. "Winter is Coming: Europe's Deep Freeze of 1709." *National Geographic History* (January – February 2017): 18-21.

Schurz, William Lytle. *The Manila Galleon*. Manila: Manila Conservation Society, 1985.

—"Mexico, Peru, and the Manila Galleon." *The Hispanic American Historical Review* 1, no. 4 (November 1918). 389-402. Jstor.org.

Scott, William Henry. *Pre-Hispanic Source Materials for the Study of Philippine History*. Quezon City, Philippines: New Day Publishers, 1984.

Seton-Karr, Walter Scott. *Selections from Calcutta Gazettes of the Years 1784-1797*. Vol 2. London: Longmans, Green, Reader and Dyer, 1865. Google Books.

Sobel, Dava. *Longitude*. New York: Walker and Co., 1995.

Sommervogel, Carlos, SJ and Augustin de Backer, SJ. *Bibliotèque de la Compagnie de Jésus, Nouvelle* Édition. Vol. 2. Bruxelles: Oscar Schepens, 1891. HathiTrust.

—*Bibliotèque de la Compagnie de Jésus, Nouvelle* Édition. Vol. 4. Bruxelles: Oscar Schepens, 1893. HathiTrust.

—*Bibliotèque de la Compagnie de Jésus, Nouvelle* Édition. Vol. 7. Bruxelles: Oscar Schepens, 1896. HathiTrust.

Tachard, Guy, SJ. *Second Voyage du Père Tachard et des Jésuites Envoyés par le Roy au Royaume de Siam*. Amsterdam: Pierre Mortier, 1689. Google Books.

Tarnas, Richard. *The Passion of the Western Mind*. New York: Ballantine Books, 1993.

Tavernier, Jean-Baptiste. *Tavernier's Travels in India*. Vol. 1. Translated by Valentine Ball. New Delhi: Asian Educational Services, 2004. Google Books.

Toussaint, Auguste. *History of the Indian Ocean*. Translated by June Guicharnaud. Chicago: The University of Chicago Press, 1966.

Tylenda, Joseph N., SJ, *Jesuit Saints and Martyrs*, Chicago: Loyola University Press, 1984.

Udías, Agustín, SJ. *Jesuit Contribution to Science, A History.* Chp 2.2. (Provided by the author, pre-publication, 9/15/2014). Springer, 2015.

Verma, Sandeep Kumar. "Currency System in Pondicherry under the Rule of the Compagnie des Indes Orientales, 1674-1761." *International Journal of Applied Research* 1, no. 8, Part C (2015): 110-116. Allresearchjournal. com

Viswanathan, Gauri. *Outside the Fold: Conversion, Modernity, and Belief.* Princeton, New Jersey: Princeton University Press, 1998.

Vregille, Pierre de. *L'Observatoire du Collège de la Trinité, à Lyon.* Paris: Victor Petaux, 1905.

Waldinger, Maria. "The Long-Run Effects of Missionary Orders in Mexico." *Journal of Development Economics* 127 (Online version, July 2017): 355-378.

Weber, Henry. *La compagnie française des Indes: 1604-1875.* Paris: Arthur Rousseau, 1904. Google Books.

West, Robert C. "Early Silver Mining in New Spain. In *Mines of Silver and Gold in the Americas*, edited by Peter Bakewell. New York: Routledge, 2020.

White, John. *History of a Voyage to the China Sea.* Boston: Wells & Lilly, 1823. Google Books.

Zupanov, Ines G. "The Historiography of the Jesuit Missions in India (1500-1800)" In: *Jesuit Historiography Online.* Last modified: November 2016. Brillonline.com.

INDEX